Javier Laviña,
Michael Zeuske (Eds.)

The Second Slavery

Sklaverei und Postemanzipation
Slavery and Postemancipation
Esclavitud y postemancipación
Escravidão e Pós-Emancipação

herausgegeben von
edited by
editado por

Michael Zeuske
(Universität zu Köln)

Javier Laviña
(Universitat de Barcelona)

Dale W Tomich
(Binghamton University)

&

Rafael de Bivar Marquese
(Universidade de São Paulo)

Vol. 6

LIT

The Second Slavery

Mass Slaveries and Modernity in the Americas and in the Atlantic Basin

edited by

Javier Laviña and Michael Zeuske

LIT

This book is printed on acid-free paper.

Cover image: Victor P. Landaluze, "El Mayoral" (1881)

Gefördert im Rahmen des DFG-Projektes: "Out of the Americas: Sklavenhändler und *Hidden Atlantic* im 19. Jahrhundert" (ZE 302/18-1 „Sklavenhändlerprojekt").

Grupo de investigación sobre culturas indígenas i afroamericanas

Este trabajo se ha llevado a cabo con el proyecto HAR2009-09766

Bibliographic information published by the Deutsche Nationalbibliothek
The Deutsche Nationalbibliothek lists this publication in the Deutsche Nationalbibliografie; detailed bibliographic data are available in the Internet at http://dnb.d-nb.de.

ISBN 978-3-643-90367-9

A catalogue record for this book is available from the British Library

Klosbachstr. 107
CH-8032 Zürich
Tel. +41 (0) 44-251 75 05
Fax +41 (0) 44-251 75 06
E-Mail: zuerich@lit-verlag.ch
http://www.lit-verlag.ch

LIT VERLAG Dr. W. Hopf
Berlin 2014
Fresnostr. 2
D-48159 Münster
Tel. +49 (0) 2 51-62 03 20
Fax +49 (0) 2 51-23 19 72
E-Mail: lit@lit-verlag.de
http://www.lit-verlag.de

Distribution:
In Germany: LIT Verlag Fresnostr. 2, D-48159 Münster
Tel. +49 (0) 2 51-620 32 22, Fax +49 (0) 2 51-922 60 99, E-mail: vertrieb@lit-verlag.de

In Austria: Medienlogistik Pichler-ÖBZ, e-mail: mlo@medien-logistik.at
In the UK: Global Book Marketing, e-mail: mo@centralbooks.com
In North America: International Specialized Book Services, e-mail: orders@isbs.com
e-books are available at www.litwebshop.de

Contents

Introduction: African slaves and the Atlantic: a cultural overview[1]

Catherine COQUERY-VIDROVITCH

As late as the beginning of the 2000s, French and Francophone people – white speople, who were supposed to be slave traders‘ inheritors and black people, some of whom were of slave descent - were full of shame when facing the issue of slavery. The condition was no better in Africa, where a history of local slavery was not yet recognized. A common taboo resulted in common ignorance. This began to publicly change, especially in the Francophone world, with a now famous law, known as Taubira‘s law, named after the French Guyanese deputy, Christiane Taubira, who struggled to have it voted into law in 2001 by the French Parliament, proclaiming that slavery was a crime against humanity. Of course the law mainly addressed colonial French slavery, which was only suppressed in 1848 in French islands producing sugar cane (namely, Martinique, Guadeloupe and La Réunion). Since then, francophone research started in spite of many hesitations among historians, both African and French ones, hesitations which are only now on the decrease. The present paper aims at presenting the current state of research, namely what are the new francophone trends of knowledge about slavery and slave culture, according to recent historical research, as well in Africa as elsewhere. I will analyze three major points: firstly, proposing a few general remarks on slavery, which probably was a generalized labor system everywhere in the ancient pre-mechanized world, as well in Africa as elsewhere. Secondly, a questioning about what it was to be a slave inside African societies before the Atlantic slave trade, with new research that has well explored the topic. And thirdly, how this former slavery, transformed by the Atlantic system, resulted into a large hybridization (or cultural *metis-*

[1] A former version of part of this paper, "African slave culture and the Atlantic World in the Nineteenth Century" will be published by Chouki El Hamel and Paul Lovejoy (eds), *Confluence of Cultures or Convergence of Diasporas, forthcoming.*

sage) between African and American slave culture, the climax of it, on both sides of the Atlantic Ocean, being expressed in the nineteenth century.

Slavery always existed in old societies

Slavery has everywhere existed. It was the easiest means, in a pre-industrial society with rudimentary tools (such as a *daba* or hoe), to use men and above all women (because women were easier to submit) as literally tools of labor, rather than regarding them as human beings. Later, slavery was justified by moral reasons: for example, planters questioned whether or not Amerindian and black people had a soul; then, in the nineteenth century, Europeans theorized the inequality of races. At last, slavery was even integrated by the capitalist mode of production: as long as Western developed societies were no longer politically responsible for slaves, they maintained and used slave labor to make the capitalist mode of production work. One of the best examples is the US case: cotton slave plantations, generalized in the Deep South, enabled the development of Industrial Revolution in England, which needed cotton as a raw materials for its major basic industry. In spite of many discussions, economic historians still do not agree on whether or not slave labor was more profitable for industrial companies than for a waged labor force, at least in the first third of the nineteenth century. As a matter of fact, capitalism and this "second slavery", as historian Dale Tomich calls it[2], were tightly articulated one to the other, the condition being that developed societies no longer be directly responsible for slavery (which may be discussed for the US case). Therefore, in the nineteenth century, when the Atlantic slave trade was progressively banned in the western world, an African internal "second slavery" was organized by African businessmen and was used by the Western world to afford tropical

2 Dale Tomich & Michael Zeuske, eds, "The Second slavery: Mass slavery, World-Economy, and Comparative Micro-Histories", *Review. A Journal of the Fernand Braudel Center,* part I, special issue, 31:2, 2008. On Dale Tomich's Second Slavery: Anthony E. Kaye, "The Second Slavery: Modernity in the Nineteenth Century South and the Atlantic World", *The Journal of Southern History*, August 2009, LXXV, 3, 627-650.

raw materials demanded by their industries (oil seeds, tinted woods, ivory, later rubber), as much in Africa as was the case in the US South.

Second remark: The invention of slaves as "black" is relatively recent. In ancient times, most slaves were white. They had been enslaved because they were strangers to the prominent culture: non-Greek people were slaves because they were barbarous; non-Arab people might be enslaved because they were not Muslim. Black slaves, growing in number from the ninth century onwards, were first used by Arab and Indian merchants, trading from sub-Saharan Africa to the Mediterranean world and the Indian Ocean. The specificity of the Atlantic slave trade was to systemize the colour-bar. In the eighteenth century, in French, the word *nègre* (from *niger*, black in Latin) had become synonymous with *slave*: from thence, beyond the Atlantic Ocean, only black Africans were made slaves, and any black African was thought of as made to be a slave.

Last remark: in many historical societies, the growing use of slaves went hand in hand with the emergence of a politically and economically viable State. This was true for the Roman Empire; this probably was the case for ancient Egypt. This proved to also be the case for the medieval Muslim empires. Why not enlarge to Sub-Saharan States? This has been well studied for so-called interlacustrine kingdoms, which appeared from the sixteenth century, such as the best studied of them, the Buganda kingdom.[3] Small or large, an African State was made powerful and relatively wealthy thanks to a double activity: on one side, its internal subsistence economy was enriched by the adoption of American crops (corn, cassava, beans. . .)[4]; the emergence of a powerful state was greatly encouraged when the state power controlled the production and long distance trade of a wealthy mineral, such as iron, gold or copper: such were the medieval Sudanese empires of West Africa or central Luba and Lunda empires; on the other side, annual wars were usual. The political and economic system was well adapted to environmental conditions, with the combination of crops and war fitted with

3 Henri Médard et Shane Doyle (eds), *Slavery in the Great Lakes Region of East Africa,* Eastern African Studies, (James Currey. Oxford; Fountain Publishers: Kampala; EAEP; Nairobi; Athens: Ohio University Press, 2007.

4 Jan Vansina, *Paths in the Rainforests: toward a History of Political Tradition in Equatorial Africa,* (Madison, Wis.: University of Wisconsin Press, 1990).

the succession of rainy and dry seasons. During the dry season, cultivation was over, and the people followed their chiefs at war out of their borders, aiming at bringing back home their booty: cows, women and slaves. This model may be found nearly everywhere, as well in Central Africa (interlacustrine states) as in Equatorial Africa (Kongo kingdom). It was the same in Western Africa, ensuring, before the Portuguese‘s arrival, the making of Benin-City or of the Kongo kingdom, then the growth of slave trading states, such as the Asante empire or the Abome kingdom.

Therefore, African slaves, an inferior and overexploited part of African people, have nevertheless been a well-integrated group inside a given society before the Atlantic slave trade. They, too, were a kind of inferior casted people bound to endogamical rules. Slaves were uprooted, taken away from their ancestral origins, and so direct familial descent. In a number of societies, women were more frequently enslaved than men, but they might be adopted by their masters‘ ancestors through marriage. This was never the case for male slaves, who were no longer able to ensure their own ancestors‘ cult: slaves and their descendants were slaves forever. Till today, peoples‘ surnames, i.e. in Senegambia, may inform on their ancestors‘ social status, and this often stands as a social problem.

What is to be a slave in Africa?

How can we understand what it was like to be a slave in Africa, in the eighteenth or in the first half of the nineteenth century, before being sold to European or American Atlantic slave traders? It probably was the most intensive period of slave trading all over Africa. Slaves were sold towards the Mediterranean Sea through the Sahara, massively "produced" by the Western Sudan Sahelian jihads (Uthman dan Fodio, al-Hadj Umar...); they were sold northwards down the Nile River, and eastwards to the Red Sea and Indian Ocean and the Omani and Zanzibar sultanate by Ethiopian, Swahili, Arab (such as Tippu Tip) and African (such as Rabih) traders. The north Atlantic contraband trade and above all, the Brazilian and Portuguese south Atlantic trade (authorized by the British, south of the Equator) remained as important as the "licit" trade of the eighteenth century. Besides, slaves were used inside Africa, as well as to be exported abroad; sacrifices of slaves for religious reasons and kings' funerals probably increased all over these centuries[5]. It sometimes happened that several hundred or even a few thousand slaves accompanied their master to his new home. These customs have been described in the cases of the Dahomey and Asante kingdoms, but were also common in Igboland and at the enthroning of chiefs in central Africa (such as for Bakongo and Bakuba). In central Africa slaves were also the first to be sacrificed, in cases of witchcraft, crime, or debt. Several slaves were sacrificed at the burial of the Orunga chief in 1847;[6] his people were major slave traders and accounted for half the population in Gabon. These rituals aimed at exerting social control over a growing slave population. For example, in 1881, the 400 titleholders in Asaba (Igboland) each sacrificed a slave when they were invested with their title. There was also an Igbo custom such that, in case of need, a family could offer the god a slave (*osu*), who then became the property of the priest in charge of the god's altar. Therefore African slavery and African slave trade were definitely imbricate, African trading networks being multiple and connected. Historian Marcia Wright demonstrated it in the core of the continent (today north-west Tanzania) with female slaves' life-stories, when for example, Bwanika found herself traded once in a caravan going westward on the Atlantic road, then escaped by good chance, but was again traded in a caravan going eastward to the Indian Ocean.[7]

Although Bwanika was of aristocratic origin (she had been given as a young girl to a local warlord), most traded slaves previously were already slaves in their own societies. During annual wars, many captured slaves were not prisoners of war, they were booty: soldiers following at war their chiefs or kings usually were free men or even noble people whose capture was negotiable against exchange or payment (as it was used across the Mediterranean sea between Arabs and Christian sailors and

5 C. Coquery-Vidrovitch, "La fête des Coutumes au Dahomey : historique et essai d'interprétation", *Annales*, 1969, 4,: 696-716. E. Terray, "Le pouvoir, le sang et la mort dans le royaume asante au XIXe siècle", *Cahiers d'Etudes africaines,* 1994, Volume 34, 136, 549-561.

6 K.D. Patterson, *The Northern Gabon Coast to 1875* (Oxford: Clarendon Press, 1975): 53.

7 Marcia Wright, *Strategies of Slaves & Women : life-stories from East/Central Africa* (New York : L. Barber Press ; London : J. Currey, 1993).

traders). Human booty came from raided villages or fields, where women enslavements were appreciated and usual, but enslaved men were above all, those who were not negotiable: that means former poor or already enslaved people. Unfortunately, we know little about African slaves' first generation (most African American slaves who wrote their life stories were already born on the other side of the Atlantic ocean), except for women: a number of life-stories are female life stories, locally collected by missionaries; they were from poor and deserted old women with no other chance of survival than to be converted and hosted by Christian missions. Nevertheless a few stories tell us that the difference was tiny between supposed domestic slaves and trading slaves: such is the (?) story of Ali Eisami, who was born in Bornu in 1780 and grabbed near Lake Chad in 1810. [? Word choice? Grabbed? I had to guess enslaved.] He was successively sold for dozens of years from village to village, before arriving to the coast, at Porto-Novo in 1818[8].The idea that Atlantic slaves were already slaves before being traded across the Atlantic Ocean is important. It means that original slave cultures previously existed. As Ibrahima Thioub explains it, predatory African local systems aiming at looting slaves pre-existed the Atlantic trade[9], even if they were intensified all over the eighteenth and nineteenth centuries because of the apex of international slave trading—research suggests that at the eve of the scramble for Africa, at least half of African people were locally enslaved, and probably more in west and central Africa, while the percentage was much lower beforehand [10].

What we may call an *African slave culture* definitely is a cultural process, which made several cultures meet and change at different stages of history:

– First, slaves were or had been made slaves in a given African society, because of an internal war or looting. They were already uprooted, and

[8] H.F.C. Smith et al., "Ali Eisami Bazimbe of Bornu", In Philip D. Curtin (ed.), *Africa remembered. Narratives by West Africans from the Era of the slave Trade* (Waveland Press, 1967): 199-217.

[9] Ibrahima Thioub,. " L'esclavage et les traites en Afrique occidentale. Entre mémoires et histoires ", in Adame BA KONARÉ (dir.), *Petit précis de remise à niveau sur l'histoire africaine à l'usage du Président Sarkozy* (La Découverte, Paris, 2008), 201-214.

[10] Paul Lovejoy, *Transformations of Slavery. A history of Slavery in Africa* (Cambridge University Press, 1983):199-216.

put with other slaves, sometimes coming from other corners of Africa, far from their birthplaces. This was their first change

- then, they were sold, or again plundered, and had to travel, sometimes for several weeks or more, from deep in the interior to the coast, where again they were sheltered in special barracks, meeting all their way along this journey, a lot of other African people coming from diverse cultures, whom they did not speak the language of; they again had to adapt, all the more so, as there was also a substantial coastal trade in slaves.
- once on board on the ships crossing the Atlantic Ocean, again they had to meet many other nationalities, and again to exchange cultures and languages.

They were neither stupid nor mute: all their way along to the sea, they wanted to understand what was happening, where they were going, what would be their fate. When waiting for weeks or months to be shipped on board, they listened to any news, of which they heard a lot, since a number of them were used in the forts as slaves and domestic servants, where news was circulating.

Therefore, confluence of cultures occurred from the very beginning, as it was in the Americas (which is not my field), when slaves landed in the harbors and were sold at market, had to turn, sometimes far away inside the continent, into African Americans, as in the African hinterland, when hybridazations began long before slaves arrived to the coastal barracks. Of course, in some cases, slaves that landed to a given American area were mainly recruited only from the near hinterland of one port or from a set of closely neighboring ports, as Walter Hawthorne recently explained for Guine slaves exported to coastal Amazonia.[11] Nevertheless, they were locally and regionally mingled between several mini-groups (such as Papel, Balanta, Bijago, Banyun, Brame, Mandinka, Floup or Fula):[12] even within small areas, there were cultural differences from group to group (Hawthorne gives the example of people occupying a zone within tens of miles of the ports of Cacheu and Bissau). Mintz and Price rightly demonstrated that, most of the time, the slave trade resulted in randomizing

[11] Walter Hawthorne, *From Africa to Brazil. Culture, Identity and an Atlantic Slave Trade,* 1600-1830, (Cambridge: Cambridge University Press, 2010).

[12] Hawthorne: 11.

Africans coming from more diverse places, as it did for Africans shipped in the Caribbean: they were not one cultural group, but were thrown together into multicultural "crowds".[13] Therefore creolizations were manifold, with exchanges of influences and counter influences, as well in Africa as in Americas: it is in Amazonia that *Upper Guinea* was built as a common space, with deportation as a catalyst to fashion a dynamic regional Guinean "nation", enhancing cultural similarities, while, beforehand, these small groups were mainly raiding one another. Inside Africa, on a larger scale, caravans of slaves coming from the hinterland were long; and slaves also waited for a long time in the coastal entrepôts before shipping on board. Slaves time together in transit was central to their making of new cultural links. Creolizations began early.

Such connections interfered everywhere, and the mingling of cultures needs more multicultural studies: the direct Atlantic culture is pretty well studied; Joseph Miller did it for Loanda, Verger and Cameiro da Cunha did it for Afro-Brazilians,[14] while Nigerian Christian Saros, coming from Sierra Leone and who settled in Abeokuta, also were well studied, such as *signares* in Senegal.[15] But who studied how these diverse influences combined with one another *inside* Africa, as in, for example the meeting of Saros with Islam arriving from northern Nigeria? Because of the slave trade networks, it became possible for people, as well in Africa as in Americas, to wear protective amulets honoring ancestral spirits, and, at the same time, to hide under their clothing other amulets coming from the Muslim religion, while attending a multi-ethnic masses celebrated by Catholic priests in the coastal forts.[16] A huge complex of African-Arab-European-Brazilian interconnected cultures was in the making inside Africa long before the late nineteenth century European conquest.

---

[13] Sidney W.Mintz and Richard Price, *The Birth of African-American Culture: an Anthropological Perspective* (Boston: Beacon Press, 1992).

[14] Mariano Cameiro da Cunha & Pierre Verger, *From Slave Quarters to Town Houses. Brazilian Architecture in Nigeria and the People's Republic of* (São Paulo, Nobel Edusp,1985).

[15] George E. Brooks, "*Signares* of Saint-Louis and Gorée: Women entrepreneurs in 18th century Senegal", in N. J. Hafkin et E. G. Bay eds, *Women in Africa* (Stanford, 1976): 19-44

[16] Hawthorne: 10.

Language is very important: one speaks as he or she thinks, but conversely one thinks as he or she speaks, and so languages evolved immensely. Languages are precious culture-making tools. Most of the time, slaves had to discover a number of new languages, to become as multilingual as possible, and to create common languages to communicate with their new masters, fellow travelers and shipmates. They also had to create new common connections with other African strangers. Religion was a strong means of recognition: known in Americas as *Vaudou*, it resulted from the meeting of a number of local cults, which conglomerated all along these ways, the name of which varying in Africa according to local cultures and languages. That is the reason why, as Hawthorne argues, spiritual beliefs were among the most stable aspects of African American culture over time and across space: although many aspects of spiritual belief and practice originally differed from group to group, all the African slave diasporas agreed to hold a common "set of overlapping beliefs that changed little over time":[17] all believed that there was one creator who seldom interacted in daily life; that spirits inhabiting the earth interacted with humans and affected them for better and worse; that a number of natural substances contained supernatural powers, and that some people were more "gifted" than others to manipulate them and to please them with gifts and sacrifices. Therefore even if cults might differ according to their varied African origins, they nevertheless re-created abroad traditions aiming at unifying the members of varied groups and not as dividing them. When African people landed in American ports, several months or several years after their first breakaway, they often were drowning from a great variety of widely dispersed ports, from Mombasa or Mozambique to Lagos or Elmina. They had already changed a lot. And they had to face a new dramatic change: Europeans and American traders and masters intended to differentiate and classify them, according to their given origins, their "tribes", their scarifications, and their supposed ethnical qualities. These new definitions resulted in introducing and hardening new rigid categories, which distorted much more complex previous realities socially, psychologically and mentally. African slaves became cultural creators who drew on many African

[17] Hawthorne: 22

and non-African cultural forms to create something new: this process of cultural creativity under oppression did not only occur in Americas, as Mintz and Price insisted on, it began far away, inside Africa. Therefore the so-called "native African culture" described when slaves arrived at Americas was a Western "invention" of African culture, similar to the "invention of Africa" realized for Africa itself by travelers, missionaries and colonial anthropologists.[18]

Cultural hybridizations: an historical approach

A number of researches enhances how early this convergence of cultures occurred, either in Americas (which is not my field) or inside Africa. Jean Comaroff studied it during the eighteenth century in southern Africa.[19] Thornton insisted on the early contamination of Christian concepts in the sixteenth-century kingdom of Kongo,[20] Peter Mark discovered the early cultural hybridization between Senegambia people and Portuguese, between the sixteenth and eighteenth centuries: later, British and French traders and colonizers were surprised to discover, inside West Africa, a great number of black people still calling themselves "Portuguese" in spite of their blackness and local roots.[21] Pierre Verger, in his turn, studied the Afro-Brazilian culture in neighboring areas. Such connections interfered everywhere; nevertheless, they often did not appear as obvious for researchers who do not necessarily compare their knowledge to other specialists' knowledge, dealing with the same people but in another time, or studying other people in different spaces or cultures open to similar influence: for example, specialists of the Senegambian Atlantic trade usually do not pay attention enough to the trans-Saharan trade; or conversely, while African people from

18 See Valentin Mudimbe, *The Invention of Africa, & The Idea of Africa* (Bloomington, Indiana University Press, 1988 & 1991).

19 Jean Comaroff. *Body of power, spirit of resistance : the culture and history of a South African people,* (Chicago: University of Chicago Press, 1985).

20 J. K. Thornton, "Religious and Ceremonial Life in the Kongo and Mbundu Areas, 1490s-1850s", in Linda M. Heywood (ed.), *Central Africans and Cultural Transformations in the American Diaspora* (Cambridge University Press, 2001): 71-90.

21 Peter Mark, *Portuguese Style and Luso-African Identity. Precolonial Senegambia, Sixteenth-Nineteenth Centuries* (Bloomington: Indiana University Press, 2002).

Senegambia were aware of, and sometimes practiced both trades: specialists of African Islam and specialists of the Atlantic world did not meet to compare and question the interrelationships between the Islamic Mediterranean Sahel culture and the Portuguese Atlantic culture, although both of them co-existed and interpenetrated each other inside Western Africa for centuries. Or specialists did not think to question a possible relationship between Luso-African people, such as those studied by Peter Mark in Senegambia,[22] and Afro-Brazilian people who developed later in neighboring areas, as studied by Pierre Verger or Camheiro da Cunha in the eighteenth and nineteenth centuries.[23]

These hybridizations have existed since the beginning of the story. They varied according to a differentiated periodization in Atlantic-space building. Two great periods have to be distinguished: before and after the crossing of the Atlantic to the Americas.

The Atlantic as a Luso-African lake in the fifteenth century

From 1415, when Portuguese settled in Ceuta in Morocco, to 1492, when Christopher Columbus discovered Haiti, and to 1498, when the Portuguese made it around the Cape of Good Hope, a transatlantic slave trade did not yet exist; for nearly one century, the Atlantic space was only a Luso-African lake[24]. All over the century, there were many costly expeditions along the African coast. African slaves were not yet exported to Americas, but imported to Portugal, as well as slaves from North Africa had been imported beforehand and still were imported:[25] In Portugal, in the nineteenth cen-

---

22 Peter Mark. *Portuguese Style.*

23 Pierre Verger, *Flux et reflux de la traite des nègres entre le golfe du Bénin et Bahia de todos os santos du 17° au 19° siècles* (Paris, Mouton,1968). Manuela Cameiro da Cunha,*Negros, Estrangeiros : os escravos libertos e sua volta à Africa* (São Paulo, Nobel Edusp, 1986). Cameiro da Cunha & Verger. 1985. *From Slave Quarters to Town Houses.*

24 Armelle Anders, Histoire de l'Afrique lusophone, Paris, Chandeigne, 1994.

25 Antonio de Almeida Mendes, "Les réseaux de traite ibérique dans l'Atlantique nord (1440-1640)", *Annales*, July-August 2008, 4: 739-768.

tury, there were at least 300,000 slaves; there were at most 40,000 slaves in France at the end of the eighteenth century.[26]

The fifteenth century was a major transitional moment, rebalancing between the former Mediterranean and the later Atlantic systems, while Portuguese were, at the same time, well aware of the presence along the African coasts of Muslim merchants whom they had known beforehand in North Africa: a major change, but made possible thanks to the continuity between previous Mediterranean networks and new markets. Previous slaves imported in Southern Europe came from North Africa across the Mediterranean Sea. The stream did not disappear, and went on provisioning Portugal and Portuguese islands, while new Portuguese expeditions along the Atlantic coast were made possible, thanks to financing by previous money makers off the Mediterranean trade. For financing these expeditions was not a miracle. Bankers and investors were not new ones: they were professionals from Genoa or Venice, previously enriched with trade across the Mediterranean Sea, including exchanges and the slave trade between the South of Europe and the Maghreb powers. Therefore there was a Mediterranean interference, which ensured continuity as well as change.[27]

Along the Atlantic coast, Portuguese were not at first looking for slaves, but for gold. It is the reason why they first settled along the western coast that they nicknamed, the *gold coast,* creating there their major port, St George of the Mina (São Jorge da Mina which was to become Elmina). African gold was part of a sailing trade from coast to coast, when Portuguese sailors offered their African partners a number of varied products in exchange for their gold: a few manufactured goods, local foodstuff, and of course, slaves, bought and sold from port to port to their clients. Africans were well aware or these varied products: they asked Portuguese to provide them with Moroccan crafts (and also horses) rather than with shoddy goods of a lesser quality imported from Europe. With the African gold, Portuguese also bought slaves for themselves and, discovering sugar cane which had arrived in Africa from the East and Egypt (where sugar-cane plantations

---

26 Sue Peabody, *‚There are no Slaves in France'. The Political Culture of Race and Slavery in the Ancien Regime* (Oxford University Press, 1996).

27 Antonio de Almeida Mendes, " De la Méditerranée à l'Atlantique : les traites modernes en perspective ", *Les Anneaux de la Mémoire,* 13, 2010: 287-306.

already existed), they began to create and organize in neighboring islands their first sugar cane plantations: in Madeira, the Canaries, and above all in Saõ Tome islands.[28]

As early as the time when the Portuguese sailed along Senegambia coast, they found evidence of the relative importance of African Islam and the Arabic world. They were aware of African Islam and Muslim traders there. Ca' da Mosto, a Venetian traveler, protected by Henry the Navigator, visited twice the Senegal area in 1454-55, and well describes the early presence of Islam and the importance of *malams*. He met Africans selling slaves and gold as well to Muslim traders, coming from the North and connected with the Mali emperor, as to their European partners[29]. Of course the Portuguese knew about Arab slave trading. Conversely, on the African side, they practiced it, too, and Berber culture and *metissage* were important. In other words, neither the Portuguese slave trade nor Arab or Berber slave trade functioned separately in Africa South of the Sahara, at least in the Sahel area. From the beginning, they were connected. This is culturally important, because we don't only have to study Euro-African cultural hybridization, but also and at the same, time Berber-Euro-African cultural blending. Therefore, there was not only an encounter between Europeans and Africans, but also between Christian and Muslim influences, and traders coming from North Africa, who were connected with Africa south of the Sahara as well as with Europeans. From the beginning, cultural influences were complex.

The Atlantic space and culture after 1492

On the African side, the cultural blend became more and more enriched by these diverse contacts, which intensified through the centuries; all the more so as African gold was used to finance the first transatlantic expe-

---

[28] Marian Malowist, "Les débuts du système de plantations dans la période des grandes découvertes, *Africana Bulletin*, Varsovie, 10, 1969: 9-30.

[29] Alvise Ca' da Mosto, *The voyages of Cadamosto and other documents on Western Africa in the second half of the fifteenth century*, translated and edited by G. R. Crone (London: the Hakluyt Society, 1937).

ditions towards Brazil.[30] From the seventeenth century onwards, the presence of Muslim traders coming from the north to the Western African coast became more and more important. In the eighteenth and nineteenth centuries, European slave traders, invited by King of Dahome, or by the *Asantehene* of Kumasi in their capital cities, were directly competing with Muslim traders coming from the North.[31] Foreign Muslims were as many as European traders at their courts, especially trading in slaves during the long custom festivals organized every year for several weeks in their capital cities.[32] In Kumasi, there was a special district reserved for Muslim foreigners who enjoyed a special right to trade, while Asante people were forbidden to freely do the same because of their king‘s monopoly.[33] Interferences of trade involve interferences of culture. Thence, we have to question interferences between the Atlantic trade and the trans-Saharan trade, which provisioned the Diula and Hausa traders from the Niger river as far as the African coast. We have to question the chronology and history of these interactive diffusions of cultures, which were not just bilateral, but tri-lateral or more.

I attempted to do it on one example: the history of the making and adoption in coastal western Africa of the so-called "colonial style" embodied by the model of the veranda house, the diffusion of which all along the West African coast, generalized all over the nineteenth century. Its origin is much older, and it appears very complex. Not only was the model adopted when the first Portuguese appeared (such as in Goa as well as in Mozambique island or in Salvador de Bahia in Brazil), but it generalized

---

30 Joseph MILLER, " Slavery and the Financing of the Atlantic World ", Lecture on *Debt and Slavery: the History of a Process of Enslavement,* McGill University, Montréal, may 2009: 7-9.

31 This appears from a number of descriptions by European traders. See i.e. C. Coquery-Vidrovitch, "Le blocus de Whydah et la rivalité franco-anglaise au Dahomey (1876-1878)",*Cahiers d'Etudes Africaines,* II, 7, 1962: 373-419.

32 C. Coquery-Vidrovitch, "La fête des Coutumes au Dahomey" : historique et essai d'interprétation", *Annales* 4, 1964: 696-716. Emmanuel Terray, "Le pouvoir, le sang et la mort dans le royaume asante au XIXe siècle", *Cahiers d'Etudes africaines,* 1994, Volume 34, 136: 549-561., op.cit.

33 Ivor Wilks, *Asante in the Nineteenth Century: the structure and evolution of a political order* (Cambridge University Press, I975).

in Africa. The Yoruba case is revealing, because it allows an understanding of the complexity of the cultural blend. Three major authors studied the itinerary of such diffusion, without connecting their respective research. On one side, Peter Mark studied the Luso-African model[34], then Pierre Verger and a number of other authors, insisted on the Afro-Brazilian model. On the other side, Antony King splendidly studied the Indian bungalow model, which was first imported from India to England, and thence was encouraged in Nigeria by Lord Lugard.[35] None of these authors thought of crossing these diverse influences, while they obviously met and mingled inside Africa. Thinking about these diverse links, you may come to a final hypothesis[36].

The former colonial model probably originated from the Algarve province, South of Portugal, where most Portuguese sailors came from. Algarve houses were poor housing, most of them chalk whitened, and the first Portuguese settlers imported the model to Africa (Peter Mark). Luso-Africans early adopted it. The key characteristic of members of this acculturated community was not that they knew how to read and write a European language, as the colonizers later thought, condescendingly. It was that they had implicitly made a choice. They were all raised in an urban culture and hoped to speed up the evolution toward a more advanced technology than that of their own cultural heritage, going along with a Christian, Muslim or, later, humanist spirit that would allow them to elaborate a civilization also respecting their views and lifestyle. The group was relatively important, but scattered all over the coastal areas of West Africa; G. Brooks estimates that Luso-Africans, most of them quite africanized, might

---

34 Peter Mark. *Portuguese Style.*

35 Anthony D. King, *The Bungalow. The Production of a Global Culture* (London, Routledge and Kegan Paul, 1984).

36 For the details of this study, see C. Coquery-Vidrovitch, "Luso-Africains et Afro-Brésiliens du XVIè au XIXè siècle", *Afrikanische Beziehungen, Netzwerke und räumliche Dimensionen – Spatial dynamics, Exchange and Networks in Africa – Dynamiques spatiales, réseaux et échanges africains,* Laurence Marfaing & Brigitte Reinwald eds (Hambourg, LIT Verlag, 2000): 61-70. Also publ. in: *Le Portugal et l'Atlantique,* Arquivos do Centro cultural Calouste Gulbenkian, XLII, Lisbonne-Paris, 2001: 155-168. Brigitte KOWALSKI, *L'héritage architectural afro-brésilien sur la Côte des esclaves* (mémoire de l'École du Louvre, 2004).

have numbered 2 million in the seventeenth century (including the Cabo Verde islands).[37] These people were usually urbanites, and were remarkably well integrated into larger societies, which is probably why they had a strong influence on urban African architecture. Indeed, this group seems to have spread the Portuguese style far into the interior. Unfortunately, no remains exist in Africa before the eighteenth century (and most of present day houses were only built in the nineteenth century); nevertheless visitors left earlier descriptions. This model of housing was called "lodge", which came from the Portuguese *loja* (large store). There are no traces left of dozens or perhaps hundreds of lodge houses, such as this one on the Gambia river, which was built of adobe and straw by Francis Moore in 1733, which already had a veranda (*alpendre* in Portuguese). It seems to be one of the first known examples of what would become the standard house for traders from the end of the century on. Perhaps it can be linked with an analogous but much larger building, such as in Cape Coast Castle, described by Barbot in 1682.[38] This might be the link between the Portuguese fort, Afro-Brazilian veranda house, and English bungalow that I will mention again later.

Then the African model crossed the Atlantic, where it was progressively adapted and enlarged in Brazil, as early as the sixteenth or seventeenth century, even if local designs attest it only for the eighteenth century. The typical veranda house had a four-sided roof, made of local stuff (thatched roof). Thence, this former Luso-African model evolved towards a more elaborated architecture, which was improved by Brazilian planters. It progressively gave birth to a solid square house, with a balcony or veranda ensuring good ventilation, adapted to a hot climate. Possibly a few thousands Afro-Brazilians coming back since the eighteenth century diffused the *sobrado* model,or Brazilian-style home. The masters used the first floor, and the slaves lived on the ground floor. A side influence has existed with the Dutch occupation of Brazil: from the 1630s, the north of Brazil was occupied by the *Western Indies Dutch Company* whose Governor Joahan

[37] George Brooks. *Eurafricans in Western Africa. Commerce, social status, gender, and religious observance from the 16th to the 18th century* (Western African Studies: Ohio University Press and Oxford: J. Currey, 2003).

[38] A.W. Lawrence. *Trade Castles and forts of West Africa* (Standford, Cal., Stanford University Press, 1964).

Maurits of Nassau, very fond of arts (1637-1644), had two painters come from the Netherlands to copy a number of landscapes and housing, which they did on the spot and when coming back to Europe. They were precious and praised documents. At the same time, the first Dutch settlers arrived to The Cape (1852): thence a possible influence on a similar model known as typical Cape-Dutch housing style.

A major return was the coming back to West Africa, from Saint-Louis to Loanda, of so called Afro Brazilians, most of them relatively wealthy free *metis* people (more than former slaves) who re-imported the model to the African coast. There, especially among the Yoruba, this architecture flourished on the Benin coast and in the near hinterland, and early met with the bungalow model, generalized by the British. The nineteenth-century urban house became a large, square, two-story house with many windows and a veranda running all around the internal walls, usually rather isolated from neighboring buildings. The expansion was very rapid, and towards the end of the nineteenth century, most Yoruba houses, as well in cities as in the countryside, replicated the model rather than the former native huts scattered in a common courtyard.

Of course these architectural combinations were helped by the know-how of many craftsmen, carpenters, masons, etc. who often were former slaves trained in Brazil and brought to Africa. They brought back with them their knowledge and trained African apprentices who, in their turn, expanded their techniques in the hinterland. The diffusion of this complex style, made of multiple "Portuguese- African-Brazilian-English" encounters, resulted from the Atlantic system which, for centuries, managed to favor exchanges and influences between people, techniques and financial tools, intensified by international and interregional contacts and *metissage*. This cultural melting-pot went hand in hand with globalization of the economy: the pre-colonial nineteenth century was the moment when progressively, especially in West African societies, the former slave trade economy was superseded by merchant capitalism.[39] The veranda house also became the symbol of an emerging African urban upper middle class whose growth

[39] Jacques Gubler, "Architecture and colonialism. A Historical Safari", *Lotus international,* 26: 5-19, 1980.

would be stopped by early colonial imperialism. Reshaped and adopted by the colonial powers, it gave birth to a so-called "colonial style" which, in fact, was borne much earlier with the Atlantic world.

The end of the British Atlantic slave trade or the beginning of the big slave robbery, 1808-1850

Christian CWIK

University of the West Indies
Trinidad and Tobago[1]

Introduction

The second slavery emerged during the 19th century, exactly in the era of the abolition of slave trade and slavery. Despite abolition policy, officially 3,444,500 million African slaves were sold between 1801 and 1867 by slave traders of different nations to the Americas.[2] If we estimate at least a million more smuggled slaves during the same period, like the German historian, Michael Zeuske, calculated on the bases of his own work with Spanish documents, these almost 4.5 millions of slaves covered approximately 40% of the whole slave trade. How could this be, when at the same time, the

[1] Christian Cwik received his Ph.D. from the University of Vienna, a post-graduate diploma in Latin American Studies (Austrian Latin America Institute) and holds a M.A. degree in History and Philosophy from the University of Vienna where he was lecturer from 1999-2001 and 2010-2011. He is lecturer at the History Department at the University of the West Indies, St. Augustine in Trinidad and Tobago as well as lecturer in Cologne, Dresden in Germany, Vienna and Graz in Austria and at the Pablo de Olavide University in Sevilla, Spain. Between 2012 and 2013 he was visiting professor at the department of history at the University of Havana. Between 2010 and 2011 he was professor at the Department of History at the University of Erfurt in Germany. From 2009 to 2011 Christian Cwik was Professor at the Department of History at the University of Cartagena in Colombia and between 2006 and 2008 at the Department of Political Sciences and Government Studies at the Venezuelan Bolivarian University and at the Diplomatic Academy Pedro Gual in Caracas.

[2] ELTIS David, The Volume and Structure of the Transatlantic Slave Trade: A Reassessment. In: The William and Mary Quarterly 58, 1: New Perspectives on the Transatlantic Slave Trade (2001) p. 44.

British were the ones who controlled the abolition of the Atlantic slave trade through their squadrons and royal agents?[3]

Even the British, who already ended their own transatlantic slave trade on March 25, 1807, still received African slaves in their colonies afterwards.[4] With the exception of some islands in the Indian and Pacific Ocean, the British at this time possessed mainly colonies in the Caribbean. Almost all colonies were based on a sugar economy and necessarily needed slave labour force. The questions remain: from where did the slaves come, and who dealt with slaves, when it already had been forbidden?

Finally the British abolished slavery in their colonies in 1834, but didn‘t abolish their sugar economy, which ensured that the demand for slave labour still remained. But who substituted the missing slave labour force?

Of course it is not possible for this paper to answer all of these questions. Thus in this paper, I will concentrate on two specific questions: Firstly, how did the British manage to control of the prohibited transatlantic slave trade, while at the same time, receive masses of African slaves to their Caribbean colonies? And secondly, how did they substitute the missing slave labour force during the long process of abolition of slavery? This paper will also present an overview of the British way to the second slavery.

The notion of the second slavery was conceived in the late 1980s by the historian, Dale Tomich, from the Fernand Braudel Center for the Study of Economies, Historical Systems and Civilizations at Binghamton University, New York. His works, like *Through the Prism of Slavery: Labour, Capital, and World Economy* and *Slavery in the Circuit of Sugar: Martinique and the World Economy, 1830-1848,* together with Tomich‘s and Michael Zeuske‘s, *The Second Slavery: Mass Slavery, World-economy, and Comparative Microhistories,* are the basis for further investigations.

The abolition process in the British colonies is well elaborated by scholars like Robin Blackburn, Seymour Drescher, Thomas Clarkson, Magde Dresser, Roger Anstey and many others. Although the fact that the topic of

---

3 47° Georgii III, Session 1, Cap. XXXVI. An act for the abolition of the slave trade [25th March 1807]. www.pdavis.nl/Legis_06.htm (consulted on August 4th 2012).

4 Williams Eric, History of the people of Trinidad and Tobago. New York 2002, p. 75.

mixed commissions and African indentured labourers is well known, the work of Leslie Bethell is still essential.

Great Britain on the way to Capitalism

The so-called turn to "Free Labour Ideology" (FLI), based generally on Adam Smith's work *An Inquiry into Nature and Causes of the Wealth of Nations*, published in 1776, was responsible for the development of anti-slavery policy. The modern world was a "world of commerce", creating a network of interdependence and resting upon the joint modern voluntary wage labour of a great multitude of workmen.[5] As stated by Smith:

"The experience of all ages and nations, I believe, demonstrates that the work done by slaves, though it appears to cost only the maintenance is in the end, the dearest of any. A person, who can acquire no property, can have no other interest but to eat as much and to labour as little as possible. Whatever work he does beyond what is sufficient to purchase his own maintenance can be squeezed out of him by violence only and not by any interest of his own"[6]

The British were greatly motivated by economic self-interest, as the rapidly increasing sugar economies of Brazil and Cuba, the two major markets for the sugar trade at the time, were competing against the established British West Indian colonies of Jamaica and Barbados with increasing effectiveness.[7] But how could the British manage this change of work conditions in the tropical colonies, when Smith seemed only interested in the urban cluster of North America, not in the plantations of the West Indies?

At the same time some personalities of the British and American upper class with political and economical influence, asked for changes in the British slavery policy. One of the demands was the abolition of slavery and

5 SMITH Adam, Lectures on Jurisprudence. Indianapolis 1982, p. 185; DRESCHER Seymour, Abolitionist Expectations: Britain. In: Slavery and Abolition. Special issue: After Slavery. Emancipation and its Discontents (editor: Temperley Howard), 21, 2 (August 2000), pp. 41-66 here p. 42.

6 SMITH Adam, Wealth of Nations. Indianapolis 1981, pp. 22-23.

7 DRESCHER Seymour, Capitalism and Antislavery: British Abolitionism in Comparative Perspective. New York 1987.

the return to indentured labour. The judgment of Lord Mansfield, in the famous Sommersett Case in 1772, supported the abolitionists.[8] Thomas Jefferson prohibited the importation of slaves for resale during the process of independence of Virginia in 1778. Only those settlers who emigrated with their own slaves were not punished by law. Slaves who arrived illegally to Virginia were free.[9]

The generation of great British abolitionists, like William Wilberforce, James Ramsey and Thomas Clarkson, founded in 1787 the Committee for the Abolition of the Slave Trade. During the Napoleonic War, the British Parliament, after more than a decade of debate, finally passed the "Act for the Abolition of the Slave Trade" (but not slavery itself) on March 25, 1807 throughout its dominions and outlawed any further involvement in it by British citizens. Great Britain was preceded in this action by the United States Congress, which, for different reasons, passed a similar law on March 2, of the same year, which would take effect on January 1, 1808.

The Abolition of the transatlantic slave trade under the government of Grenville-Fox referred only to Great Britain, and here, only in regards to its transatlantic slave trade from Africa to the Americas. During the Napoleonic wars, Britain prohibited the importation of African slaves to its colonies, proclaiming that

"all manner of dealing and trading in the Purchase, Sale, Barter, or Transfer of slaves, or of Persons intended to be sold, transferred, used, or dealt with as slaves, practiced or carried on, in, at, to or from any part of the Coast or Countries of Africa, shall be, and the same is hereby utterly abolished, prohibited, and to declared to be unlawful" (Article I) as well as they have to pay for every such Offence

[8] "The state of slavery is of such a nature that it is incapable of being introduced on any reasons, moral or political, but only by positive law, which preserves its force long after the reasons, occasions, and time itself from whence it was created, is erased from memory. It is so odious, that nothing can be suffered to support it, but positive law. Whatever inconveniences, therefore, may follow from the decision, I cannot say this case is allowed or approved by the law of England; and therefore the black must be discharged" LOVEJOY Paul E., Transformations in slavery: a history of slavery in Africa. Cambridge 2000, p. 290; ANSTEY Roger, The Atlantic Slave Trade and British abolition, 1760–1810. London 1975, p. 5.

[9] SELBY John E., Higginbotham Don, The Revolution in Virginia, 1775–1783. Williamsburg 2007, p. 158.

the Sum of One hundred Pounds of lawful Money of Great Britain for each and every slave so purchased, sold, bartered, or transferred, or contracted or agreed for as aforesaid ...".[10]

London also made it legal for the Royal Navy to confiscate the ships, the equipment and the goods (mostly slaves) of the enemies. The vast majority, over 95% of all vessels captured under the anti-slave trade treaties that Britain had secured from Portugal, Spain, the Netherlands and Brazil between 1819 and 1871, were taken by ships of the Royal Navy. Under British rule, established mixed commissions were responsible for the condemnation of over 600 slave vessels and the "liberation" of 160,000 slaves. Most of the so-called "Liberated Africans" lived on further as peasants in villages in Sierra Leone, Jamaica, the Bahamas and Trinidad. Only Britain exercised the right of search outside its own territorial waters. Warrants to search ships suspected of illegal slaving activities were issued to British warships at all foreign stations, which became part of the network of mixed commissions. As Robin Blackburn wrote in his article, "Emancipation & Empire, from Cromwell to Karl Rove": "The Atlantic slave trade had created large scale slave raiding and trading complex. With its end, large numbers of slaves were available on the African market at low prices."[11]

From the English to the British slave trade, 1550 - 1807

From the beginning of the 16th century, English merchants were involved in the illegal Atlantic slave trade. Most of them co-operated with Lançado pilots, who knew very well the African and American coasts since the days of conquering. English merchants from Plymouth like William Hawkins and later his son, John as well as his cousin Francis Drake, supplied Spanish and Portuguese ports in the Americas with slaves. The Portuguese learned from local merchants how to trade slaves along the African coast and drew on this trade to establish sugar plantations. During the first third of the 17th cen-

---

[10] 47 Georgii III, Session 1, cap. XXXVI. An Act for the Abolition of the Slave Trade, [25th March 1807.] http://www.pdavis.nl/Legis_06.htm (7.11.2012).

[11] BLACKBURN Robin, Emancipation & Empire, from Cromwell to Karl Rove. In: Daedalus, On Imperialism, 134, 2 (Spring, 2005), pp. 72-87, here p. 74.

tury, the English started to found own their colonies in the Americas. Now the English slave traders operated legally for their own colonies. In 1672 the royal Stuarts established the Royal African Company (RAC), which became a monopoly for the English slave trade between Africa and the Americas. For the next 17 years the RAC founded many slave depots on the Western African shores and sold between 95,000 and 100,000 African slaves to the Americas.[12] During the last decade of the 17th century, the English slave trade advanced and became one of the most important financial supports of their economy. In 1698 the RAC lost their monopoly and new private slave trading companies, like the well-known company of the slave trader Edward Colston from Bristol, developed. Because of the rise of many different slave-trading companies, the English business with African bodies quickly increased.[13]

In1707 the Empire of Great Britain emerged and strengthened its position as the first Atlantic colonial power, with its victory in the war of the Spanish succession in 1714. One of the British goals of this war was to take hold of the Asiento de negros treaty, whichexisted from 1543 up to 1834. Until the British received the Asiento in 1713, the Spanish fit out the French *Compagnie de Guinée et de l'Assiente*. The Asiento de negros treaty became a key for the economic and political success in Atlantic commerce because of its guarantee to be the only legalized slave trader in all Spanish colonies. During the negotiations of the peace treaty of Utrecht on March 26, 1713, the kings of Spain and Great Britain signed the *Asiento de negros*. Through the official character of the agreement, the *Asiento de negros* became a sort of early international law. In July of 1713 the two Atlantic powers signed a commercial treaty to reinforce the relations between them.[14] The treaty guaranteed the British many economic advantages over

[12] ELTIS David, BEHRENDT S., RICHARDSON David, KLEIN Herbert S. (eds.), The Trans-Atlantic slave trade - a database on CD-Rom. Cambridge 1999; MICKLETHWAIT John, WOOLDRIGE Adrian, The Company: A Short History of a Revolutionary Idea. New York 2003; DAVIES Kenneth Gordon, The Royal African Company. New York 1999.

[13] DRESSER MAGDE, Squares of distinction, webs of interest: Gentility, urban development and the slave trade in Bristol.1673–1820. In: Slavery & Abolition: A Journal of Slave and Post-Slave Studies. 21, 3 (2000).

[14] Article XII of the treaty of Utrecht July13th 1713. A Collection of Treaties be-

the Spanish crown. In1711 the South Sea Company was founded by the British Secretary of the Treasury Lord Robert Harley and the investor Sir John Blunt and others. The South Sea Company lent Spanish King Philipp V the amount of 200,000 pesos, with a run-time over 20 years. Although both kings were each participating with a quarter of the profit of the South Sea Company, the dependency as debtor weakened the Spanish crown. In 1716 the Spanish agreed to a 30-years run-time of the *Asiento de negros* for the South Sea Company.

The Spanish permitted the South Sea Company the annual importation of 4,800 pieces of India (piezas de India)[15], which corresponded to an amount of 144,000 slaves during a period of 30 years. Moreover the Spanish Crown allowed the South Sea Company to send a 500-ton heavy ship (Navío de Permiso) to visit the annual fair of Portobelo, Cartagena de Indias and Veracruz, where it had the right to sell goods tax-free.

During 25 years the South Sea Company managed altogether 96 voyages, where it sold 34,000 slaves of whom 30,000 survived the voyages across the Atlantic (11% mortality rate).[16] After the big bubble burst of

tween Great Britain and Other Powers, George Chalmers, Printed for J. Stockdale, 1790: http://en.wikisource.org/wiki/Peace_and_Friendship_Treaty_of_Utrecht_between_Spain_and_Great_Britain#ARTICLE_XII (July 3rd, 2012).

15 A Piece of India, was a unit of value in the slave trade in West Africa through the Cape Verde Islands during the 16th to 18th centuries. One piece was the value of a healthy male or female slave between 15 to 25 years of age. Slaves between 25 and 35, and between 8 and 15 years were valued at 2/3 a piece. Slaves outside this age range and those infirm were valued lower. The piece was used to establish quotas and tariffs.

16 CARSWELL John, The South Sea Bubble. Cresset Press. London 1960; DICKSON P. G. M., The Financial Revolution in England: A Study in the Development of Public Credit, 1688-1756. London 1967; DONNAN Elizabeth, The Eighteenth Century, Documents Illustrative of the History of the Slave Trade to America, 2. Washington, DC 1931; GARBER Peter M., ‚Famous First Bubbles'. In: Journal of Economic Perspectives, 4 (1990), pp. 35-54; HABBAKUK John, Marriage, Debt, and the Estates System: English Landownership, 1650-1950. Oxford 1985; MANNING Patrick, ‚Migrations of Africans to the Americas: The Impact on Africans, Africa, and the New World'. In: Slave Trades, 1500-1800: Globalization of Forced Labour, ed. by Patrick Manning. Aldershot 1996, pp. 65-82; NEAL Larry, The Rise of Financial Capitalism: International Capital Markets in the Age of Reason. Cambridge 1990; PORTER Roy, English Society in the Eighteenth Century. Middlesex 1984; SORSBY Victoria G., ‚British Trade with Spanish America under the Asiento, 1713-1740' (unpublished doctoral thesis, Univer-

1720, the South Sea Company had its greatest economic success. The slave trade flourished like never before. In 1732 the books of Liverpool harbour recorded 101 slave traders, one of London 135, with even Bristol recording 150 slave traders.[17] The English port cities became rich and invested the capital of the slave trade and the sugar industries into the improvement of the trade infrastructure. They founded different joint-stock companies, which financed the construction of a sophisticated network of roads, canals, aqueducts and tunnels in England and some of their colonies. Between 1750 and 1820 the British extended their network of waterways on the British Islands from 5000 to 6600 km. Without doubt the triangular slave trade pushed the development of the Industrial Revolution and strengthened the capital based economy:

> By 1750 there was hardly a trading or manufacturing town in England which was not in some way connected with the triangular or direct colonial trade. The profits obtained thereby provided one of the main streams of that accumulation of capital in England which financed the Industrial revolution[18]

Until the year 1750 the South Sea Company possessed the *Asiento*, except during periods of war between Spain and Great Britain — 1718-1721, and 1727-1729 — when the treaty was suspended. During these periods of war, the British increased their slave smuggling activities through interlopers from different countries, not only from Great Britain. The illicit trade was much more lucrative and nobody could stop it any more. The relations between Spain and Great Britain suffered from these illegal practices. Several small-armed conflicts followed up until the case of Captain Jenkins in 1739,

---

sity of London, 1975; SPERLING John G.,The South Sea Company: An Historical Essay and Bibliographical Finding List, In: The Kress Library of Business and Economics, 17. Cambridge, MA 1962; STECKEL Richard H., JENSEN Richard A., ‚New Evidence on the Causes of Slave and Crew Mortality in the Atlantic Slave Trade'. In: Journal of Economic History, 46 (1986), pp. 57-77; THOMAS Robert Paul, NELSON BEAN Richard, ‚The Fishers of Men: The Profits of the Slave Trade'. In: Journal of Economic History, 34 (1974), pp. 885-914.

17 FRANCO José Luciano, Comercio clandestino de esclavos. La Habana 1980, p. 42.

18 WILLIAMS Eric, Capitalism and Slavery, Richmond, Virginia. University of North Carolina Press, p. 52.

where the situation collapsed completely and a larger conflict, the "Jenkins ear war" or "Guerra de Asiento" (1739-1742) broke out.

The treaty of the palace of Buen Retiro in Madrid in 1750 concluded the *Asiento* for the South Sea Company. The Spanish Crown paid a transfer fee of about 100.000 pound sterling to quit the Asiento with Great Britain.[19] After 37 years of legal British slave trade to Spanish America, the British slave traders continued as "free traders" (though called by the Spanish,smugglers), when they sold their slaves to the Spanish colonies. Most of these long distance merchants had long experiences as free traders and became rich. Some of them invested their money in the sugar estates of Jamaica, Barbados and Nevis, where mechanization revolutionized work.[20] But it was the island of Jamaica, where this development reached a level never before seen. Between 1751 and 1800 the sum of 582,075 slaves arrived on the small island of Jamaica.[21] If we compare this with the arrival of 131,030 slaves to the British Mainland of North America during the same period, we comprehend the importance of Jamaica for the British colonial economy at this time. Only the French colony of Saint Domingue, with the arrival of 593,030 slaves, and Southeast Brazil with 655,090 arrived slaves, topped Jamaica by quantity.

The so-called "free trade" of the British supported the illegal Atlantic slave trade during the second half of the 18th century. The African kingdom

---

19 POSTLETHWAYT Malachy, The Universal Dictionary of Trade and Commerce. London, 1751, fol. (3rd edit. London, 1766, fol.; 4th edit. London, 1774, fol.); CLARKSON Thomas, The History of the Rise, Progress and Accomplishment of the Abolition of the African Slave Trade by the British Parliament. Vol I. London 1808. http: //www.gutenberg.org/files/12428/12428-8.txt (Zugriff: 3.7.2012); GARDINER DAVENPORT Frances, PAULLIN Charles Oscar (eds.), European Treaties Bearing on the History of the United States and its Dependencies (4 vols., Washington, 1917-1937), IV, pp. 79-80.

20 About the mechanization of sugar estates in Jamaica see the daily journals of Thomas Thistlewood, who was the manager and owner of properties in Western Jamaica. BECKLES Hilary, Centering Woman: gender discourses in Caribbean slave society. Ian Randle Publishers. Kingston 1999, pp. 38-58; Hall Douglas, In Miserable Slavery: Thomas Thistlewood in Jamaica, 1750-1786. London 1987;SHEPHERD Verene, Livestock, Sugar & Slavery: Contested Terrain in Colonial Jamaica. Kingston 2009.

21 ELTIS et al. (eds), Trans Atlantic Slave trade data base.

of Dahomey profited very much from this new kind of slave trade. From 1770 on they sold annually slaves worth 250.000 pounds sterling.

The American War of Independence (1776-1783) was, too, a consequence of the struggle for hegemony in the Atlantic slave trade between France and Great Britain. Because of the war in the Atlantic, the legal supply with African slaves stopped and the illicit trade flourished like never before. Now nobody could stop the demand of free trade and by royal order of May 28, 1795, the Peruvian ports of Callao and Paita next opened to free and direct Negro traffic by sea; and finally, following successive extensions of time,[22] Guayaquil and Panama were granted the same privilege in a royal *cedula* of April 22, 1804.[23] The so-called "illegal slave trade" became legal and the prices for slaves went rapidly down.

Mixed commissions or how the British robbed slaves

With the beginning of the 19th century, Great Britain started to manipulate the slave market to stop the expiry of the price for slaves. The solution to this problem was the abolition of the slave trade, which included the birth of a new illicit slave trade. The first European power to formally declare the abolition of the transatlantic slave trade was Denmark in 1792. The implementation of this law took time until 1803. In 1807/08 followed the abolition of the US-American and the British Atlantic slave trades as a consequence of the Napoleonic war as well as the First Barbary War.[24] During the congress of Vienna 1814/15, the British government propagated the abolition of the transatlantic slave trade and assured its new colonies, which were robbed from the Dutch, like Essequibo, Demerara, Berbice, the French, like Tobago and the St. Lucia, and from the Spanish, the island of

22 Francisco de Saavedra to the viceroy of the Rio de la Plata, Aranjuez, April 12, 1798, D.H.A., VII, pp. 145-146.

23 About the prolongation of slave trade: Cedula Real (Madrid, 1804). This cedula is printed in D.H.A., VII, pp. 281-287.

24 ROJAS Martha Elena. "Insults Unpunished" Barbary Captives, American Slaves, and the Negotiation of Liberty." In: Early American Studies: An Interdisciplinary Journal. 1, 2 (2003), pp. 159-186; PFEISINGER (2005), p. 65. TAVARES (1988), p. 91; GERSON (1975), p. 9; JACOB (1974), p. 209.

Trinidad. Only the new Kingdom of the Netherlands signed the abolition of the slave trade in Vienna in 1814, followed by France and Portugal in 1815. In 1817 Spain agreed to sign, but only for its trade north of the equator, as Portugal agreed to two years before. In 1820 Spain also guaranteed the end of its slave trade south of the equator. Now the legal slave trade was almost finished, and the illicit slave trade flourished like never before. But the Brazilian Empire, founded in 1822, undermined the British policy and intensified its slave trade with African kingdoms and Portuguese colonies in Africa.

One of the most important consequences of Britain's campaign for the abolition of the transatlantic slave trade in the 19th century was the establishment of several International Tribunals. They adjudicated upon vessels seized on suspicion of trading in African slaves after the trade had been declared illegal.[25] Therefore Britain signed treaties with Portugal, Spain, the Netherlands, Brazil, the US and several Latin American Republics. In November of 1824 Britain signed an anti-slave trade agreement with Sweden with the right of search, but because the slave trade was no longer carried under the Swedish Flag, they didn't established any Anglo-Swedish mixed commission. For the period of 1819 to 1871, we found mixed or joined commissions in Freetown, Luanda, Cape of the Good Hoop, St. Helena Boa Vista (Cabo Verde), Rio de Janeiro, Paramaribo, Spanish Town (Jamaica), Havana and New York. The commissions were responsible for the condemnation of over 600 slave vessels and the "liberation" of almost 160,000 slaves. At the Foreign Office records, PRO, slave trade series (F.O.84) in London, we can find the correspondences of British officials of the different mixed commissions as well as in the archive of the mixed commissions in Freetown (F.O.315), Cape Good Hope (F.O.312), Spanish Town (F.O.314), Havana (F.O.313) and Rio de Janeiro (F.O.128, 129, 131).[26]

To prevent slave vessels from illegally crossing the Atlantic, the British government used ships of the Royal Navy. They also claimed the right to visit and search vessels from other countries on the high seas. The US

---

25 BETHELL Leslie, The mixed commissions for the Suppression of the transatlantic slave trade in the nineteenth century. In: Journal of African History, VII (1966), pp.79-93 here p. 79.

26 Foreign Office records, PRO, Slave trade series (F.O.84) London.

and France initially refused this British stipulation of the anti-slave trade agreements, but Portugal (July 28, 1817), Spain (September 23, 1817) and the Netherlands (May 4, 1818) signed the convention under which it was agreed that, outside ports and roadsteads and beyond the cannon-shot of shore batteries, ships of war of either power, furnished with the necessary special warrants, might visit and search merchant vessels of either power suspected on reasonable grounds of having on board African slaves. Yes, except for the Royal Navy, there was no other navy that had the capacity to for anti-slave trade patrol. It was further agreed that the captured ship would be taken for adjudication before one of two mixed commissions, one placed in the British Territory in West Africa and the other, across the Atlantic in Spanish, Portuguese or Dutch territory.

The composition of the mixed commissions included a commissary judge and a commissioner of arbitration from each nation. Further, a secretary or registrar was appointed by the government in whose territory the commission was situated. The commission decided on the trading practices of slave ships, whether the cargo was legal or illicit, and also on the legality of ship seizure. Further, the commissions decided whether to liberate captured cargo, i.e. slaves, or else acquit and restore both vessel and slaves. However, the commissions were given no jurisdiction over the owners, master or crew of a condemned vessel: individuals were to be handed over to their own authorities for trial and punishment in their own courts and according to their own laws. Since 1819 there was an Anglo-Spanish Commission in Havana and an Anglo-Portuguese in Rio de Janeiro, and since 1820, an Anglo-Dutch Commission in Paramaribo in Guyana. The Foreign Office in London, which was responsible for the commissions, in 1820 founded its headquarters for the mixed commissions in the Sierra Leone's port city, Freetown. It was in Sierra Leone, where the British Government established in 1807/08 a Crown colony, because of the bankruptcy of the Sierra Leone Company. Thus, in Freetown, a Vice-admiralty court already existed, which dealt with British and, occasionally, foreign slave ships captured by the Royal Navy during the Coalition Wars. They assumed belligerent rights to stop and search the ships of all nations, and whenever they came across a slave trader, they further assumed that their own abolition law applied, and thus confiscated vessel and captives alike.

Sierra Leone advanced as a colony for liberated Africans and received quickly slaves from condemned ships. But on the other hand, the disadvantage of Freetown was that it was especially dangerous for the white British commissary judges; a lot of them died at their posts.[27] Even though Freetown was in control of overseeing the illegal slave trade, it was far away from the centres of slave trade, such as in the Bights of Benin and Biafra and after 1839, even further south, in the delta of the Congo. Some British officials proposed to move the mixed commission from Freeport to the island of Bioko, formerly Fernando Pó, to control the Niger Delta. In 1828 the Spaniards permitted the British Captain W. F. W. Owen to construct suitable buildings for a mixed court on the island. Nevertheless, Madrid refused to transfer to Britain its sovereignty over the island because they suspected the abolition of slaves there.[28]

With the independence of Brazil in 1822 the new South American Empire went on stage and in 1826, signed its first Anglo-Brazilian treaty, where the Brazilian slave trade became illegal, thereafter officially designating it as piracy. Thereby Brazil incorporated the Anglo-Portuguese convention of 1815 and 1817 — with the right of search — word for word. Thus the Anglo-Portuguese mixed commission, which was established in Rio de Janeiro in 1819, became Anglo-Brazilian in the period of 1828. In 1830 the Brazilian government, represented by ambassador Mello Mattos in London, called unsuccessfully for a cancellation of the treaty because of the piracy stipulation (F. O. 84/111). The mixed commission in Rio de Janeiro continued legitimately until March 1845.[29]

Another problem was that a majority of slave traders used flags of other nations that were not part of the treaty, so the British Foreign Secretary Lord Palmerton demanded a new piracy act against them. In 1839, the final breakdown of negotiations with Portugal for a new anti-slave trade treaty happened. The treaty was designed to give the British navy the powers it

---

27 BETHELL (1966) p. 81.

28 ONWUKA K., Trade and Politics in the Niger Delta, 1830-1885. Oxford 1956, p. 55-60.

29 About the correspondences see Mello Mattos to Aberdeen, 4. October 1830, F.O. 84/111, Foreign Secretary Lord Palmerston to Mello Mattos, 10 December 1830 F.O. 83/111 and also based on a order of the Law Officers from 28 July 1831 (F.O. 83, Great Britain and General) on 16 August 1831, F.O. 84/122.

needed to suppress the extensive slave trade to Brazil and Cuba, which was being carried out on under the Portuguese flag. As a result the British Government decided to carry out its repeated threat to take matters into its own hands and treat slaves ships flying the Portuguese flag ‚summarily and by its own authority as Pirates and Outlaws‘.

In 1831, the US and France refused to co-operate with the British and founded their own national courts. The Latin American Republics of Argentina (1839), Uruguay (1839), Chile (1839), Bolivia (1840), and Ecuador (1841) signed treaties conceding the right of search, under which captured ships were to be taken before courts of mixed commissions, but waived their right to establish mixed commissions in their own territory. In fact only two ships of Latin American slave traders, ever came for the mixed commission in Sierra Leone; both were from Uruguay and in the years, 1851 and 1861.[30]

In the case of Brazil, Lord Palmerston used secret service funds to bribe Brazilian politicians (including the negotiator of the anti-slavetrade treaty), subsidize Brazilian newspapers to print anti-slave-trade material, and hire a network of spies around the Atlantic world. Finally, in 1850, Palmerston authorized the navy to invade Brazilian waters and destroy the property of slave traders, a clear casus belli.

The British preventive squadron only seized a small proportion of slave ship voyages, which annually crossed illegally the Atlantic to the Americas, mainly to Brazil and Cuba. New research at the Schomburg Center for Research in Black Culture in New York City published on its website that

> of 6,921 voyages known to have been involved in the slave trade after 1807, 1,799 (about 22 percent) were interrupted when the ships were captured, and all but 233 of these detained ships were taken by the British navy. Many were empty and were condemned for carrying slave-trading equipment rather than slaves.[31]

If we take a look to the distribution of cases between the different courts during the period of 1819 to 1845, we see that the mixed commissions in

[30] BETHELL (1966), p. 81.

[31] http://abolition.nypl.org/essays/suppression/4/ (July 8, 2012)

Sierra Leone were the most successful institutions[32]:

Sierra Leone[33]:
Anglo-Spanish commission: 241
Anglo-Portuguese commission: 155
Anglo-Brazilian commission: 111
Anglo-Dutch commission: 21

Havana: 50
Rio de Janeiro 44
Paramaribo 1 (1823)

In Freetown, the British commissioners found themselves sitting alone because the officials of the other nations often quickly perished in Sierra Leone. On the other hand, in cities like Havana and Rio de Janeiro British commissioners didn't have the most agreeable lives because of angry groups of merchants and anti-imperialistic movements, which regarded the rights of the commissioners as a violation of sovereignty. The officer who made the capture first had to make an affidavit before the registrar of the court, and then hand over any papers found on board, while describing the condition of the ship and the number of slaves. The British commissioners naturally tended to be more hostile towards the slave trade as their foreign colleagues. As Portugal and Brazil traded legally south the line (until 1839), it was priority to discover if the slaves had been shipped from prohibited areas. Condemnation started, if the ship was clearly equipped for slaving purposes: shackles, handcuffs, spare planks for a slave deck, open hatches, unusual quantities of fresh water, food, disinfectant or sometimes they incriminated because of the smell alone.

When the commission decided in favour of acquittal, the ship, the cargo and any slave on board were generally restored at once to the owner, when he claimed before. Damages were not included. If the vessel was condemned by the mixed commission, the British Government refused any

[32] Statistic results of the annual reports to the Foreign Office in London by British commissioners. BETHELL (1966), p. 84

[33] The peak was in 1839 when 62 cases held. Ibid.

claims of compensation. The vessels condemned were publicly auctioned, so the local British merchants in Sierra Leone bought very cheap ships and equipment. Some were bought on behalf of the slave traders, since sometimes the original owners and re-entered the trade. Some of the ships, the Admiralty confiscated and converted into cruisers for anti-slave-trade patrol. The proceeds of the sales were divided between the two governments of the mixed commission.

But what did Britain do with the liberated slaves from the condemned vessels? In accordance with the anti-slave treaties, they delivered liberated slaves over to the government in whose territory the commission sat and employed them there, as free labourers or servants. But in practice, the majority of the liberated slaves were reduced to slavery because of the bad conditions of apprenticeship. Until the emancipation act of 1833, slavery in British colonies still existed and the so-called Liberated Africans who were removed to the British Caribbean came to the colonies slaves or later, as indentured servants. Another group became low-wage municipal workers in Brazilian cities. The least fortunate were spirited away to Cuban sugar plantations and effectively remained slaves or, worse, were sold a second time after being kidnapped from the Sierra Leone village where they had been resettled. The great majority did escape this fate, however, and their personal details are recorded in huge registers of "Liberated Africans", in archives in Freetown, Rio de Janeiro, and London. It is a fact, that many of the British actions were illegal. After the end of war, Great Britain broke even the nascent dictates of early-nineteenth-century international law because it continued to detain French and Spanish slave vessels quite illegally.

In Sierra Leone, liberated slaves were registered, as at King's Yard, as British citizens and sent to live and work in villages near Freetown. After the British curtailed the villages in Sierra Leone, they "persuaded" them to "immigrate" to the West Indies. According to K.O. Laurence's research, between 1840 and 1867 the British imported exactly 8,854 "Liberated Africans" to Trinidad, 14,060 to British Guiana, 11,391 to Jamaica and 5,027 to the British Windward Islands.[34] France also imported 16,380

[34] LAURENCE Keith Ormiston, Immigration into the West Indies in the 19th century. Caribbean Universities Press. London 1971, pp. 10-19, p. 26, p. 36, pp. 39-45, p. 57.

to the French Caribbean. If we compare this sum of "indentured labour" with the East Indians and Chinese during the same time (1840/67), we have to realize that the 55,712 Africans represented the largest group.

The Bahamas connection

In 1811 the British government started an experimental system of apprenticeship in its colonies. Until the year 1826, approximately 1,400 liberated Africans, who were liberated from foreign slave owners, landed in the Bahamas. Until the end of slavery in the British colonies in 1838, perhaps 6,500 liberated Africans had reached the islands of the Bahamas. The liberated Africans willingly filled the temporary shortage of unskilled labour caused by the export of slaves to the sugar islands. The freed captives of 1811, almost 100% male, were housed in military complexes. Repatriation was said to be out of the question. A collector started quickly to distribute the liberated Africans. A fifth was recruited into the second West India Regiment, the local detachment of the Royal Artillery and the naval flotilla on station, while the remainder was apprenticed as labourers for seven years (renewable for a further seven) or as a domestic for fourteen years. Around a quarter of the first apprentices were employed by the Crown.

Local whites claimed that all liberated Africans were ignorant and troublesome and signed petitions against fresh importations, whenever a slave ship and its cargo appeared before the Vice-admiralty court. For example, when a Spanish slaver was wrecked at Green Turtle Cay, Abaco, in 1816, and a proposal was made to free the three hundred Africans it was carrying in New Providence, certain "People of Nassau" petitioned Governor Charles Cameron. They claimed that the Liberated Africans already in New Providence were the most "worthless and troublesome class of black people in town of Nassau, where unluckily they are nearly all centred".[35] The liberated Africans did not associate with the other Negroes because of their unique status as neither slave nor free; they misbehaved at work and leisure because they knew that they would be eventually be fully freed; and they

[35] CRATON Michael/SAUNDERS Gail, Islanders in the stream. A history of the Bahamian people. From the ending of slavery to the 21st century. Vol. 2, Athens 1998, p. 6.

had no desire or need to work properly for their masters, behaving in a superior manner because they felt they were protected by the Crown and had no loyalty to the colony. On the other hand, the white class asserted that the newcomers depressed the labour market because they were working for almost nothing and would displace more Creole labourers. Most of the liberated Africans proved at least as industrious as slaves, because of their skills learned in Africa, like the Iboes and Yoruba, who were ingenious craftsmen, traders and organizers. African recruits have left no direct testimony about their willingness to emigrate.[36]

Conclusion

During the 19th century in Europe increased the demand for sugar, coffee and cotton, even though the bad working conditions of the plantation industry and slavery, in general, were well known. In 1867, he Austrian explorer, circumnavigator and diplomat Carl von Scherzer published a statistic, though a worldwide comparison, that is similar to the statistic arrived at by Dale Tomich (presented by the colloquium at the University of Cologne) on the sugar production of Cuba, Jamaica and Guyana,. Scherzer, comparing the worldwide sugar production in 1849, 1857 and 1859, asserted that Cuba's production increased from 220.000 to 415.000 tons, followed by the British colonies, which produced in 1849, 259.700 tons that then increased to 460.000 tons; Mauritius followed with 120.000, and India with 160.000 tons.[37]

The difference between the consumer (Europe) and the producer (America, Africa, and Asia) opened a new discourse on "Civilization versus Barbary". The British decision of 1807 about the end of the transatlantic slave trade seems to be an outcome of a long discussion about human rights,

---

[36] NORTHRUP David, Freedom and Consent in the Recruitment of African Labour. In: GAMES Alison, ROTHMAN Adam (eds.), Major Problems in Atlantic History: Documents and Essays. Boston 2008. pp.443-447 here p.446.

[37] SCHERZER Carl von, Statistisch-commerzielle Ergebnisse einer Reise um die Erde, unternommen an Bord der österreichischen Fregatte Novarra in den Jahren 1857-1859. Brockhaus. Leizig-Wien 1867.

but on closer inspection, it was just the outcome of the transition process from mercantilism to capitalism. Bodies and, especially, the human bodies of Africans were the most important capital of the 19th century and depended on the terms of trade akin toother "goods". The robbery of slaves from illegal slaves shipping vessels was by no means new. We know this practice from the period of the famous privateers during the 17th century. But the robbery of the 19th century was somewhat different because the slave ships were declared by British law as illegal, and the slaves robbed by them were liberated (kidnapped) in the name of the law. As "free labourers" but also as "liberated slaves", the British sold or assigned them to their own colonies or to foreign colonies, like Cuba and Puerto Rico or to the Empire of Brazil.

Peasant or Proletarian: Emancipation and the struggle for Freedom in British Guiana in the shadow of the Second Slavery

Wazir MOHAMED

Ph.D. Assistant Professor of Sociology
Indiana University East, Richmond, Indiana, USA
November 2012

Introduction

Former slaves of Guyana (British Guiana), who acquired miniscule parcels of land and moved into villages in the vicinity of sugar plantations, while maintaining a working relationship with the plantation system, have been mischaracterized in the main body of literature and writings dealing with the post emancipation period (after 1838) as having constituted themselves into a peasantry.[1] The main body of historical literature and historical analysis that emerged in the early and mid- to late-twentieth century sought to shape the understanding of the outcome for ex-slaves after emancipation in British Guiana as having constituted themselves into a peasantry.[2] Hence the concept "peasant" has found common usage in the literature as students of history have attempted to designate and categorize those former slaves who moved into what is commonly known as the free villages.[3]

1 Guyana, Guiana, and British Guiana are used interchangeably in this essay – The colony British Guiana became Guyana after political independence in 1966. Guyana is bordered on the East by Suriname (Dutch Guiana), on the South by Brazil, on the West by Venezuela, and on the North by the Atlantic Ocean.

2 See among others the works of Lowell Ragatz. The Fall of the Planter Class in the British Caribbean. New York: The Century Co, 1928; Jay R Mandle. The Plantation Economy. Philadelphia: Temple University Press, 1973; Rawle Farley. "The Rise of a Peasantry in British Guiana." Social and Economic Studies, 2, 4 (1957): 87-103.

3 The concept "free villages" is commonly used in the literature to designate contiguous (abandoned plantations cooperatively bought by ex-slaves) settlements primarily over

This essay joins with newer scholars who have attempted to correct the analysis of the historical record. In particular, Walter Rodney (1978 and 1981) and, to a lesser extent, Douglas Hall (1978) in separate studies sought to correct and inform the analysis of the historical record.[4] This is important for several reasons, the most pertinent being the need for students of history to learn to decolonize their minds by emphasizing the reading of history from the standpoint of the toilers, and not from that of the oppressing ruling classes. Secondly, the re-reading is relevant as we try to locate the historical and structural reasons and factors that account for the divided society of British Guiana (renamed Guyana at the time of political independence from Great Britain in 1966). A distinguishing feature of Guyanese society is the easily observable and easily perceptible levels of inequality between the descendants of slaves, the descendants of indenture, and the ruling classes. Inequality based on race/ethnicity and class is reflected in the organization of its villages and towns and, indeed, of the society. Thirdly, based on these divisions in the society, the re-reading is important to correct the historical anomaly out of which the perception arises, which informs the sub-culture, that the African people (descendants of slaves) are somewhat economically unequal in relation to East Indians (descendants of indenture) because they are "lazy."[5] I have addressed the root of this division in other places and will not dwell upon it here.[6] But while I do that, it is important to point out in

---

the years 1838-1848 in the vicinity of sugar plantations where ex-slaves (Africans) organized living arrangements from where they attempted to establish trade union like activity.

4 Walter Rodney, "Plantation Society in Guyana," Review 4, 4 (1981): 643-666; Douglas Hall, "The Flight from the Estates Reconsidered: The British West Indies, 1838-42," The Journal of Caribbean History 10&11 (1978): 7-24.

5 The concept "lazy" has taken on common cultural usage in many of the former slave colonies to answer the question as to why peoples of African heritage are at the bottom of the social ladder in the Americas. In the context of Guyana the use of this word to describe the African population was introduced in the colonial literature to account for poverty in the "free villages" after 1850. Note is made that this word was not part of the literature that accounts for the progress in the "free villages" over the period 1838-1848.

6 Indentured labor was brought in large numbers from India to supplement and downgrade the ability of Africans to bargain for decent wages and conditions in the sugar plantations after slavery ended. The phrase East Indians (Coolies in the Colonial Period) is commonly used to designate the descendants of indenture in Guyana.

passing, that the first time a peasantry was allowed — and I emphasize the word *allowed* — was in the first decade of the twentieth century, when an East Indian rice peasantry was permitted to develop, as the local economy was being diversified away from the sugar monoculture in the aftermath of the global sugar crisis, which began in the mid 1880s.[7] Fourthly, from this backdrop, the re-reading takes on more importance because it forces us to acknowledge and account for the role and local impact of the second slavery on the divergent outcomes for labor (African and East Indian) in one of the new sugar producing colonies.[8]

The primary point of departure between newer studies, that is those that examine history from the point of view of the people, and those that adopted the analysis of the planter class with respect to the relations between labor and capital in British Guiana, have to do with the extent to which ex-slaves or labor separated themselves from plantation labor and the plantation economy. The data does not support the claim of earlier scholarship that ex-slaves in British Guiana separated and broke off economic (labor/capital) relations with the plantation economy. They could not; the planter class and labor were required by the ecological determinant, backed up by land laws to inhabit the same physical space that is the coastal enclosure. The destiny of African labor was thus tied to their interaction with capital within the bounds of the plantation economy and plantation system.

7 The concept "East Indian Rice Peasantry" is used deliberately to express the racial/ethnic/cultural/economic division that was constructed as the economic diversification was permitted for the first time in the colony – The East Indian population was able to benefit from this change of policy for two reasons. Firstly, the colonial authorities had to find an answer to the glut in the labor market created by the global sugar crisis which began in the mid 1880s. And secondly, to answer this problem, the land market was liberalized to allow the East Indian population to acquire land at very cheap rates in areas outside the enclosure (the coastal area or the plantation zone from the sea dam to the crown dam was the main and only precinct of permitted habitation until the 1897 land laws). Inequality in access and ownership of land between the African and East Indian populations is related to the land laws that created the enclosure, and land laws that served to break the enclosure. The enclosure was constructed through land laws to protect the interest of the sugar planters to keep labor rates cheap in the period of local competition in the global sugar market driven by the second slavery.

8 The concept "African" is used interchangeably in this essay to designate the descendants of slaves. At times the word African, and at other times the word ex-slaves is used.

The plantation system operated within what I describe as a sort of "coastal enclosure." The pertinence of this term is related to the fact that the planter class operated within this area; but not only did they operate in this area, they debarred through enforcement of land laws any significant movement of the African population out of this zone.[9]

The coastal enclosure or plantation space was not only a physical enclosure bounded by the sea from in front and floods from behind, it was also an economic and political enclosure bounded by the sugar monoculture, and the political control the sugar barons exercised over government.[10] The maps below were retrieved from David Rumsey's historical map collection, which features John Arrowsmith's depiction of land usage in a section of Guyana's coastline in 1838. And secondly, a map of the organization of habitation along the Atlantic coastline of Guyana taken from Walter Rodney's History of the Guianese Working People is included here to help in explaining the problems of ecology, which was effectively used in the period of the second slavery to create the physical, economic, and political enclosure until the end of the nineteenth century. Note the contiguous relationship between sugar plantations and village settlements. Also, take note of the pressure of water from in-front and behind, and how physical barriers to independent economic activity are impossible, in such circumstances, if monoculture is imposed on the economy, as it was between 1838 and 1897, through law-making and political control. The first map helps to explain, through the shaded areas on the Atlantic Coast, the way in which the economy was hemmed into a small area. The second map helps us to see the division between plantations and villages living in proximity to one another, as well as their relationship to the ocean and the pressure of water from the interior.[11]

---

9 For description of land laws passed to keep the African population within the coastal plantation enclosure see Allan Young. The Approaches to Local Self-Government in British Guiana. Longman, Green & Co. ltd, 1958: 10; also see British Guiana Colonial Ordinances No. 4 of 1851, Nos. 1 & 2 of 1852, and No. 33 of 1856.

10 For details on the struggles to create and maintain this enclosure, or plantation space – see Walter Rodney. History of the Guianese Working People, 1881-1905. London: Johns Hopkins University Press, 1981: 1-19.

11 John Arrowsmith, Map of British Guiana from the latest surveys of Schomburg et al., retrieved from www.davidrumsey.com/luna/servlet/detail/Rumsey; Walter Rodney 1981:

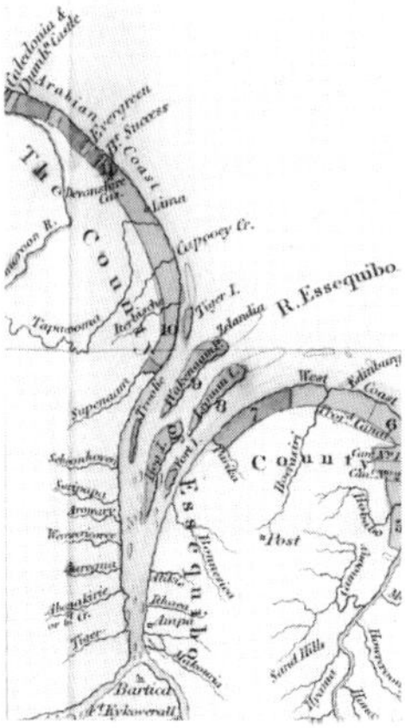

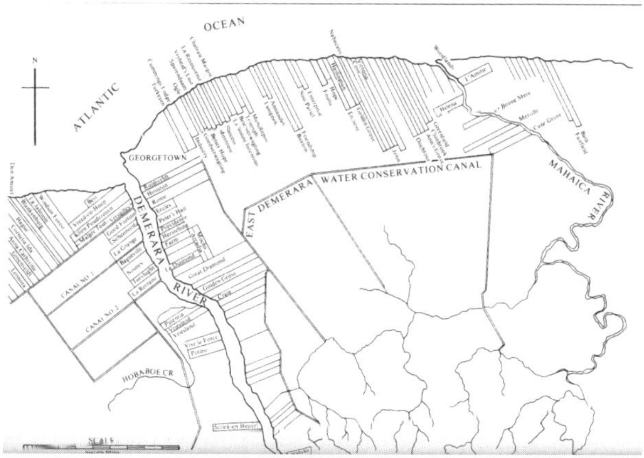

It is from this ecological background that the planter class was able to organize to gain the upper hand. The post-emancipation struggle for control was thus located within these enclosures, where the economy was driven by the sugar monoculture. After emancipation, the ex-slaves were forced, by dint of ecological circumstance and the political economy governing the enclosure, to organize their freedom within these constraints.

Hence, one of the major points of departure between the outcome for Africans in post-emancipation Guyana and those in the older colonies of the British Caribbean was the nature and character of their relationship to plantation labor. In Guyana, the relationship to plantation labor was governed by the control over land and resources by the sugar monoculture economy; whereas in the older colonies, the relationship to plantation labor was determined by the diversification of the sugar economy, and the opening up of land beyond the plantation zone to former slaves.[12] There is no evidence that suggests significant levels of diversification away from sugar's domi-

8

[12] The evidence of diversification in places such as Jamaica and St. Vincent brings out the difference between outcomes between Guyana and the old colonies. In the old colonies the ex-slave populations were engaged as small landed proprietors in the production of new tradable commodities, such as Logwood, Mahogany, Coconuts, Arrowroot, Beeswax, Honey, Fustic, and so on. For analysis on diversification and participation of ex-slaves in the export economy see Eric Williams. From Columbus to Castro. New York: Random House, 1970: 338-339

nance of the economy of British Guiana between 1838 and 1900.[13] On the other hand, there is overwhelming evidence that suggests there was growing competition between former slave communities and the plantation system in the overall economy in the older colonies. The point here is that while there was a precipitous movement of ex-slaves away from plantation housing over the period 1838-1848 in British Guiana, this cannot be confused or construed, as the old literature does, with movement away from availability for continued work on plantations. In the formative literature, movement of ex-slaves away from plantation housing in British Guiana in that period has been construed and, hence, constructed as their counterparts in the other land-endowed colonies of the British West Indies (case in point Jamaica) have been, that is, as having constituted themselves into a peasantry.

Rodney and Hall, speaking through the historical data, explained that in British Guiana, what was witnessed was "residential withdrawal," not withdrawal from availability for plantation labor. Writing in the late 1970s, these scholars separated themselves from others, such as Gisela Eisner (1961), Woodville Marshall (1968 and 1972), Rawle Farley (1953 and 1956), Alan Adamson (1972), and Jay Mandle (1973) all of whom sought to analyze the post-emancipation rupture between the former slaves and the plantation as a total "flight from the plantation," and, hence, the arrival and baptism of those who organized independent village settlements, while maintaining the desire to labor on the plantations, as having constituted themselves into a "peasantry."

The formative literature thus gave birth to the construct, "Guyanese Peasantry," without regard to the specificity of the local economy as it responded to global change and how this changed labor/capital relations; it also paid little or no attention to the local ecology and how ecology aided the planter class in their attempts to limit the scope for independent economic lives away from plantation labor. The motion and activity of former slaves in Guyana and the older land-endowed colonies are locked together

---

13 Alan Adamson. Sugar without Slaves. New Haven: Yale University Press, 1972: 215. See export tables for British Guiana between 1838 and 1904. There is no evidence in these tables that suggest ex-slave participation in an independent diversified economy because diversification was not significant. The ex-slave economy in British Guiana was subsumed in the plantation economy driven by sugar.

in this theoretical frame, without consideration for their specific roles and places in the reconfigured world market for sugar, a market driven by slave labor. It must be noted that though Guyana and Jamaica are former British colonies, the rural relations that developed after emancipation in each place resulted from and were connected to the specific world-economic conjuncture of the nineteenth century and each colony's relation to the developing structures of the global sugar market, which was being driven by the second slavery. Rural relations (labor planter relations) in Jamaica and Guyana began to diverge around 1815 and continued on that path through the remainder of the nineteenth century, as the global impact of the second slavery became the motor for change in each local sugar-producing area.[14]

After 1815 as Jamaica continued to lose its competitive edge to Cuba and as its internal economy became more diversified away from the sugar monoculture, British Guiana became a sugar monoculture economy and thus emerged as an active player (albeit minor player) in the developing sugar revolution of the nineteenth century. As a result, ex-slave/planter relations that developed in British Guiana were more akin to slave/planter relations in Cuba, and much different from those that developed in Jamaica and some of the other old colonies of the British West Indies. From this reference point, labor/planter relations in British Guiana must be understood with reference to the growth of slavery in Cuba and other new sugar colonies; which in the context of a unified world market for sugar, required the colonial planter class to reorganize the plantation labor process in order to cheapen labor. British Guiana is an anomaly; it is unique; it was not a mirror image of its West Indian counterparts. Its plantation history in the nineteenth century was different from the older colonies of the West Indies, with the exception of Trinidad and Tobago.

From this backdrop the label "peasant" ought to be examined from the backdrop of the divergent plantation history. The label "peasant" must be discussed from the experience of rural labor in its relationship to the plantation system, not in relationship to the notion "abundant land," as proposed in the formative literature. Mere presence, not accessibility, of abundant

[14] For analysis on the divergent development of Jamaica and Guyana vis a vis local sugar production in response to global change, see Dale Tomich. Slavery in the Circuit of Sugar. Baltimore: The Johns Hopkins University Press, 1990: 24-25.

land in British Guiana has been given credence and is connected to the idea of peasant growth. Availability and access to abundant land in the older colonies, as Eisner (1961) and Marshall (1968 and 1972) rightly point out, played a role in the growth of peasant development. But despite the presence of abundant land, post-emancipation outcomes for ex-slaves in British Guiana differ significantly from that which obtained in other areas of the region. Even though land was abundant in British Guiana, the control that the planter class exercised over arable land between 1838 and 1897 acted as a roadblock to the progression of the evolution of African villagers into a peasant class.

With this background in mind, the succeeding sections of this essay do two things: Firstly, they discuss the construct plantation ascent and/or decline and what this has meant for ex-slaves in British Guiana. And consequently, how plantation ascent and decline affects the meanings attached to the term, "Peasantries," as it relates to British Guiana and to the older West Indian colonies after emancipation. It is demonstrated that in each case, whether we speak about Guyana, Barbados, and/or Jamaica, the relative health of the plantation system in each location was determined and had an enduring influence on how those proto-peasantries of slavery, as Sidney Mintz has characterized them, were reconstituted after 1838.[15] This is done as a means of focusing attention on the decline thesis and the potency of this school of thought, as well as its relevance as a meter to measure historical outcomes in the different locations. In my view, each local experience must be isolated for investigation and analysis. One size does not fit all. It is in this connection that I reiterate that rural relations, which developed in British Guiana, ought to be contrasted with the rise of the "second slavery" in Cuba.

Secondly, noting that the plantation system in British Guiana was not in

[15] See Mintz, Sidney. "Slavery and the Rise of the Peasantries." in Roots and Branches, edited by Michael Craton. Toronto: Bergamon Press, 1979; Mintz, Sidney W. Caribbean Transformations. New York: Columbia University Press, 1974; Mintz, Sidney. "Decrying the Peasantry," Review 6, 2 (1982): 209-225; Mintz, Sidney. "The Question of Caribbean Peasantries: A comment." Caribbean Studies 1 (1961): 31-34; and Mintz, Sidney. "A Note on the Definition of Peasantries," The Journal of Peasant Studies 1 (1973): 91-106.

decline — rather it was on the ascent as the historical record demonstrates — I argue that those who Sidney Mintz described as the proto-peasants were not reconstituted into a peasantry in this colony, as the old literature would have us believe.[16] In British Guiana, the proto-peasants of slavery were reconstituted into what Walter Rodney describes as a rural proletariat.[17] Noting that after emancipation, in many places those ex-slaves, the African Creoles who Sidney Mintz describes as the proto-peasantry during slavery, were, to use his phraseology "reconstituted" into "peasantries." Mintz's conception, "peasant," and its historical relevance to Guyana and to the West Indies, are discussed against the empirical evidence of the everyday existence of the African Creoles after 1838 in British Guiana. The empirical evidence bucks such a linear categorization. From this backdrop, the emergence, meanings, and relevancy of the terms, "Peasantry" and "Guyanese Peasantry," are scrutinized. Special emphasis is placed on Rawle Farley's adaptation of the terminology, "peasant," in his work to conceptualize the emergence of the small, rural landholders class in Guyana.[18] This is necessary because, as mentioned before, the early conceptualization of this class as peasants serves as the foundation to the general body of early literature on the rural British Guiana that emerged.

The adoption of such a linear approach is of limited utility to a deeper comprehension of the character and nature of the transformations that emerged among and within Guyanese rural society. With that in mind, the generalized predominance of the decline thesis in scholarly works on the British Caribbean and its relevance to the history of Guyana after emancipation is fair game. The workability of the decline thesis which placed

---

16 Evidence in support of plantation ascent is located in the construction of the economy of British Guiana as a sugar monoculture, and the steady expansion of sugar production and exports between 1818 and 1887. The evidence of increase from 16,521 tons in 1815 to 131,127 tons debunks the decline thesis. See Deerr, Neol. The History of Sugar.2 vols. London: Chapman and Hall, 1949-50.

17 Rodney, Walter. "Plantation Society in Guyana," Review IV, 4 (1981)

18 Rawle Farley's work has been used to construct the idea that those who developed the free villages constituted a peasantry. See Farley, Rawle. "Rise of a Peasantry in British Guiana," Social and Economic Studies 2, 4 (1954): 87-103; and Farley, Rawle Egbert Griffith. "Aspects of the Economic History of British Guiana 1781-1852." PhD diss., University of London, 1956

Guyana within the realm of the socio-historical analysis of the old British West Indian Colonies, is problematic because the conception, "peasant," was misplaced or fused as analysts tried to extrapolate the relationships that developed as ex-slaves in British Guiana attempted to establish some form of autonomy within the ambit of planter dominance over the colonial state and economy. These analysts have treated British Guiana as though it was one of the countries within the West Indian Island chain, which began their long road of "decline" in the 1770s. The experience of plantation sugar in Guyana after 1815 cannot and ought not to be frozen in the economic, political, and social experiences of the geographic space called, the West Indies.

Plantation Rebirth in Guyana and the Decline Thesis

The now famous decline paradigm is the most persistent theme that has served as a guide to an understanding of the history of the West Indies. This interpretation was first put forth by Lowell Ragatz in his 1928 publication, *Fall of the Planter Class in the British West Indies,* and was later joined by Eric Williams in *Capitalism and Slavery*. These scholars promoted the view that the abolition of slavery was a consequence of the economic underdevelopment of the slave plantation system. In this light, their scholarship was based on the platform that slave abolition was a direct and natural outcome of the outmoded structure of the slave plantation system in the West Indies. They argued that by the mid-1770s, the slave plantation, which had served the British Empire well, was faltering and could not be sustained in the long term. Having established this approach to the understanding of the growth of anti-slavery within the British ruling class, they contended that the abolition decision was economic, rather than political and humanitarian. While this theory has been the subject of comparison, analysis and dispute, these will not detract me from the task at hand.[19]

[19] The most vociferous critic of Ragatz and Williams is Seymour Drescher, who explained that far from declining the plantation economy of the old sugar colonies, especially Jamaica grew in the short term between the period of the American Revolution and the time of slave abolition. See Seymour Drescher, Seymour. Econocide: British Slavery in the Era of Abolition. Pittsburgh: University of Pittsburgh Press, 1977; Seymour

My concern with this theory is its lack of transparency, with regards to the historiography of sugar in colonial British Guiana. Despite the ascent of the sugar plantation system, these scholars paid very scant or little attention to British Guiana. Rather, they seemingly suggested that British Guiana suffered the same fate as the older colonies. Williams (1945), in particular, suggests that although British Guiana made significant advances, such advances were inconsequential, and hence, the colony is lumped with historical outcomes of the old colonies.[20] British Guiana is, therefore, inaccurately placed in the context of the general wave of decline of the sugar plantation system, which had been the prevalent condition within the old Windward Island colonies. The broad parameters of this thesis do not fit what happened in British Guiana. Having said that, it is necessary to note that because of this blinded-sided approach to historical analysis, the growth and rebirth of the plantation system in British Guiana has been dealt with in a tangential and incidental manner. As Walter Rodney points out, some scholars of Guyanese history, and even West Indian scholars, have been found wanting because they disregarded the local context or response to global change and adopted the generalized notion that the sugar plantation system in British Guiana was in decline, although it was on the ascent. For Rodney, the old scholars did not examine the crucial question, that is, "whether the ex-slaves... could create a new way of life... whether labor could free itself from some of the absolute controls characteristic of slavery."[21] The answer to this question, he explained, "was resolved to the advantage of the planters and to the detriment of the ex-slaves in the years after emancipation."[22]

Drescher. Capitalism and Antislavery: British Mobilization in Comparative Perspective. New York: Oxford University Press, 1986; Seymour Drescher. From Slavery to Freedom. New York: New York University Press, 1999.

20 Eric Williams, "The Historical Background of British Guiana's Problems," The Journal of Negro History 30, 4 (1945): 357 381. Although he acknowledges Guyana's potential for sugar production and its contribution to the sugar revolution after 1850, Eric Williams maintained the view that the colony's development was stunted by the labor shortage. He failed to come to account for the rise of the sugar industry in Guyana in the wake of its decline in the old Caribbean. He linked Guyana to the economy and politics of the West Indies.

21 Rodney 1981: 646.

22 Ibid

Without paying enough attention to the attempts to cheapen labor in British Guiana as a means of meeting the demands for competition posed by slave produced sugar in the global economy, older scholars accepted the general view of decline and ruin, which was peddled by the colonial ruling class. Hence, the class location of ex-slaves and their relationship within the wider Guyanese economy and polity has been placed in the context of the rise of the "peasantry," the term which gained general acceptance over time to describe non-plantation rural labor. This literature assumes that the Guyanese economy was being diversified. It assumes that there was uniformity in the growth of the non-plantation sector in all land-endowed colonies. British Guiana does not fit the mold of Jamaica and other land-endowed colonies, which presented the openings for economic diversification and for proto-peasant reconstitution as the plantation system declined.

The misplacement of British Guiana within the plantation decline tendency and or thesis does not do justice to history, nor to theory. The dilemma of early West Indian scholars, such as Lowell Ragatz and Eric Williams, was their linear approach to the understanding of social history. This approach to history has infected thinking and the thought process, over all, with the idea that labor adaptations, which emerged across the Caribbean, can be painted along similar lines, such as in, where land was in abundance, a peasantry developed, and where it was scarce, the plantation system remained dominant. This mantra did not hold for British Guiana. The adoption of such a linear approach of earlier scholars to the evolution of the proto-peasantry fits into the approach found in the thought process of the planter class of the Caribbean in that formative moment after emancipation. Such a generalized understanding of the outcome for labor, as Rodney explained, "have essentially a class perspective in historical terms," which the literature that emerged adopted and peddled as "common truths," and as "universal truths."[23] Based on these generalizations, scholars of the decline thesis categorically present analyses that give weight and meaning to the growth of peasantries, which results, as it were, in filling the vacuum left by the "declining" planter class in the Caribbean. In doing so, they failed to account for the ways in which capital was being reconstituted in places

[23] Ibid

such as British Guiana at the very moment of West Indian decline, and the ways in which the reconstitution of the plantation system was consumed in the process of the recalibration of capital. And likewise, the ways in which labor itself was being cheapened to meet the demands of capital.

Significantly, while later scholars, for instance, Jay Mandle (1973) in *Plantation Economy* and Alan Adamson (1972) in *Sugar Without Slaves,* gave detailed accounts of the recalibration of capital and the rebirth of the plantation system in Guyana, they failed to contradict the linearity inherent in the understanding of West Indian history. Notwithstanding the evidence of plantation rebirth in British Guiana, these scholars assumed that land acquisition by ex-slaves to form the "free villages" constituted the development of a peasantry. Closer readings of the factors that led to the availability of land and of old and abandoned plantations for purchase by ex-slaves vary between the colonies. These variations are especially significant between what obtained in Jamaica and in British Guiana. While the availability of land had become commonplace in Jamaica by 1850, in British Guiana this market had dried up in significant ways after 1850. A good gauge of the differences in economic outlook between Guyana and Jamaica can be gleaned from the number of estates that were being placed on the auction block because of bad debts. It is noted that while Jamaica and most of the old colonies fell under the Encumbered Estates Act and Court because of the number of properties that were either abandoned or had accumulated hefty mortgages, which had become bad debts, in British Guiana, this occurrence was not as prevalent. In British Guiana the availability of abandoned estates and estates for sale by any means had virtually disappeared by 1854.[24]

Due to the turn-around in the sugar industry, most of its estates became solvent after 1854.[25] There are significant variations and differences

24 Adamson 1972: 173-175

25 Solvency was possible due to the rise of the use of technology. Estates which could not afford to make technological improvements were amalgamated and swallowed up into larger holdings. While the total number of sugar estates declined from 173 in 1853 to 105 in 1884, this decline represented an increase in the average holding under cultivation by a single estate which increased from 256 to 757 acres. R.W. Beachey, The British West Indies Sugar Industry in the Late 19th Century Westport: Greenwood Press, Publishers, 1957, 32-33 & 40-45; Adamson Sugar Without Slaves: The Political Economy of British Guiana, 1838-1904 (New Haven: Yale University Press, 1972: 160-213; C.O

between these two colonies. This is gleaned from a closer reading of their plantation and labor histories. The state of decay in Jamaica was related to it having entered a period of prolonged crisis after 1815.[26] This state of decay was consequent on the fact that by 1815 Jamaica had already lost its place as the premier sugar-producing colony within the world economy to Cuba.[27] As an old colony, its sugar production regimen could not keep pace with the newer sugar colonies. Its sugar factories were in a state of disrepair, and it could not generate the needed capital to reconfigure them with efficient machinery. While land was available for the expansion of production, the terrain precluded the growth of competitive estates. The terrain in most inland locations did not permit for the introduction of the plough, which carried up the cost of production. Added to this was the high cost of internal transport from estates to port, which made the price of Jamaican sugar prohibitively expensive in relation to other areas within the world economy.[28] This situation was exacerbated in the first decade after emancipation, in the wake of the labor problem and the rise of free trade, both of which magnified the problems faced by the already crisis-ridden plantation sugar economy. In the face of emancipation and the growth of free trade, the capitalist class in Britain, within the banking system, was uncertain that the plantation system in Jamaica was salvageable and, hence its sugar plantation system was starved for capital.[29] After 1815, the writing was on the wall: the sugar plantation system of Jamaica was at the end of the road. A peasant class emerged in Jamaica in the wake of this development.[30] It de-

116, Blue Books of Statistics.

26 The decline of the Jamaican plantation sector did not have to await emancipation. Emancipation served to hasten the process of decline. See Beachey 1957: 1-39; Eisner, Gisela. Jamaica, 1830-1930: A Study in Economic Growth. Manchester: Manchester University Press, 1961: 195-201; Ragatz 1928: 286-383; Hall, Douglas. Free Jamaica. New Haven: Yale University Press, 1959: 81-120; Dale Tomich. Through the Prism of Slavery: Labor, Capital, and World Economy. Lanham: Rowman & Littlefield, 2004: 80 & 110-119; Tomich 1990.

27 Tomich 1990: 23-25.

28 Hall 1959: 81; Tomich 2004: 80 & 110-119.

29 Eisner 1961: 195-200.

30 See the rise of the peasantry in Jamaica in Hall 1959 and Eisner 1961.

veloped because of the vacuum created by the declining plantation system. On this score, the proponents of the decline thesis are on target.

In British Guiana, there was a counter trend to the decline thesis; plantation production of sugar was on the ascent. Having said that, it cannot be denied that there was some level of crisis in the colony, resulting from emancipation and free trade. This is reflected in the momentary decrease in sugar production over the ten-year period, 1838-1848.[31] Two factors account for this momentary downward shift in the fortunes of the sugar planters in Guyana. Firstly, in this period the planter class was forced to retire, albeit temporarily, the accustomed command they had established over labor. Secondly, having lost command over labor, they had to contend with the impact of the sugar duties act, which equalized duties on slave and free produced sugar in the world market. However, because of Guyana's propensity for sugar production, the planter class was able to ride out these problems through the employment of the mechanisms of labor and land control they successfully implemented after 1848. Through the imposition of these mechanisms, the prior growth pattern in sugar that the colony experienced between 1815 and 1838 was re-established after 1850. Quite unlike the experience of Jamaica, through these mechanisms, a cheap and available workforce was constructed in British Guiana to complement the technological changes that were being introduced to enhance sugar production. As a result of these changes, the process of decline and decay, which marked the first ten years of emancipation, was halted and planter dominance over labor and the economy was re-established. After 1850, smaller estates were amalgamated and consolidated into large holdings, which demanded an increase in labor and technology.

As such, the complexity of the situation of Guyana cannot be confused by the downward process of decline that gripped the plantation system in Jamaica and other old colonies. Decline was not a permanent condition in Guyana. As Adamson (1972:164) points out, the situation in British Guiana was complex, and the record shows that there were "simultaneous pro-

[31] Over this period sugar production in Guyana and Jamaica dropped significantly. A significant difference between Guyana and Jamaica was that the decline trend in Jamaica was steady, while in Guyana it was momentary. The sugar industry in Jamaica was affected by its lack of propensity for further competition.

cesses of growth and decay... at work" in this colony. While this dual process of growth and decay was unfolding in British Guiana, in the old sugar colonies, plantations were being abandoned, bankrupted, and sold at execution. In British Guiana, such sales and abandonment resulted in the growth of sugar, whilst in the older sugar colonies; it culminated in the downgrading of the sugar economy and the growth of diversified economies. Hence in British Guiana, the sugar economy rose in the wake of its decline in the older colonies. In British Guiana, large sugar plantations emerged out of the crisis of the plantation economy. Adamson (1972:160) reports that what took place was "a change of ownership" and that this change was "so extensive as to constitute a revolution." The idea of decline encapsulated in the language of abandonment and sale of plantations did not constitute the same outcome, nor did it mean the same thing in British Guiana as in Jamaica and other land-endowed old colonies of the British West Indies. Neither Ragatz nor Williams paid much attention to the empirical evidence of what took place in British Guiana between 1838 and the early 1850s, the bleakest period of the sugar industry in the nineteenth century. Had they done that, they would have noted that out of the 201 estates sold at execution, 175 of them or approximately 60 percent of these holdings were transferred to new owners and amalgamated (Adamson 1972: 160-161). From the standpoint of capital, British Guiana came of age in the 1850s. What developed after the crisis of the 1840s were capital-intensive and technologically savvy sugar plantations. The age of the small sugar planter came to end, and British Guiana entered and became a player in the changing Atlantic Sugar economy of the nineteenth century. Decline scholars miss this trend completely.

What is striking about early scholarly literature is its cautious hesitancy in dealing with the counter trend of British Guiana as against the rest of the old West Indies Ragatz is lackluster and completely disregards the ascent of sugar in British Guiana, instead placing it in a sea of decline along with the rest of the West Indies; and Williams (1945: 357-381), while acknowledging the attributes of British Guiana for the propensity to produce sugar, dismisses the evidence and lumps the colony within the decline paradigm. His approach was informed, as he sees it, in the shadow of the colony's intractable labor problem. He thus (Williams 1945: 357-381 and 1970:361-

373) downplays the rebirth of the plantation system in British Guiana from the standpoint that they could not compete with Cuba. In so doing, Williams overemphasized the quantitative value of Cuban production over Guyanese and West Indian production. In his work, Cuban production statistics are used to downplay the potency of growth in British Guiana, which pales in comparison, but nevertheless occurred. In his works, Williams fails to address the phenomenal growth that took place internally, despite the labor shortage. He also fails to grasp the fundamental changes that had taken place in British Guiana, with regards to the cheapening of labor and how this redounded in the increases in sugar production between 1850 and 1887.

Unlike the older plantation colonies covered extensively in Ragatz's seminal work, the planter class in British Guiana, driven by market forces, was able to regroup and reorganize in the free trade era, accounting for the ascent. British Guiana's golden age as a plantation society began around 1815, at precisely the moment when the plantation system of the old colonies was saying their last hurrah. The ability of each colony to meet the requirement for competition within the world sugar market determined the extent to which the power of the plantation system declined or grew in the Caribbean. As the experience of Jamaica brings out, plantation decline was related to its inability for competition. Its inability for competition weakened the capacity of the plantation system to create and maintain coercive tactics to keep labor attached, and this gave rise to new patterns of social relationships. On the other hand, British Guiana's capacity for competition was enhanced by the ability of the plantation sector to maintain and deepen coercive control over labor. There was a direct correlation between the outgrowth of new social relationships between planters and ex-slaves and the power of the planter class in each location. Each location presented its own logic. In some locations, the power of the planter class increased, while in others, the power declined.

When each case is isolated for study, different sets of social relations can be found. For instance, in Barbados the power of the planter class increased after emancipation through their monopoly over land. In Barbados the social relationships, which were forged under slavery between slaves and masters, did not increase with freedom, as the experience of the Windward Islands brought forth. They were negated in freedom. This was possible because of the ability of Barbadian planters to compete in the world sugar economy after emancipation. Their ability to compete was created through the fact that the planter class had almost complete control over land on the Island. In Barbados and other Islands of the Leeward Caribbean with high population density the former slave garden plots were confiscated and all ex-slaves were made to rely on wage labor for their sustenance. In these colonies of high population density, in relation to land space, wages were the lowest.[32] Ex-slaves in these places had no bargaining power. Slaves and ex-slaves in Cuba shared a similar experience. In Cuba, as the capacity for sugar competition grew, so did the monopoly of the plantations over land and labor, which limited the possibility for labor diversification.[33] In contrast to the history of Cuba and Barbados, in Jamaica and the Windward Islands, the planter class was saddled with encumbrances; despite the fact that land was available for expansion, the sugar economy could not expand to compete in the world economy. In these colonies, it became impossible for the plantation system to maintain and increase its control over the society and diversification of the economy was a natural outcome. As such, it could be argued that formal diversification of the Jamaican economy in the latter half of the nineteenth century was a natural outcome of the interplay between labor and capital. [34]On the other hand, by 1852, sugar had become the primary staple of British Guiana, and diversification became impossible. While the Jamaican economy was engaged in a natural process of diversification, in British Guiana, diversification of staple production was discontinued after 1852. Sugar, after having overtaken the production and export of coffee and cotton between 1803 and 1838, took control of the reins of power in the colony. Therefore, British Guiana did not follow a similar trajectory as Jamaica and some of the other West Indian colonies. While their economies were being diversified due to their lack of propensity to compete in the sugar market, the Guyanese economy consolidated and grew around the production of sugar.

---

32 William A. Green, British Slave Emancipation: The Sugar Colonies and the Great Experiment 1830-1865. Oxford: Clarendon Press, 1976: 197

33 Like Barbados in Cuba sugar slaves were denied access to their provision grounds as the sugar revolution took off after the imposition of free trade in the 1840s.

34 Verene Shepherd. Slavery Without Sugar.Gainesville: University of Florida Press, 2002

The decline thesis does not hold for British Guiana; in the nineteenth century, it did not experience a similar phase of diversification in its economy, nor in its political system.[35] While the economy of the old colonies was going through its processes of diversification, the plantation system of this colony was being retooled for sugar production and competition in the world economy. It was caught up in the web of free trade. It provided the fillip British capital required for the enlargement of sugar production within the empire. British capital, having turned its back on the old West Indian colonies, shifted its emphasis to British Guiana and other colonies, such as Mauritius, which had the capacity for engagement in the commodity trade in sugar. As such, its sugar industry was reorganized and modernized. Its technological capability, its labor recruitment, and its labor process were brought in line to match that which obtained in other producing areas, such as Cuba.[36] Reorganization and modernization of the sugar economy of British Guiana involved the establishment of labor recruitment and labor management mechanisms, which matched its technological capability for competition with the new sugar producing areas. The mechanisms employed were in keeping with the increasing demands of competition within the world sugar economy for cheap labor. The standard that was established by the legal and illegal slave trade to Cuba fuelled that country's capacity to cheapen the price of sugar on the world market. While British Guiana's technological capability matched what existed in Cuba, its labor recruitment and management had to be constructed to match the growth of the slave trade and slave production. In effect, the second slavery, the expansion of slavery in Cuba, drove the changes that occurred in British Guiana. In this stead, there exists some degree of historical convergence between Cuba and British Guiana. This convergence has to do with the degree to which the cost of slave production of sugar in Cuba drove the necessity to

35 No semblance of representative government arose in Guyana until 1928 with the constitutional reform which brought with it the Crown Colony system of government.

36 The reorganization and modernization involved and included the shedding of unwanted plantation real estate, amalgamations and mergers of existing plantations, employment of new technologies-such as the vacuum pan which was introduced in the 1830s and which was fully utilized across the sugar industry by the 1870s. Beachey 1957: 61-80 and 118-136.

cheapen labor in British Guiana, so that it could compete and survive in the world economy.

Given this convergence, while the decline thesis fits the older plantation colonies, it does not fit British Guiana. As earlier stated, the divergence between British Guiana and the old West Indian colonies calls into question the linear approach of the literature of West Indian rural society, which presents the view that in colonies where land was available, the proto-peasantry of slavery were reconstituted into a peasantry in the post-emancipation period. From this standpoint, having explained that the plantation system in British Guiana was not in decline, the next section of this paper examines the issues of conception, and explains why the proto-peasants of slavery were reconstituted into what Walter Rodney describes as a rural proletariat. In this stead, in this section special emphasis is placed on Rawle Farley's adaptation of the terminology, "peasant," in his work to conceptualize the emergence of the small rural landholders in Guyana. This is necessary because, as mentioned before, the early conceptualization of this class as peasants serves as a foundation to the general body of early literature on the rural British Guiana that emerged. It also calls into question the construction and placement of British Guiana within the paradigm that land availability was equal to the growth of a peasantry. Because the transformations in British Guiana were more complex than such generalizations permit, it is necessary that I examine in some detail the conceptual framework, within which so labeled peasant development is discussed. A major issue in this discussion is whether or not the Free African villages of the village movement that erupted between 1838 and 1848 can be construed as having constituted themselves into a peasant class.

The Free African Villages cannot be construed as having constituted a peasant class

The construction of planter prosperity and/or decline in British Guiana hinged on the labor question, rather than on other sources of viability. Hence, the manner in which the plantations organized to deal with labor is pertinent to the discussion on whether the Ex-Slaves who established the Free African Villages can be construed as having evolved into a peasantry. The answer to this question lies in an understanding of the evolution of planter/labor relations. Labor, though "free" after emancipation, had to contend with the terrain, the environmental factors, and the invigorated sugar economy, which all combined to shape the decisions and choices of the former slaves. Despite acknowledging that the village movement came to a standstill and retrogressed after 1852, early scholars of Guyanese social and economic history persisted with the earlier declaration that the villagers who owned, lived, and planted small parcels of land constituted the "Guyanese Peasantry."[37] In so doing, scholars, beginning with Farley, failed to take into consideration that the material conditions in the colony after 1850 did not permit the African villages the space — political, social, and economic — to develop and evolve into a peasantry. As earlier pointed out, this was the beginning of the period of planter prosperity. Scholars, such as Farley, did not merely accept the planters' view that Africans abandoned the plantations; they followed through on this misconception by formulating the theory that Africans left the plantations to establish a peasantry.[38] A misconception such as this has arisen in the historiography because of the history of the slave period, wherein slaves had been permitted the "luxury" of providing for their subsistence through provision ground cultivation. Due to this development during slavery, Sidney Mintz coined the phrase "proto-peasants," to categorize slaves who were engaged in subsistence cultivation to meet their needs.

37 There have been many scholarly discussions on the evolution of a "peasantry" in Guyana. But Farley's work in particular is testimony to this line of thinking. While other scholars, namely Adamson and Mandle in their works posit the rise of an African peasantry, they are merely parroting Farley's work. Farley's work is used as foundation by these scholars to understand and speak about the history of the relations which developed between ex-slaves and the plantation labor process. Farley's work mistakenly follows the argument of the scholarship on Jamaica and other old colonies of the British Caribbean which prefaces the growth of peasantries on the demise of the plantation system. Farley's work was established in the framework of the assumption that across the British Caribbean the plantation system entered a period of decline after emancipation. With regard to Guyana it is possible to argue that this was technically correct-due to the number of plantations which were sold, abandoned and or absorbed into larger holdings between 1838 and 1848.

38 Rodney, Walter. "From Niggeryard to village," Georgetown: Red Thread Women's Press, 1988

Beginning with the assumption that all things were equal and that there was a smooth transition from subsistence production through provision grounds during slavery to small-holder peasant farming after slavery, Rawle Farley develops and propounds the conception Guyanese Peasantry. He thus located the peasant origins of British Guiana in the context of provision ground cultivation of the slave period. This approach was taken without regard for the manner in which the plantation system was reshaping slave labor and its relationship to provision grounds even before slavery ended. Without attending to this history and the actual conditions of inherited experience, he locates his post-emancipation "peasantries" in the colony as the "reconstitution" of the proto-peasantry of slavery (Farley 1964: 52-61). This approach mirrors the generalized conceptualization of Woodville Marshall (1968 and 1972) who also assumes that "the proto-peasantry" of slavery was reconstituted into "peasantries" in each place where land was available and ex-slaves had established villages. Without a complete examination of the conditions of existence, of labor, and of living arrangements as Walter Rodney outlined in 1978, Farley (1954, 1955, and 1956), Adamson (1972), Mandle (1973), Marshall (1968 and 1972), and other early scholars adopted the assumption "peasantries" as a useful term to describe all these groups across the Caribbean.[39] In the case of Farley, he used the term peasantry to describe the economic activity of ex-slaves who resided in proprietary villages on the front lands of plantations and in communal villages contiguous to plantations. He adopted this term despite the recognition that it did not match the conditions on the ground. Indeed, Farley says as much: "the holders of plots of land in Guiana were by force of circumstance more wage earners."[40] Hence, while recognizing that ex-slaves were not peasants, but wage earners, he maintained in his later work this categorization. Farley's work is blinded by the generally common colonial slave history of Guyana and the British Caribbean. From this angle, he argues that the his-

39 Rodney1981: 643-666. The assumption peasantry as Rodney surmised in his lecture at the Braudel Center at Binghamton University in 1978 arose out of the neglect of these scholars to arrive at workable theoretical categories through thorough going examinations of the conditions of life of the people concerned.

40 Farley 1956: 229.

tory of Guyana is linked to that of the British Caribbean.[41] This, I believe, was his cardinal mistake.

This analysis, in my view, suffers from a few basic misconceptions. While Farley establishes the category "peasantry" as a useful tool of analysis in identifying the independent activity of ex-slaves, he lost complete sight of the ongoing sugar revolution that was fuelling plantation rebirth. He thus failed to recognize the extent to which the village economies, in themselves, evolved and were being absorbed into the plantation labor process, becoming appendages of the plantation. In this context, while he accounts for the rapid growth of African villages in the 1840s, he fails to account for their rapid decline after 1850. Growth and decline occurred over a relatively short period. While acknowledging the decline of the "peasantry" of Guyana as a consequence of the rebirth of plantation sugar coupled with the control planters exercised over the state, there is no systematic discussion in Farley's work as to how this happened. Thus, his account for the rise and decline of the independent "peasantry" is closeted within the confines of the period 1838 and 1852. He operates on the assumption that the villages and, in his terms, the peasantry, developed in the context of plantation decline, and stagnated in the context of plantation ascent. This period was more complex than that. The so-labeled decline of the plantations, as discussed earlier, was related more to labor shortage and to the struggle for better wages and conditions than to encumbrances, as in Jamaica. The decline of the villages was connected to the defeat of African labor with the institution of the indentured contract, and to the needs of the plantations for a reserve army of labor. It was linked to indentured immigration and the ways in which the planter class used indentured labor as a weapon to discipline and control the ex-slave population. Consequently, while connecting the rebirth of the plantation system to the demise of the "peasantry," Farley fails to explain why after 1852, the African villages were a picture of widespread desolation and neglect (Farley 1953:87-103). He also fails to explain the factors that negated the so-called "peasantry" only after a decade.

---

41 Rawle Farley, "The Rise of Village Settlements in British Guiana," Caribbean Quarterly 10, 1 (1964): 52-61; Eisner 1961: 210-236; Hall 1959: 157-207

Farley is not alone in this approach. His work has been used as the foundation in the work of other scholars. In *Sugar Without Slaves,* Alan Adamson acknowledges, as Farley did, that a "peasantry" came into being with the following caveat: that "as the peasantry was forming, it was beginning to differentiate." This differentiation did not include laborers — those who never left the plantations and who, by 1850, had continued to live on plantations. He did not consider them to be part of the "peasantry" (Adamson 1972:39-41). These laborers accounted for 19,939 still resident on the plantations in 1850, compared to 42,755 laborers who, by then, had left plantation residence and were residing in villages (Adamson 1972:39-41). Among the "peasantry" were those ex-slaves who had bought lands within existing plantations; primarily on the front lands, those who had become landed proprietors on estates, and who continued to labor on estates, either as day laborers, or in company with others in task gangs (Adamson 1972:39-41). Secondly, there were those who had purchased entire estates, and who had established communal villages in proximity to plantations, and who continued to offer their services as laborers to plantations. Despite acknowledging that most of these villagers had continued to work as laborers on the plantations, he called them peasants. There is very little evidence if any that these villagers were able to or had established any level of independent subsistence away from plantation labor. On the contrary, the three scholars who wrote on this period acknowledge that those they called peasants declined in the face of plantation ascent and failed to exist as independent subsistence producers after 1852. It would be correct, in my view, to assume that these scholars based their conception on the notion that village life equaled a peasantry. They assumed that availability and access to land through which village life was formulated meant that these rural people could be construed as a peasantry. In this stead, despite the growth of the plantation system, Farley (1958:87-103) notes that, Peasant freehold and village development were possible only because of the existence of one basic condition and that was the abundance of land over and above what could be developed by the existing population.

Farley thus based his assumption on the fact that because British Guiana was land endowed; this meant the possibility for a peasantry. Through the prism of abundant land, Guiana is thus equated with other places with abundant land where peasant development did occur. Case in point, Jamaica, but the history of Jamaica is different from that of Guiana. One important fact that brings out the difference is that while Jamaica had abundant land, peasant development based on abundance of land was backed up by other factors, such as the declining power of sugar and of the planter class.[42] Another important factor has to do with slave participation in the internal economy. In Jamaica slaves had built up a strong internal market, which though present in Guiana, was comparatively very weak.[43] This weakness was reflected in the fact that the plantation history of Guiana was short, relative to that of Jamaica. Also the slave population was small in Guiana, relative to Jamaica. Jamaican slaves had a longer period to build the internal market and allied mechanisms of support for their efforts at freedom. This accounts for the minor role of the internal market at the end of slavery in Guiana as a fillip to propel the struggle between ex slaves and plantations in the rise of a peasantry. In Jamaica the village economy represented a real threat to capital and was able to open up a diversified export market, while in Guiana, this was far from possible. In Guiana, the first time a diversified export market was opened, it was not by Africans, but by East Indians, who established the production and marketing of rice at the end of the nineteenth century.[44] The ex-slaves of Guiana at emancipation lacked the tools, which in Jamaica, had contributed to the weakening of the role of the plantation system in the society. The cardinal weakness of the scholar-

---

42 Eisner 1961: 210-236; Hall 1959: 157-207

43 Sidney Mintz, "The Jamaica Internal Marketing Pattern: Some Notes and Hypotheses," Social and Economic Studies 4 (1955): 95-103; Mintz 1974: 180-224. In Guyana the marketing base for slave and ex-slave subsistence produce was extremely weak. This was due to the relatively small population base and the fact that almost everyone outside of the small European group was involved in production of one sort or the other. In addition the sugar economy did not permit for the expansion of the export economy to accommodate other crops

44 Note is taken that the East Indian Rice Peasantry developed in the wake of the crisis which enveloped the world cane sugar industry. The growth of the East Indian Rice Peasantry in this context resulted as compensation to pacify plantation labor. In this stead land was given to East Indians in Lieu of their return passages. While in the middle of the nineteenth century colonialism denied the possibility for growth of the African Creole Peasantry, at the end of the century it afforded the mechanisms for the construction of an East Indian Peasantry.

ship of Farley, Mandle, and Adamson is their reliance on the understanding of history which says that at the time of emancipation labor withdrew from plantation labor to form a peasantry in land-endowed areas of the West Indies. While this may be true for some areas of the region, it was certainly not the case in Guiana. This approach to the understanding of the social history did not arise from empirical evidence, but from supposition. The consequence of this supposition was the painting of the African population of British Guiana with the peasant brush.

Furthermore, the consequence of this historical divergence and misreading of the empirical evidence of the actions, intentions, and economy of the African population in the 1840s has led these authors to define them as peasants. The withdrawal of ex-slaves from plantations into villages and their subsequent supposed transformation into a peasantry cannot be treated in the same manner across the British West Indies. This phenomenon, we argue, cannot be painted in the same general way that the literature paints the relations between planters and ex-slaves in the West Indies. Each local condition presented a different and varied relation within the world economy and should be treated as such. In British Guiana, the movement of ex-slaves away from plantation labor and the plantations, generally, was not as stark as in other colonies. In British Guiana, the movement of ex-slaves away from plantation labor was not dramatic as the literature suggests; it was gradual. The evidence suggests that as late as 1850 at least one third of the laboring population of 19,939 ex-slaves were still resident on plantations. This was even after the massive withdrawal, following the sugar strike of 1848. Withdrawal of labor from plantation residency occurred over a ten-year period and grew in intensity as the planter class increased their demands for continuance of tenancy to be tied to continuous labor on plantations. In such a climate, the withdrawal of labor from plantations in British Guiana was more or less withdrawal from plantation residence. This is the position of newer scholarship. In this light, Walter Rodney (1981 and 1988) and Douglas Hall (1978) in more recent, but separate works, have called for reconsideration as to whether the thesis that ex-slaves were fleeing from the plantation is accurate, and whether ex-slaves were fleeing from plantation labor or from plantation housing.[45] These scholars argue that movement from the plantation was not as stark as the old literature has expressed it. In decrying the notion that movement from the plantation represented the growth of a peasantry, they used empirical evidence to demonstrate that by 1840, a small proportion of ex-slaves in British Guiana, having removed themselves from plantation housing, ruptured the plantation dominance over them and their mobility and had begun to use their labor power as a bargaining chip to negotiate their freedom to earn better wages. Movement and withdrawal, prior to 1848-49, was not about separating themselves from the plantation labor process, but was a conscious aspect of the struggle to improve wages and working conditions. Rodney thus points to the successful strike of 1841, when there was no competing group of available labor in the colony; and their defeat in the strike of 1848, when indentured contract labor was introduced in competition with them and for their place on the plantation (Rodney 1981:643-666). Rodney's intervention in the debate is instructive from the standpoint that the act of movement from estate residence increased the bargaining position of the ex-slaves; and that this bargaining position was jeopardized with the introduction of "captive" competing labor, who by virtue of their contract, and by virtue of the magnitude of the immigration project, became one of the important catalyst in the cheapening labor.

It is from this standpoint important to note that the formative literature, upon which Adamson (1972) and Mandle (1973) based their arguments, presents the relative decrease in output for sugar in the colony between 1838 and 1848 as a consequence of withdrawal of African labor from the plantation. In paying attention to shortfall in volume of production, they failed to point to the nature of residential withdrawal. Their failure is that they account for the shortfall in production in terms of a peasantry, not as the growth of such factors as the ex-slaves reclaiming life's virtue, as rebuilding culture, as organizing families, and as establishing spaces for organizing freedom.[46] The point of departure between Rodney and Hall with the

[45] Douglas Hall, "The Flight from the Estates Reconsidered: The British West Indies, 1838-42," The Journal of Caribbean History 10&11 (1978): 7-24; Rodney 1981: 643-666

[46] The organization of the villages into cultural and family units is discussed in the fol-

others on this score is that old scholarship did not consider the dual nature of relations that emerged between families and capital in the 1840s. They assumed that withdrawal and establishment of villages naturally meant the birth of a peasantry. As such, they did not make the connection between such acts as the withdrawal of women and child labor, and the continued ties by able-bodied males in their capacity as free labor with the plantations as a continuance of the struggle between labor and planter. In so doing, they contributed to the imprecision that exists with regards to categorization, and which continues to serve as foundation for on-going studies, as well as for the establishment and promulgation of policies to enhance development projects. It is necessary to note, in this respect, that the imprecision which gave rise to the term, "Guyanese Peasantry," was first given credence by Rawle Farley, who produced the first major scholarly work on this period of Guyanese history that examined the relationships between the Creole Africans and land. Though recognizing the imprecision of the usage of the term "peasants" in his work, Farley did nothing about it. This is in spite of having come to the recognition in his PhD dissertation (1956:229-230) that the Creole Africans who were owners of small plots of land, "were by force of circumstances more wage earners than peasants and, as such their fortunes were still bound up with the fortunes of the sugar industry."

This terminological and theoretical imprecision has continued to inform the major body of historical and analytical literature and, hence, the social and cultural body politic of Guyana.[47] An unintended consequence of this imprecision is the fact that it has served over time as foundation for establishing parallels between the understandings of the outcomes of the Creole African Labor force of other West Indian colonies and those of the wider Caribbean with those of Guyana. It has also blurred the divergence and divisions at the social, economic, and political levels between the outcomes of African Creoles and the East Indian Indentured Immigrants in Guyanese society. While sections of both of these population groups have been labeled

---

lowing works: Rodney 1981: 31-89; Raymond T. Smith, "Land Tenure in Three Negro Villages in British Guiana," Social and Economic Studies 4 (1955); Raymond T. Smith, The Negro Family in British Guiana: Family Status and Social Structure in the Villages. New York: Grove Press, Inc. 1956

47 Mandle 1973; and Adamson 1972

peasants, the East Indians have moved ahead economically in the society by virtue of wider and more pronounced access to land.[48] Noting that while this divergence is not discussed in this paper, it would be remiss if I do not mention in passing that this disparity in access to land is perhaps a major source of the ongoing internecine tension and conflict, which envelopes relations between these two major population groups.[49] It is also important to note that disparity in access and, hence, in ownership to land has also not informed the debate with regards to land. The debate on the other hand, has been informed by closeness to land, rather than ability to create independent life from the land. This discrepancy between closeness and ability is captured by Walter Rodney (1981:60) in his *History of the Guyanese Working People, 1881-1905*, in which he aptly conveys that "rural wage earners in Guiana in the nineteenth century were so close to the land that they have often been imprecisely designated as peasants." Having made this argument, Rodney suggested that such inaccuracy in the theoretical categorization of the African descendants of slavery in post-emancipation nineteenth century Guyana was related to scholarly inattention to the details of everyday life of these people.[50] In pinpointing this flaw, he opined that the relations of production, which produced closeness to land, did not permit the growth of a diversified economy, and the creation of a peasant class.

48 Note that while the Creoles in Guyana were being kept in subjection in the villages, with land holdings ranging from one quarter to five acres; in the last quarter of the nineteenth century and beyond East Indians were given plots of land in lieu of their return passages to India, and were afforded the possibilities to lease or purchase large tracts of Crown Lands which had been out of reach of the African population between 1830 and 1890. See Carl. B. Greenidge, Empowering A Peasantry in a Caribbean Context: The Case of Land Settlement Schemes in Guyana, 1865-1985. Kingston: The University of the West Indies Press, 2001. Also see Dwarka Nath, A History of Indians in Guyana. London: Buttler & Tanner Ltd, 1950; Peter Ruhomon, Centenary History of the East Indians in British Guiana, 1838-1938. Georgetown: Guyana National Printers, 1988

49 Ethnic and Racial conflict between these populous groups have been growing with intensity since the mod 1950s a full ten years before the culmination of British Colonial rule.

50 Rodney1981. 643-666

Proto-Peasants evolved and became a Proletariat and the Rural Proletariat

The issues which confronted the African Creole population after emancipation was whether they would be permitted the space to create for themselves a new life either as a peasant class, or as workers. The crux of the confrontation, which developed in the years following emancipation, was whether or not, and to what extent, the freed slaves were able to create a new life. And to what extent the conditions permitted them to engage with capital on their own terms. The economic and political climate of planter dominance allowed them the leverage to restrict the growth of any class that could challenge their hegemony in the society. In the context of planter hegemony over the political economy of the colony, "slaves became plantation workers immediately after slavery."[51] But unlike Cuba or Barbados in the same period, plantation workers in British Guiana also pursued the land market that had opened up as coffee, cotton, and the small sugar plantations were abandoned. Such land purchases were either on or adjacent to existing and prosperous plantations. Through this process, land purchases for housing and subsistence were integrated with plantation labor. This situation gave rise to the concept, "permanent hybrid of peasant and proletarian" (Rodney 1981:218), used to describe the condition of the largest group of laborers within the African population.

This group was characterized by the permanent "overlap" between peasant-like activity or village subsistence, wage work, and being unemployed. The integration between village subsistence, plantation wage labor, and the unemployed has received much attention, especially from Sidney Mintz (1982:209-225) and Walter Rodney (1981:218) and, to a lesser extent, Richard Frucht.[52] These scholars paid attention to the details of everyday life and tried to make sense of the way the freed Africans through attachment to land whether through purchase or through historical relations with the land, were reaching for independence from continued serfdom.

[51] Rodney 1981: 218; and Sidney Mintz, "Decrying the Peasantry," Review 6, 2 (1982): 209-225

[52] Richard Frucht, "A Caribbean Social Type: Neither Peasant Nor Proletarian," Social and Economic Studies 16, 3 (1967): 295-300

The tension evident in the writings of these scholars reflect the problems inherent in the condition of African labor as the plantation system grappled with the need to maximize the use of land for sugar production in the period of abolition and emancipation. Given the legal and environmental constraints, it must be recalled that ex-slaves were faced with two options as they looked at the horizon towards freedom: to create village subsistence, or bargain with the planter class for the enlargement of plantation subsistence. Through either of these processes, they were intending to escape the life of wage serfdom.

There are two points to be made in this respect. Firstly, the African workforce seemed content at the end of slavery to settle for a "proto-peasant" future, with the caveat that they be allowed to own and or lease the houses and lands they were farming and had been using for other purposes, such as burying their dead. Secondly, having taken that position, they had resigned themselves to a proletarian outlook as wage laborers on the estates. Note that the integration of the two modes of reproduction of labor in the period of slavery was being advanced in a revolutionary fashion after emancipation. In the post-emancipation setting the demand for the right to purchase and or lease the spaces of housing and subsistence was an attempt to liberate themselves as the workforce from the yoke of the planter class. It is from this standpoint that the notion, rural proletariat or the "permanent hybrid of peasant and proletarian," emerged to give theoretical teeth to the continuation of the integration of subsistence and plantation work in the post-emancipation period. This, in my view, must be understood as the reconstitution of the specific form of proto-peasant relation of Guyana. It is arguable, from this background, that the relation "peasant," the relation "proletarian," and the relation "rural-proletarian" developed and kept pace with the extent to which one relation superseded the other. As such, the African population, who while in slavery Mintz categorized as proto-peasant, in the context of the class struggle that ensued in the period between 1838 and 1848, felt and looked like a "modern proletariat;" and for the remainder of the century while sugar maintained its dominance, they constituted what can be described as the "rural proletariat" (Rodney 1981:217-222).

Conclusion

The construction of the African workforce after 1850 in British Guiana into the sphere of neither/nor, that is neither peasant nor proletarian, was not determined by the paucity of opportunity for industrial labor, or by the paucity of land.[53] The evolution of the African Creole workforce into the rural proletariat was determined by the extent to which capital was advancing, and as it advanced, its control over the productive resources was deepened through varying and variable social forms. The deepening of control by capital in Guyana was not accompanied by the parallel deepening of the proletarianization of labor. The domination of capital over African labor after 1850 was accompanied by three conjoined processes: subsistence (if possible), wage labor (if available), and unemployment (a semi permanent condition of life). It was the combination of these three processes that pushed scholars, like Walter Rodney, to designate the African population as the "rural proletariat." The condition, rural proletariat for definitional purposes, therefore, is a hybrid group of rural people who, though attached to the land, were involved in a dual-natured system of social reproduction. These are folks who worked part-time on the plantation for money wages that were supplemented by subsistence production whenever and wherever possible from the little land they owned, and/or rented.[54] When the relations that developed in the post-emancipation setting are explored, several questions arise. For instance, were the ex-slaves capable of establishing a complete

---

53 Frucht 1967: 295-300. It was being conditioned by the confluence of the world sugar economy and slave labor in one zone which influenced the conditions of labor in Guyana. The experience of African Creole labor in Guyana was different than that of their counterparts in Cuba. Though Cuba and Guyana were producing and competing in the world sugar market, the "proto-peasant" dimension in Cuba disappeared. Despite the presence of abundant land, the measurement for the growth of the peasantry, what could be regarded as a proletariat developed within the slave mode. On the other hand as capital lost control over the productive resources in some colonies as in Jamaica there was more movement towards the growth of the peasant dimension. In Guyana, a colony with abundant land, with immense possibilities for growth, a majority of African Creoles emerged and is described by Rodney as the "rural proletariat".

54 Note is made in this regard that although the African villagers owned land. On many occasions they could not farm these lands because of inundation from the Atlantic. In such circumstances they rented small parcels from the sugar estates.

break from the plantation? Did they have enough land, and were they capable of creating a fruitful life from the land, given the environmental factors? The land laws inform us that while some of them were able to acquire land, the parcels they were able to acquire were too miniscule and were more a drag than a benefit in the quest for independence. Note is also made in this score of the vagaries of the harsh environmental conditions, which further compounded the problems of the African population in their attempts to use the land. On this score, it should also be noted that for many decades at least, until the mid 1880s, they could not access the required capital, nor get assistance from the state to create functional farms as reliable subsistence and economic units. As a result they became a rural proletariat.

The End of the "Second Slavery" in the Confederate South and the "Great Brigandage" in Southern Italy: A Comparative Study

Enrico DAL LAGO

National University of Ireland, Galway

Methodological Introduction

Current studies on the U.S. South have moved increasingly toward an emphasis on comparative and transnational dimensions, leading to a better appreciation of the New World and Atlantic contexts of the rise and fall of American slavery, when seen also in its connection with the Old World. In this respect, the best available research at the moment – pioneered particularly by David Brion Davis, Robin Blackburn, Peter Kolchin, Shearer Davis Bowman, Mark Smith, and a few other scholars – focuses increasingly on hemispheric, transnational, and transatlantic perspectives on the American South, when compared not just with Latin America or the Caribbean, but also with Europe, within a Euro-American and world context of economic, social, and political transformation, as in the work of Edward Rugemer, Brian Schoen, Sven Beckert, and Timothy Roberts. More importantly, the idea of a "second slavery" – that is, of a new, aggressively capitalist form of enslavement in the U.S. South, Cuba, and Brazil in the nineteenth century, initially argued by Dale Tomich and then proposed also by Michael Zeuske, Anthony Kaye, and others – has done a great deal to open new perspectives of comparison between different, but related, forms of labor exploitation in the New World and Europe.[1]

[1] See especially David Brion Davis, *Inhuman Bondage: The Rise and Fall of Slavery in the New World* (New York, 2006); Robin Blackburn, *The American Crucible: Slavery, Emancipation, and Human Rights* (London, 2011); Peter Kolchin, *Unfree Labor: American Slavery and Russian Serfdom* (Cambridge, MA, 1987); Shearer Davis Bowman, *Masters and Lords: Mid-Nineteenth Century Prussian Junkers and U.S. Planters* (New

In respect to the terminal part of the history of American slavery, though, scholarly studies tend to focus on comparisons of the end of the "second slavery" and its aftermath in the U.S. South and in Cuba, as in Rebecca Scott's work, or in the U.S. South and in Brazil, as, for example, in a famous article by William Freehling.[2] Only a few works – first and foremost, Steven Hahn's 1990 *AHR* article, and Michael L. Bush's seminal synthesis, *Servitude in Modern Times* (2000) – have broadened this perspective in order to make comparisons between the end of the "second slavery" in America and of forms of unfree labor in Europe, or else they have focused their analysis specifically on emancipation in the U.S. South and in Russia, as in the case of several of Peter Kolchin's essays.[3] And yet, in order to understand correctly the wider world context in which the end of the "second slavery" in the United States occurred during the Civil War, it would be important to keep in mind – in line with current scholarship – that the American Civil War was essentially a phenomenon of national con-

York, 1993): Mark Smith, "Old South Time in Comparative Perspective", *American Historical Review* 101 (1996); Edward Rugemer, *The Problem of Emancipation: The Caribbean Origins of the Civil War* (Baton Rouge, LA, 2008); Brian Schoen, *The Fragile Fabric of Union: Cotton, Federal Politics, and the Global Origins of the Civil War* (Baltimore, MD, 2009); Sven Beckert, "Emancipation and Empire: Reconstructing the World Wide Web of Cotton Production in the Age of the American Civil War", *American Historical Review* 109 (2004), 1405-1438; Timothy Roberts, *Distant Revolutions: 1848 and the Challenge to American Exceptionalism* (Charlottesville, VA, 2009); Dale Tomich, *Through the Prism of Slavery: Labor, Capital, and the World Economy* (Lanham, MD, 2004), 56-74; Dale Tomich and Michael Zeuske, "Introduction, The Second Slavery: Mass Slavery, World-Economy, and Comparative Microhistories", *Review* 31:2 (2008), 91-100; Anthony Kaye, "The Second Slavery: Modernity in the Nineteenth-Century South and the Atlantic World", *Journal of Southern History* 75:3 (2009), 627-650; and Enrico Dal Lago, *American Slavery, Atlantic Slavery, and Beyond: The U.S. "Peculiar Institution" in International Perspective* (Boulder, CO, 2012), 63-91.

2 Rebecca Scott, *Degrees of Freedom: Louisiana and Cuba after Slavery* (Baton Rouge, LA, 2005); William W. Freehling, *The Reintegration of American History: Slavery and the Civil War* (New York, 1994), 176-219.

3 See Steven Hahn, "Class and State in Postemancipation Societies: Southern Planters in Comparative Perspective", *American Historical Review* 95:1 (1990), 75-98; Michael L. Bush, *Servitude in Modern Times* (Cambridge, 2000); and particularly Peter Kolchin, "Some controversial questions concerning nineteenth-century abolition from slavery and serfdom" in Michael L. Bush, ed., *Slavery and Serfdom: Studies in Legal Bondage* (London, 1996), 42-68.

solidation similar to, and comparable with, other phenomena that occurred in Europe at the same time, as several scholars have pointed out.[4]

In fact, given these premises, it would make a great deal of sense to compare the American Civil War with a similar epochal phenomenon of national consolidation that affected in its entirety a system of labor in a European country. Therefore, I argue that we will be able to understand better the nature and meaning of the American Civil War and the end of the "second slavery" in the United States if we place them clearly within a Euro-American context. Specifically, I intend to do so by comparing the Civil War and Emancipation in the U.S. South with a particular and contemporaneous military and socio-political European movement of national unification – the making of the Italian Kingdom during the *Risorgimento* – and the subsequent five-year period of civil warfare (1861-65), known as "Great Brigandage," in southern Italy, or the Italian *Mezzogiorno*.

Agrarian Elites in the U.S. South and Southern Italy, 1815-1860

The point of departure of the present investigation is the recognition that, in different ways, the American South and southern Italyplayed key roles in the formation of American and Italian national identities. From the beginning of the nineteenth century, through the crucial decade of the 1860s and beyond, these two souths – both peripheral agricultural areas within a nineteenth-century world economy centered upon industrialized England and the industrializing northeastern United States – expressed particular regional cultures.[5] The foundations of these regional cultures lay in specific socio-economic systems – based, in one case, on slaveholding and, in the other case, on landowning – while the regions' political influence went far beyond their borders and affected the development of the nations

4 See especially Thomas Bender, *Nation among Nations: America's Place in World History* (New York, 2006); Carl J. Guarneri, *America in the World: United States History in Global Context* (New York, 2007); and Ian Tyrrell, *Transnational Nation. United States History in Global Perspective since 1789* (New York, 2007).

5 For the wider context, see especially Immanuel Wallerstein, *The Capitalist World-Economy* (New York, 1979), 1-36; and Immanuel Wallerstein, *The Modern World-System*, Vol. IV: *Centrist Liberalism Triumphant, 1789-1914* (Berkeley, CA, 2011).

of which they were, or became, part. Within the two southern regions, between 1815 and 1860, agrarian elites – American slaveholders and southern Italian landowners – played key roles, specifically in socio-economic terms, by presiding over the production and movement of valuable agricultural commodities and by exploiting large masses of mostly landless laborers – American slaves and southern Italian peasants – although in very different ways and degrees.[6]

In short, even though in command of very different agricultural systems – one mostly characterized by centuries-old *latifondi*, while the other one comprising mostly recent plantations – both American slaveholders and southern Italian landowners in the first half of the nineteenth century confronted themselves with the forces of economic modernization, unleashed in one case by America's "market revolution" and in the other case by Italy's "commercial revolution". Both these movements toward economic modernization were products of a general restructuring of the world economy consequent to the long wave of England's Industrial Revolution – a restructuring that, in the U.S. South, Cuba, and Brazil, led to the rise of the "second slavery", while in Russia it led to a renewal of the "second serfdom". In practice, in both the American and the Italian cases, economic modernization prompted by the restructuring of the world economy affected the agrarian elites by leading to a general strengthening of their more recently formed sections, the U.S. cotton planters and Italy's bourgeois landowners, while it also led to a flourishing of agronomic activities by resident slaveholders and landowners.[7]

---

6 See Enrico Dal Lago, *Agrarian Elites: American Slaveholders and Southern Italian Landowners, 1815-1861* (Baton Rouge, LA, 2005), 28-96. See also William Scarborough, *Masters of the Big House: Elite Planters in the Nineteenth-Century South* (Baton Rouge, LA, 2003); Richard Follett, *The Sugar Masters: Planters and Slave in Louisiana's Cane World, 1820-1860* (Baton Rouge, LA, 2005); Salvatore Lupo, "I proprietari terrieri del Mezzogiorno" in Piero Bevilacqua, ed., *Storia dell'agricoltura italiana in età moderna e contemporanea*, Vol. II: *Uomini e Classi* (Venice, 1990), 105-150; and Marta Petrusewicz, *Latifundium: Moral Economy and Material Life in a Nineteenth-Century Periphery* (Ann Arbor, MI, 1996).

7 See Dal Lago, *Agrarian Elites*,98-179. On "second slavery" and "second serfdom", see especially Tomich, *Through the Prism of Slavery*; Tomich and Zeuske, "Introduction, The Second Slavery", 91-100; and Dal Lago, *American Slavery, Atlantic Slavery, and Beyond*, 95-122.

As the nineteenth century reached the end of its first half, though, and the two elites grew in power and influence, strains in their relationship with their respective national governments – the American Union and the Bourbon Kingdom of the Two Sicilies – started to increase in intensity, eventually leading to open confrontation in both cases in two particular instances: in the American case, in the 1819-21 Missouri Crisis and in the 1848-50 sectional conflict over slavery, while, in the southern Italian case, in the 1820-21 and in the 1848-49 Revolutions. Though the two national governments survived the crisis, the power the elites accumulated, which reflected in their prominent roles in the social and political life of their local communities, led to their increasingly harsher resistance to the centralizing policies of those governments and to the governments' perceived attempts to threaten established traditions of local autonomy, in one case through the imposition of anti-slavery measures, while in the other case through the imposition of a strongly centralized administrative system. After 1850, therefore, in both the United States and southern Italy, the political confrontation between the agrarian elites and the national government escalated in intensity, with two regions in particular – South Carolina and Sicily – taking the lead of the two movements of opposition to the American Union and to the Bourbon Kingdom.[8]

Agrarian Elites, Nation-Building and Civil War in the Two Souths, 1860-1862

The two parallel processes of confrontation between peripheral elites and centralizing national governments reached their peak in both cases in the years 1860-61, when, in extreme attempts to protect their regional autonomy, the two elites detached themselves entirely from the politics of the American Union and of the Kingdom of the Two Sicilies, leading in one

[8] See Dal Lago, *Agrarian Elites*, 180-270. See also, within the very vast bibliography, William Freehling, *The Road to Disunion*, 2 Vols. (1990-2007); Robert Bonner, *Mastering America: Southern Slaveholders and the Crisis of the Union* (New York, 2009); Angelantonio Spagnoletti, *Storia del Regno delle Due Sicilie* (Bologna, 1997); and John A. Davis, *Naples and Napoleon: Southern Italy and the European Revolutions, 1790-1860* (New York, 2006).

case to the American slaveholders' creation of the Confederate States of America and in the other case to the southern Italian landowners' support for Italian Unification. Essentially, in the American case, slaveholders achieved their ultimate aim of nationalization of slavery by creating a nation (the C.S.A.) entirely dedicated to the protection of the "peculiar institution", while in the Italian case, southern Italian landowners achieved the ultimate aim of creating a government (the Kingdom of Italy) that protected their interests. Yet, in the course of the following five years – between 1861 and 1865 – the two newly formed nations faced comparable crises of legitimacy. These crises related to both internal and external factors. In the case of the Confederacy, internationally, the problem of legitimacy derived from the fact that the Union was the only recognized national government in America, while, internally, the elites and ordinary citizens of the South were divided both between supporters of the Union and supporters of the Confederacy and also between supporters of a strong central government and supporters of states' rights and local autonomy. In the case of the Kingdom of Italy, internationally, the problem of legitimacy derived from the overthrow of the Bourbon Kingdom perpetrated by the Piedmontese government without a formal declaration of war, while, internally, the southern Italian landowning elites and the southern people were divided between supporters of Italy and of the Savoy dynasty and supporters of the Bourbons. Both in the case of the Confederacy and in the case of the Italian Kingdom, those members of the southern elites, and also those ordinary citizens, who rejected the new nation, for different reasons, were initially a minority; yet, in both cases, the minority grew in size and influence in the course of the first half of the 1860s.

In America, in the months that passed between the secession of South Carolina on December 20, 1860, and the fall of Fort Sumter on April 14, 1861, all southerners confronted a choice between remaining loyal to the Union, or else embracing Secession and the making of a new nation. As we know, eleven states in the lower and upper South decided to secede and formed the Confederate States of America, while four border states, plus the newly formed West Virginia, remained in the Union. If it is true, though, that the reasons why the border states in the South remained loyal to the Union had a great deal to do with Abraham Lincoln's diplomacy, pressures, and anti-libertarian policies there, it is also true, as William Freehling has shown in *The South vs. the South* (2001), that the divided loyalties of those southerners had a heavier influence than we once thought on the course of the Civil War. But Union sympathizers and anti-Confederate activists were hardly confined to those states in the South. As Paul Escott has recently pointed out, on one hand, "as the war began, only a few pockets of Unionism remained in the Lower South"; on the other hand, in the Upper South, at the very heart of the Confederacy, "in Richmond itself, pro-Union sentiment, written in chalk, had appeared on walls a few days after [Jefferson] Davis's inauguration" on 18 February 1861 – what had prompted the newly inaugurated president, no differently from Lincoln, to enforce anti-libertarian policies to ensure anti-national sentiment would not spread. Yet, despite Jefferson's and the Confederate government's efforts to dispel disloyalty, pro-Union and anti-Confederate sentiment continued to exist in several areas of the Confederacy, first and foremost in the upcountry and mountainous areas – traditionally the home of fiercely independent non-slaveholding yeomen, who resented the planters and the slave system that guaranteed the latter's wealth.[9]

In the first year of the war, and until late 1862, the Confederacy showed that it was able to remain independent and, through a series of important victories, it convinced the Union government that the war for bringing back the seceded states would be long and costly. Also as a result of these initial Confederate successes, pro-Union activities and anti-Confederate sentiments within the Confederacy maintained for a while a relatively low profile, though in certain areas especially of North Carolina, Tennessee, Georgia, and Alabama, loyalties were so divided that the governors had to take fairly severe measures against either open boycotting of the Confederate government, or secret Unionist organizations, and even formation of Unionist militias. In other words, in 1861-62, anti-Confederate and Union-

[9] Paul D. Escott, *The Confederacy: The Slaveholders' Failed Venture* (Santa Barbara, CA, 2010), 14, 31; William W. Freehling, *The South vs. the South: How Anti-Confederate Southerners Shaped the Course of the Civil War* (New York, 2001). See also Paul D. Escott, *After Secession: Jefferson Davis and the Failure of Confederate Nationalism* (Baton Rouge, LA, 1978); and Aaron Sheehan-Dean, *Why Confederates Fought: Family and Nation in Civil War Virginia* (Chapel Hill, NC, 2007).

ist forces were organizing themselves; at these early stages, they took advantage of the Union's invasion in regions of Virginia, Tennessee, and, above all, Louisiana, where New Orleans was occupied from May 1862. In addition, after the enforcement of the Conscription Act of April 16, 1862, a number of disaffected young southerners – essentially yeomen who resented the planter class' exemption from military service – and deserters joined the ranks of the Unionists. By later in the same year, after the Union inflicted a resounding victory on the Confederacy at the battle of Antietam on September 17, 1862, Unionist activities – representing a combination of both political and social reasons for anti-Confederate sentiment – had gone out of control and had generated miniature civil wars with the Confederate authorities in a number of areas. In fact, by then, as Stephanie McCurry has recently written, particularly "in Jones County, Mississippi, and in Western and Central North Carolina, East Tennessee, northern Alabama, Florida, and everywhere desertion reached militarily threatening proportion, the Confederate States waged war against its domestic enemies and they did not spare women." The Confederate South's inner civil war, fought within the context of the wider Civil War, though, was about to get worse as a result of Lincoln's *Emancipation Proclamation*.[10]

The year that South Carolina seceded from the Union, 1860, was a crucial year also for the Italian *Mezzogiorno*. In that year, the process of Italian national unification accelerated dramatically its pace when Giuseppe Garibaldi and his Red-Shirts led an expedition from the North to the South, which resulted, eventually, in the collapse of the Bourbon Kingdom of the Two Sicilies, and in the later annexation of all the southern territory to the northern-based Kingdom of Sardinia, ruled by the House of Savoy. Whilst supported by the majority of the southern Italian landowners, the annexation was not, in all likelihood, welcomed by a large number of the peasant population. Opposition to Garibaldi had already led to his repression of peasant activities during his expedition, culminating in the famous episode

[10] Stephanie McCurry, *Confederate Reckoning: Power and Politics in the Civil War South* (Cambridge, MA, 2010), 117. See also David Williams, *Bitterly Divided: The South's Inner Civil War* (New York, 2010); and John C. Inscoe and Robert Kenzer, eds., *Enemies of the Country: New Perspectives on Unionists in the Civil War South* (Chapel Hill, NC, 2004).

of Bronte, where, on August 2, 1860, Garibaldi's lieutenant, Nino Bixio, ordered the shooting of five peasant rebels who had taken possession of the town, defying the landed proprietors. After the annexation of the *Mezzogiorno* to the Kingdom of Sardinia, decreed by dubiously held plebiscites on October 21, 1860, peasant activity against the process of Italian national unification increased in size and spread. It quickly found a powerful ally in the "legitimist" circles, which wished to put back on his southern throne the young Bourbon King Francis II. On September 5, just two days before the arrival of Garibaldi in the capital Naples, Francis II had decided to abandon the royal palace to spare the city – in the words of Roberto Martucci – "from the horrors of war", and to take refuge in the fortress of Gaeta, from where he had begun organizing the counteroffensive. On October 1, near the Volturno river, in Campania, ca. 30,000 Bourbon soldiers clashed against 20,000 of Garibaldi's troops and were defeated, leaving many dead and prisoners behind. Starting from that moment, while Francis II was under siege in Gaeta, the remaining Bourbon soldiers and the rebel peasants engaged in a large-scale guerrilla warfare with the purpose of undoing Italian unification.[11]

After Gaeta fell, Francis II and his court fled to Rome, from where, under the protection of Pope Pius IX, they attempted to organize the guerrilla warfare against the Italian government in southern Italy. Therefore, as the Kingdom of Italy was proclaimed in Turin in March 1861, the *Mezzogiorno* was caught in the middle of an inner civil war – comparable to the Confederate South's inner civil war – between the pro-Bourbon forces on one side and the Italian troops on the other side. From the ideological point of view, the key was in the fact that the overthrowing of the Bourbon dynasty had been perpetrated by the Kingdom of Sardinia without a formal declaration of war, and effectively there was little legitimacy involved in the process of formation of the Italian Kingdom. As a result, those who sided with the Bourbons considered themselves ""legitimist"" aiming at restoring Francis II in his rightful place. Several of them came from abroad to help, and,

[11] Roberto Martucci, *L'Invenzione dell'Italia unita, 1855-1864* (Florence, 1999), 189. See also Giorgio Candeloro, *Storia dell'Italia moderna*, Vol. 5: *Dalla rivoluzione nazionale all'Unità (1849-1860)* (Milan, 1964); and Lucy Riall, *Sicily and the Unification of Italy, 1859-1866* (Oxford, 1998).

among them, the most famous and talented was Spanish officer José Borjés. A former commander of Carlist forces in Spain, Borjés was an expert in guerrilla operations and the ideal candidate for the overall command of the pro-Bourbon forces of the anti-Italian movement, according to Francis II's advisers. On September 14, 1861, Borjés landed in Calabria, where he joined the legendary head of the largest of a number of peasant bands of brigands – Carmine Donatelli, called Crocco, the anointed leader of his 1,500 men. Together, for several months, they fought against the Italian state conquering village after village from the Italian army between the regions of Campania and Lucania, until when Crocco parted from Borjés, not wanting to move on the city of Potenza, one of the largest in the area. Left without an army, Borjés attempted to reach the Papal State, but was captured and shot by the Italian troops without a trial on December 8, 1861.[12]

In 1860-61, thus, two comparable projects of creation of nations were supported by most American slaveholders in the U.S. South and by southern Italian landowners in the *Mezzogiorno*: the creation of the Confederates States of America, and the creation of the Kingdom of Italy. Almost immediately after their birth, both nations faced, in different ways, crises of legitimacy. In both cases, the crises related to a combination of internal problems and external influences, and it was this powerful combination that led to the explosion of movements opposed to the two new nations in the form, in both cases, of guerrilla warfare fought in particular areas – especially Mississippi, Alabama, Florida, and North Carolina in the Confederacy, and Campania, Lucania, and Apulia in southern Italy – and aimed at destabilizing the new government's authority and re-establishing the old one, be it the American Union or the Bourbon Kingdom. Essentially, in both cases, the anti-national movement was both political and social, aiming at the same time also to settle grievances held by less privileged sections of the populations against those among the two agrarian elites who continued to support the new nations because they benefited the most from

12 Gigi Di Fiore, *Controstoria dell'Unità d'Italia. Fatti e misfatti del Risorgimento* (Milan, 2007), 199-201. See also Alfonso Scirocco, *Il Mezzogiorno nella crisi dell'unificazione (1860-1861)* (Naples, 1981); and Fulvio Amore, *Uccidete José Borjés: l'ordine dei Piemontesi durante la conquista del Sud. Il racconto di un'infamia (1860-1862)* (Naples, 2010).

them. Also in both cases, though for very different reasons, in 1862 the crisis of legitimacy reached a point of no return. It was not going to be long, though, before both anti-national movements would be joined by activities on a larger scale initiated and carried on by the agrarian masses of the two southern regions for different, but comparable, social, and in a sense also political, reasons.

American Slaves, Southern Italian Peasants, Civil Wars, and Social Revolutions, 1862-1865

Within the context of the two crises of legitimacy that the newly formed national governments in the Confederate South and in the Italian *Mezzogiorno* were forced to face, an essential component was represented by the numerous and widespread episodes of unrest caused by the agrarian masses during the horrific ordeals of the American Civil War and of Italy's "Great Brigandage". Even though on a different scale and in different ways, as a result of its duration and geographical extension, agrarian unrest ended up in both cases being much more than a simple military event, and affected deeply the course of the Confederate South's and southern Italy's inner civil wars, transforming the entire social structure of the two regions, particularly relationships between the agrarian elites and their slave and peasant labourers. In turn, the agrarian labourers' insurrectionary activities led to the consequent shattering of the system of labor related to the "second slavery" in the Confederate South and to the weakening of the landowning economy in the Italian *Mezzogiorno*.

Clearly, though, the labourers' revolts assumed very different aspects in the two southern regions, especially because of the crucial contribution of the Union Army to the slaves' insurrection in the Confederate South, which stood in stark opposition to the solitary fight carried on by southern Italian peasants after the defeat of the pro-Bourbon forces. In this respect, it is interesting to notice that, in the United States, some of the current debates on the slaves' contribution to the making of their own freedom during the Civil War revolve around the question of whether it is possible to say that there was a massive slave rebellion in the Confederate South, independently from the issue of the Union government's and army's roles in freeing the slaves. Conversely, in the Italian *Mezzogiorno*, the issue at stake is whether it is possible to say that the peasant rebellion witnessed during the "Great Brigandage" was, for all intents and purposes, a civil war. In both cases, the conditions that are under scrutiny are the scale, duration, and intensity, together with the modalities, of still relatively little-known phenomena – the American slaves' insurrectionary activities and the southern Italian peasants' civil war. Those conditions, in fact, for the most part, still await painstaking investigation before a final word can be said on the above issues.

In the Confederate South, slaves had already started acting from the very beginning of the Civil War, mostly by fleeing to Union camps, especially in the areas bordering the Union lines, such as Virginia and Tennessee, and in those areas where the Union had made its first territorial gains, such as the Sea Islands of South Carolina, occupied from as early as November 1861, and lower Louisiana, from May 1862. The massive scale of the phenomenon of slaves fleeing to Union camps, in turn, had forced Lincoln to find at least a temporary solution vis-a-vis their legal status, and led Congress to pass a *First Confiscation Act* in August 1861, which called for the seizure of all rebel property, including the slaves, who, by this time, began to be called "contrabands of war". Then, in July 1862, a *Second Confiscation Act* stated that all the slaves of Confederate masters were to be considered free. Finally, in September 1862, after the Union's victory at Antietam, Lincoln drafted the *Preliminary Emancipation Proclamation,* whose definitive version became the official *Emancipation Proclamation* on January 1, 1863. Justified by Lincoln as a war measure, the *Emancipation Proclamation* declared immediately, "thenceforward and forever free" all the slaves in areas under Confederate control, gave legal backing to the slaves' efforts to free themselves, and provided the Union Army with the legal power to help them in their self-liberating struggle. With the release of the *Emancipation Proclamation*, the South's inner civil war between Confederate authorities and anti-Confederate forces entered a new phase, as the slaves became now fully recognized main actors in their anti-Confederate activities.[13]

[13] Abraham Lincoln, "The Emancipation Proclamation (1863)" in Rick Halpern and Enrico Dal Lago, eds., *Slavery and Emancipation* (Oxford, 2002), 380. See also Ira Berlin

By 1863, though, the inner civil war within the white South had increased in motivation and intensity. On one hand, riots were exploding in all the major cities, first and foremost Richmond, as the fear of starvation gripped the people whose supplies were rerouted to Robert E. Lee's Army of Northern Virginia. On the other hand, in the wildest areas of North Carolina, Florida, and Mississippi, where an ever-increasing number of Unionists and deserters found their refuge, the fight kept occupied the local Confederate authorities for many months, and, in the case of the so-called "Free State of Jones" in eastern Mississippi, it came close to generating a secessionist movement from the Confederacy. Though unrelated, the slaves' own struggle for freedom inserted itself within this picture of a Confederacy that was faltering under the weight of representing a nation that was both elitist and unprepared for an industrial type of war. Ultimately, then, through their insurrectionary activities, the slaves unmasked the contradiction of a nation that fought not only for its own freedom, but also for the freedom to keep African Americans enslaved. Slaves had resisted this notion from the very beginning of the war, and, in fact, already starting from 1861, rumors of imminent slave insurrections had been heard in different places in the South – as in the famous case of slave conspiracy investigated by Winthrop Jordan in Adams County, Mississippi.[14]

More generally, as Peter Kolchin has noted, throughout the Confederacy, slaves "worked less, questioned more, and increasingly took to running away, not only singly or in pairs, as had been common before the war, but in large groups as well". By 1863, as Emancipation was proclaimed, and the Union Army, now invested with the legal power of an agent of liberation, came increasingly closer to the heart of the Confederacy, triumphing

---

et al., *Slaves No More: Three Essays on Emancipation and the Civil War* (New York, 1992), 1-76; Louis Gerteis, "Slaves, Servants, and Soldiers: Uneven Paths to Freedom in the Border States, 1861-1865" in William A. Blair and Karen Fischer Younger, eds., *Lincoln's proclamation; Emancipation Reconsidered* (Chapel Hill, NC, 2009), 170-194; and Eric Foner, *The Fiery Trial: Abraham Lincoln and American Slavery* (New York, 2010), 166-206.

14 See Victoria Bynum, *The Long Shadow of the Civil War: Southern Dissent and its Legacies* (Chapel Hill, NC, 2010); Victoria Bynum, *The Free State of Jones: Mississippi's Longest Civil War* (Chapel Hill, NC, 2002); and Winthrop Jordan, *Tumult and Silence at Second Creek: An Inquiry into a Civil War Slave Conspiracy* (Baton Rouge, LA, 1995).

at Vicksburg as well as shattering Lee's hopes at Gettysburg, the situation rapidly deteriorated beyond repair in many areas, first and foremost those regions where the local masters had left for the front, as James Henry Hammond's August 30, 1863 observations about the behavior of his slaves at Silver Bluff, South Carolina, prove: "Negroes … stealing right and left … Frank my driver escaped today and ran away". Thousands of episodes similar to this one must have happened, with massive numbers of slaves turning up in Union camps, and eventually, with many of them – close to 200,000 by the end of the war – donning the Union blue uniform. But there was more to the slaves' resistance than simply the desire to run away and perhaps join the Union Army.[15]

In his work, Steven Hahn has shown how, even before the war, slaves used mutual solidarity and kinship networks to build traditions of informal political activity through which they put up effective means to resist their masters' pretensions to exploit them. During the war, these relationships of mutual solidarity and these kinship networks were instrumental in creating the preconditions for a variety of rebellious acts, of which running away was one among many – from stealing the masters' property, all the way to setting up massive conspiracies – that went into the direction of disrupting the slave system as a whole. In this sense, emancipation, when it came, acted as a catalyst for a number of rebellious acts that now found a logical conclusion. More than thirty years ago, Leon Litwack wrote in *Been in the Storm So Long* (1979) that "the extent of black insurrectionary activity during the Civil War remains a subtle question." Thirty years later, Steven Hahn, in *The Political Worlds of Slavery and* Freedom (2008), asked if, by not acknowledging the massive – even though diverse and unconnected – number of rebellious acts in the same collective way as we acknowledge the slaves rebellious acts in the Haitian Revolution, we might have missed the largest slave rebellion that ever occurred, during the American Civil War.[16]

---

15 Peter Kolchin, "Slavery and Freedom in the Civil War South" in James McPherson and William J. Cooper, eds., *Writing the Civil War: The Quest to Understand* (Columbia, SC, 1998), 245; James Henry Hammond quoted in Carol Bleser, ed., *Secret and Sacred: The Diaries of James Henry Hammond, a Southern Slaveholder* (New York, 1981), 297.

16 Leon F. Litwack, *Been in the Storm So Long: The Aftermath of Slavery* (New York, 1979), 46. See also Steven Hahn, *A Nation Under our Feet: Black Political Struggle*

In this respect, perhaps, it would be also interesting to ask if it is possible to compare the scope, scale, and significance of the slave rebellion in Haiti in relation to the end of the "first slavery" in the 1790s with the scope, scale, and significance of the slave rebellion in the Confederate South in relation to the end of the "second slavery".

Though Hahn has been harshly criticized by some scholars, who have pointed out especially the importance of the crucial role of the Union government and of the Union army as agents of emancipation – a condition that made things radically different from the Haitian case – there is still much to be said for encouraging researchers to investigate better and deeper the slaves' multiform acts of rebellion in a number of localities within the Confederate South, particularly from 1863 onwards, and in giving these acts more significance than has been often the case. In this sense, Stephanie McCurry's recent *Confederate Reckoning* (2010) has gone some way in this direction – and, significantly, in her treatment, connections and comparisons with Haiti have a special place. However, McCurry's work really aspired to be a synthesis with a few exemplary case-studies, which, all together, could do a great deal to prove the point that a massive slave rebellion did take place in the Confederate South during the Civil War. Yet, much more research still needs to be done on this topic at the local level in several different regions and states before we can conclusively say whether this was, indeed, the case or not, or whether, perhaps, it is all just a matter of definitions and interpretations.[17]

Comparably to what happened in the Confederate South, also in the Italian *Mezzogiorno* the struggle between nationalist and counter-nationalist forces entered a new phase in 1862. In fact, by 1862, with Josè Borjés' death, the "legitimist" phase of the anti-Italian struggle in the *Mezzogiorno* was over; the peasants and brigands who collaborated with the

in the Rural South from Slavery to the Great Migration (Cambridge, MA, 2003), 62-115; and Steven Hahn, *The Political Worlds of Slavery and Freedom* (Cambridge, MA, 2009), 55-114

17 See McCurry, *Confederate Reckoning*, 239-262. For a recent exemplary treatment of social change in the Confederacy that presents a different view from Hahn's and McCurry's interpretation of the slaves' role in the Civil War, see Bruce Levine, *The Fall of the House of Dixie: The Civil War and the Social Revolution that Transformed the South* (New York, 2013).

pro-Bourbon forces would now fight their own war on their own terms with the Italian state. The conflict, derogatorily called "Great Brigandage", would be the first terrible, costly civil war in unified Italy, it would last four long years until 1865 – therefore overlapping with the American Civil War – and it would become increasingly brutal and inhuman. Crocco's life represents well the parable of those who, whether as peasants or as former Bourbon soldiers, began their anti-Italian activities in the aftermath of Garibaldi's expedition. Like Crocco, they were initially convinced that Italian unification would have brought about a more democratic form of government. Then, disillusioned, they joined the "legitimist" forces to restore a Bourbon King who, with all his faults, was not a Piedmontese conqueror, and finally they threw all their efforts behind the attempt to rid of the new Italian state, which, for them, represented little more than heavy taxes, forced conscription, and the very expression of the power of the landowners who oppressed them; in Crocco's own words, "the exploited poor answered 'also our time has come'".[18]

The Italian state responded to the inner civil war that had erupted in the *Mezzogiorno* sending an army that, by 1862, was already 50,000 strong, and by the end of the conflict would count more than 100,000 men. The enormous scale of the phenomenon and the ability of the brigands, who by then had formed hundreds of bands, all practicing very effective and brutal forms of guerrilla warfare, managed to keep the Italian Army in check, and ultimately forced the Parliament, whose members, for the most part, had no other intention than repressing the southern population, to promulgate special laws. Thus, in October 1863, the infamous Pica Law was passed and would be enforced for the next two years. It gave military authorities the power to maintain martial law in all the *Mezzogiorno* provinces – particularly Campania, Lucania, and Capitanata – where brigandage was present, leading to countless atrocities, massacres, and executions of not just brigands, but also of a large number of civilians suspected of harbouring outlaws. The final death count, according to the official documents, was of 5,212 killed; however, recently Roberto Martucci has pointed out that the

[18] Crocco's quotation is in Maria Grazia Cutrufelli, *L'Unità d'Italia. Questione meridionale e nascita del sottosviluppo nel Sud* (1975), 259.

number must have been much higher, especially if we count also the civilians, and he has proposed a number "between 18,250 and 54,750 shot or killed in other ways (suppressed, burned alive, etc.)" – a much more realistic and, sadly, extremely high figure, which reminds us that too many people died and were forgotten in the inner civil war fought in southern Italy.[19]

Similarly to what happened in regards to the slaves' actions in the Confederate South during the Civil War, in interpreting the "Great Brigandage", since the 1860s, scholars and intellectuals have divided between different views. On one hand, some of them have emphasized the political aspirations of pro-Bourbon supporters and have erroneously interpreted the popular insurgence only as part of a general "legitimist" upheaval, while, on the other hand, others have emphasized the social dimensions of the phenomenon, somewhat narrowly interpreting it simply as an example of class warfare carried on by the dispossessed masses and brutally criminalized and repressed by the new Italian state. From the 1980s, a third interpretation has also come to the fore – one that has emphasized, instead, a postcolonial interpretation of the phenomenon, shedding light particularly on the importance of hitherto mostly hidden racial prejudices by northern soldiers and civil servants against southerners. However, the increasingly accepted interpretation by a number of recent historians – among whom particularly Salvatore Lupo, John Davis, Roberto Martucci, and Gigi Di Fiore – is that the "Great Brigandage" was first and foremost an episode that, in the words of Salvatore Lupo, "assumed more clearly the character of a civil war ... because the conflict concerned only Italians."[20]

---

19 Martucci, *L'invenzione dell'Italia unita*, 314. See also Franco Molfese, *Storia del brigantaggio dopo l'Unità* (Milan, 1964); John Dickie, "A Word at War: The Italian Army and Brigandage, 1860-1870", *History Workshop Journal* 33 (1992), 1-24; and Daniela Adorni, "Il brigantaggio" in Luciano Violante, ed., *Storia d'Italia*, Annali 12: *La criminalità* (Turin, 1996), 283-319.

20 Salvatore Lupo, *Il passato del nostro presente. Il lungo ottocento, 1776-1913* (Rome, 2010), 107. See also especially Salvatore Lupo, *L'unificazione italiana. Mezzogiorno, rivoluzione, guerra civile* (Rome, 2011); Salvatore Lupo, "Il Grande Brigantaggio. Interpretazione e memoria di una guerra civile" in Walter Barberis, ed., *Storia d'Italia*, Annali 18: *Guerra e Pace* (Turin, 2002), 465-504; and John A. Davis, "Le guerre del brigantaggio" in Mario Isnenghi and Eva Cecchinato, eds., *Fare l'Italia. Unità e dis-*

Therefore, the civil war at the heart of the "Great Brigandage" of 1861-65 in the Italian *Mezzogiorno* was essentially a mass phenomenon of armed peasant revolt against, first and foremost, the Italian government and those landowners who supported it, but it had also an important political component in the "legitimist" attempt to restore Bourbon King Francis II. At the same time, though, it is also important to remember that an equally dangerous political dimension was represented by Garibaldi's August1862 expedition through southern Italy – an attempt to revive the fortunes of the Democratic Party through the envisioned conquest of Rome. Garibaldi was eventually halted at Aspromonte in Calabria, but the possibility that the southern Italian masses might have followed him, this time against the Italian monarchy, had been a very real one. In both cases, the "legitimist" and the democratic attempts, the newly formed Italian state ran the risk of witnessing a secession of the *Mezzogiorno* from the rest of the country, in a scenario reminding one of the Confederacy's secession in the American Civil War, and there is little doubt that the shrewdest members of the Italian government, well informed about contemporary events in the United States, were very well aware of this.[21]

In both the Confederate South and the Italian *Mezzogiorno*,from the point of view of the agrarian masses, the renewed conflict between the governmental centre and the peripheral elites from 1861 onwards represented a perfect opportunity to seize in order to change their condition of exploitation. Therefore, comparably to African American slaves in the Confederate South during the American Civil War, the agrarian masses in the Italian *Mezzogiorno* during the "Great Brigandage" rose spontaneously to improve their lot and end their exploitation, but at the same time joined the political and military initiatives of those governmental forces – be they the Union soldiers or the Bourbon supporters – that fought against their oppressors. In

---

unità nel Risorgimento (Turin, 2008), 738-752.

21 See Marco Meriggi, "Dopo l'Unità. Forme e ambivalenza del legittimismo borbónico", *Passato e Presente* 29 (2011), 39-56; Alfonso Scirocco, *Giuseppe Garibaldi. Battaglie, amori, ideali di un cittadino del mondo* (Rome, 2001), 293-295; and Axel Korner, "Barbarous America" in Axel Korner, Nicola Miller, and Adam I. P. Smith, eds., *America Imagined: Explaining the United States in Nineteenth-Century Europe and Latin America* (New York, 2012), 135-136.

both cases, it is clear that they did this out of convenience more than for any other reason. In the American Civil War, runaway slaves joined the Union army in increasing numbers in the latter part of the conflict, after Emancipation had been granted and the war had finally become a war for liberation, while at the time of the southern Italian "Great Brigandage", peasants joined the pro-Bourbon forces only until their aim was the same one of overthrowing Italian authority. In reality, from the beginning, African American slaves and southern Italian peasants thought and acted with a mind of their own, and with the objectives of freeing themselves from their masters in one case and freeing themselves from the landowners in the other case. In acting on these premises, African American slaves engaged in a variety of rebellious acts that, collectively, might very well one day prove to have been the equivalent of a massive slave insurrection – which, at the very least, gave a substantial contribution to the end of the "second slavery" in the Confederate South – while southern Italian peasants kept the Italian army engaged in what can only be called a civil war.[22]

Conclusion

In 1865, whereas the Confederacy did not survive the crisis of legitimacy and collapsed, together with the southern slaveholding system based on the "second slavery", under the combined military pressure from the Union and internal opposition by increasingly larger numbers among the elites and ordinary citizens, the Kingdom of Italy survived the crisis of legitimacy at the cost of strengthening the government's authoritarian character and the indiscriminate use of military force – both of which led to opposition by large strata of the southern Italian population. By 1865, therefore, two different, but comparable, processes had taken place leading to the consolidation of the United States and Italy. In these parallel processes of national consolidation, the two southern regions had played fundamental roles, since, in both regions, the different social strata had contributed in determinant, though different, ways in accelerating the movement toward creation of a free and

[22] On some of these issues, see Enrico Dal Lago, "States of Rebellion: Civil War, Rural Unrest, and the Agrarian Question in the American South and the Italian *Mezzogiorno*, 1861-1865", *Comparative Studies in Society and History* 47:2 (2005), 403-432.

integrated American nation-state and an integrated Italian nation-state – creations that, in both cases, we should see as reactions to threats posed by both centrifugal politics and internal social upheavals.

As a result, on one hand, the political actions of both southern elites ended up creating a renewed tradition of opposition to the national governments. On the other hand, while in the American South the slaves' rebellion in the wake of Emancipation was politically neutralized through its absorption into a legitimate war of liberation fought for the nationalization of freedom on the side of the Union, in the Italian *Mezzogiorno* the massive peasant revolt termed "Great Brigandage" was repressed militarily in the harshest possible way. Then, after 1865, while the revolts' aftermaths did not lead to all the changes American slaves and southern Italian peasants had hoped for – remaining, therefore, "unfinished revolutions", to paraphrase Eric Foner[23] – the situation that both the elites of the American South and of the Italian *Mezzogiorno* faced was, effectively, one of lack of power and of enduring opposition to the respective national governments. This situation continued, in both cases, until 1876, the year that signaled the end of Reconstruction in the United States and the rise of the first Left government in Italy.

[23] See Eric Foner, *Reconstruction: America's Unfinished Revolution* (New York, 1988).

Puerto Rico:"atlantización" and culture during the"segunda esclavitud"

Javier LAVIÑA

Universitat de Barcelona

Introduction

The incorporation of America into European economies opened several avenues and possiblities, already explored in the Canary Islands, which led to the destruction of the indigenous population, and the arrival of African slaves to new lands. Europe's, Africa's and the Americas' annexation into the world[1] economy is known as "atlantización." It not only produced economic effects, but also created complex social and cultural repercussions, so important and profound as to be present still today.

After their arrival to Puerto Rico, the first Spanish inhabitants received land and indigenous labor, as had occurred in other newly colonized places. This "encomienda" regime was in reality the exploitation of the native population and caused increased demand for labor, a repeat of what occured in other territories. Therefore, in 1510, Cristóbal de Sotomayor was authorized to search for Indians from outside in order to meet growing labor demands. In this regard, during the first years, Puerto Rico's colonization was like every other Spanish territory in the Caribbean, which was an extraction mining zone with few settlers dedicating themselves to agriculture. Quickly, the demographic crisis created by the deaths of large percentages of the indigenous population, made importing labor from other islands[2] and from Africa a necessity.

1 Asia se incorporó también al sistema económico mundial, aportando especias y otros productos de lujo, vide, Wallerstein, Immanuel. *El moderno sistema mundial. La agricultura capitalista y los orígenes de la economía-mundo europea en el siglo XVI*. Ed. Siglo XXI. Madrid 1979. Pags 319-488,

2 Cfr. Fernández Méndez. Eugenio. *Las encomiendas y la esclavitud de los indios de Puerto Rico. 1508-1550*.Ediciones el Cemí. San Juan Puerto Rico 1995.pag 13

Puerto Rico became a site of mass slavery, but in the early years of the colony, the weight of mining work rested on both indigenous and African slaves[3]. During the early years of colonial slavery on the island, it was quite heterogeneous, with metal extraction utilizing both indigenous labor and those enslaved and brought from the Iberian Peninsula, some of whom were not actually black. In fact, excess Muslim slave labor, coming from the Mediterranean, led the Spanish crown to decree the confiscation of Muslim slaves in the Americas[4]. This restrictive policy regarding slavery in these times, demonstrates that there was lively trade between the Old World of medieval trade and the new territories incorporated by the Crown.

Despite the little promise that extraction showed in Puerto Rico, alluvial gold mining continued for a while during the early years of colonization, with the minimal investment necessary taking place. From 1530 to 1531, 55 percent of the island‘s population was enslaved: native inhabitants accounted for 25 percent of the population, 12 percent were Indians from elsewhere, and the Spaniards were only 8 percent of inhabitants[5]. Thus, we see that a relatively important piece of the slave population was indigenous.

Nonetheless, with the depletion of mineral resources, the island began a market transformation to meet the demands of European markets, eying products like sugar and others that could boost the economy. Spanish expansion on the American continent and ensuing discovery of silver in New Spain and Peru, however, rendered the West Indies of little interest for exploitation of resources.

After this first massive surge in slavery, when the Spanish were only 8 percent of the population, Puerto Rico experienced a steep decline in investment. Without metals and with little possibility for growth, European competition left the island. The Spanish Crown focused instead on continental silver extraction and no longer devoted effort to Puerto Rican colo-

3 For the indegenous population, see Moscoso, Francisco. *Caciques aldeas y población taína de Boriquén, Puerto Rico 1492-1582.* Academia Puertorriqueña de la Historia. San Juan 2008.

4 Cardaillac, Louis. Le problème morisque en Amérique. *Mélanges de la Casa de-Velázquez.*t.12, París, 1976, pp. 283-303.

5 Moscoso, Francisco. *Agricultura y sociedad en Puerto Rico siglos 16 al 18.* Pag 9. Editorial ICP (Instituto de Cultura Puertorriqueña). San Juan 2001.

nization. The colonists were deeply isolated, and as Quintero Rivera wrote[6], little by little, the island became a wild territory with little authority, due to institutional neglect.

The Crown's power and state representation remained concentrated in two urban spaces, San Juan and San Germán. With the lack of population in the remaining territory, the interior became an important base for both indigenous and black slaves as well as for Spaniards all resisting the strict control enforced in cities.

Between 1540 and 1600, more than 6,000 slaves entered Puerto Rico to perform agricultural production, the majority of which pertained to sugar[7]. The most populated areas, according to Vila Vilar's work[8], had only 8,000 inhabitants, which gives an idea of how unattractive the area was for business and investment. Alongside the small number of inhabitants, the slave population was maintained until the eighteenth century, when the slave trade to the island began again.

Despite the Spanish Crown's lack of interest in the island in the early 1520s, Puerto Rico was one of the largest exporters of sugar[9]. Nonetheless, at the end of the seventeenth century, the Crown offered land to promote Puerto Rican agriculture, supposedly an example of the "idleness" of the island. Emigrants from the Canary Islands took advantage of this offer[10], but the small size of the plots offered were not enough to cover the heavy investments needed for sugar production. These actions thus facilitated the massive incorporation of slave labor. In fact, the economic system was based on small- and médium-sized properties. Although there were also large estates, these limited properties depended on male migration with few women

---

6 Quintero Rivera, Ángel. La cimarronería como herencia y utopía. In*David y Goliat.* 48 (nov 1985), 37-51. Sued Badillo, Jalil; López Canto, Angel. *Puerto Rico Negro.* Editorial Cultural, Río Piedras, 1986. Pags 127-137.

7 Sued Badillo, Jalil, López Cantos, Angel. *Puerto Rico Negro.* Pags 82-111. Editorial Cultural. Rio Piedras, Puerto Rico 1986

8 Vila Vilar, Enriqueta. *Historia de Puerto Rico 1600-1650.* Escuela de Estudios Hispanoamericanos, CSIC, Sevilla 1974.

9 Moscoso, Francisco. *Agricultura y sociedad en Puerto Rico siglos 16 al 18.* Pags 46-63. Editorial ICP (Instituto de Cultura Puertorriqueña). San Juan 2001.

10 López Cantos, Ángel. *Historia de Puerto Rico, 1650-1700.* Escuela de Estudios Hispanoamericanos, Sevilla 1975.

accompanying them. Thus, a large mixed class permeated colonial society, resulting in a considerable presence of free mulattoes who completed some of the tasks carried out by slaves in other Spanish colonies.

Despite the authorities' attempts to promote agricultural exports, their attempts were in vain. Subsistence farming became the economic base of the island, along with livestock that certainly had more demand abroad – both alive and dead in the form of meat. A plantation economy therefore developed in the Caribbean Islands, based on European demand for the consumption of cattle. The cattle were also needed to run the pull-mills and transport cane and sugar to shipping points. Sugar production, however, demonstrates the small number of workers, and even smaller number of slaves, involved in this agricultural activity[11].

European presence in other parts of the Caribbean eventually led the Spanish Crown to re-evaluate the value of the Puerto Rican territory. Puerto Rico had suffered several attacks by the British, and Puerto Rico's defense had failed. Nevertheless the depopulation of the territory led the Crown to enacta new immigration policy, which resulted in better success than the previous one. The low population density on the island motivated the Spanish Crown to develop a new migration policy, one that was more successful than the previous one.

From the second half of the eighteenth century, Puerto Rico managed to increase its agricultural exports, but it still was not even close to the numbers exported by Cuba.

An important part of understanding the Puerto Rican reality in the eighteenth century is the pastoral visits of bishops. We have been fortunate to have access to one of these visits, in which the bishop gives a very detailed account of his vision for the colony[12]. Of note, one of his first observations of his visit to the island tells of nearly 50 percent population growth in Puerto Rico. The total population of 7,900 – not including soldiers who lived in the garrisons – highlights how practically deserted the interior and areas outside the two major cities were.

---

[11] Moscoso, Francisco. *Agricultura y sociedad en Puerto Rico siglos 16 al 18*. Pags 109-118. Editorial ICP (Instituto de Cultura Puertorriqueña). San Juan 2001.

[12] Archivo General de Indias, en adelante A.G.I. Santo Domingo leg. 2527. Visita pastoral del obispo Pedro Martínez de Onca 14 de abril de 1760.

From 1760, the year when the bishop of Puerto Rico made his pastoral visit throughout the island, we find a series of population censuses on the island. They highlight the significant increase in population that occurred, possibly based on repopulation of Spaniards in the interior, migration from the Canaries or of those from the península. For whatever reason, in the 15 years that had passed, the population grew formidably from 7,900 to 61,929[13]. This growth was visible in towns like Utuado, worked by Fernando Pico[14]; hence, since Utuado's founding in 1733, its population growth was spectacular.

First, it should be noted that the foundation of Utuado was due to the need for some families of Arecibo to live in the interior and therefore colonize new areas, indicating that there was a relative overpopulation on the coast alongside sparse population inland, as the bishop stated in his report[15]. According to the work of Picó, cited above, Utuado's population grew from 658 inhabitants in 1765 to 1,066 in 1776[16], marking the upward growth trend in the second half of the eighteenth century. A similar situation occurred in the case of Cayey, founded in the last quarter of the eighteenth century after Coamo's disintegration. This area was devoted to the cultivation of coffee, and in this case, the slave population increased from 12 percent in 1780 to 21 percent in 1790. The growth of slaves was not only due to increased import of slaves but also to the growth of the enslaved Creole population[17].

From 1763, after the landing of the English in Havana, Puerto Rico aroused the interest of the Crown. The disaster led to the British Caribbean

---

13 According to Abad y la Sierra, Íñigo. *Historia geográfica civil y natural de la isla de Puerto Rico.* Ediciones Doce Calles, Historiador oficial de Puerto Rico. pag 251. Madrid 2002. En 1769 la población era de apenas 18.000 habitantes.

14 Picó Fernando. *Libertad y servidumbre en el Puerto Rico del siglo XIX.* Pags 19-22. Ediciones Huracán. Rio Piedras, Puerto Rico 1983.

15 A.G.I. Santo Domingo leg. 2527. Visita pastoral del obispo Pedro Martínez de Onca 14 de abril de 1760.

16 Picó, Fernando. *Cayeyanos. Familias y solidaridades en la historia de Cayey.* Pags 22-23. Ediciones Huracán, Rio Piedras, Puerto Rico. 2007

17 Torres Ramírez, Bibiano. *La isla de Puerto Rico (1765-1800).* Instituto de Cultura Puertorriqueña. San Juan 1968.Picó, Fernando. *Cayeyanos. Familias y solidaridades en la historia de Cayey.* Pags 22-23. Ediciones Huracán, Rio Piedras, Puerto Rico. 2007.

policy, and the Spanish Crown tried to protect other Caribbean possessions. Puerto Rico again became an active player in the empire. First, defense construction in San Juan revived but against construction policy that used slave labor in Puerto Rico, inmates from the Iberian Peninsula and islands were instead used.

Puerto Rico's governor and accountant asked the Crown for the introduction of black persons from foreign colonies for a period of 10 years with tax exemptions, well as other measures to stimulate plantation agriculture, such asthe importation of necessary equipment for the production of sugar and for the ownership to all occupants of Crown lands to be recognized[18]. Aguirre-Arístegu also tried, and succeeded, to revive the economy by bringing the slave trade to the island, with between 500 to 600 slaves brought per year. The contract was not quite fulfilled, at least in the early company years.

At the same time that living conditions among inhabitants improved, slave imports were more regular and supplied the local market. However, most of the slaves who entered the island did not have it as their final destination. From August 1766, a total of 12,575 slaves from Africa (Guinea) entered, of which 11,678 were re-exported. Re-export ports were in Havana, Cuba (Santiago), Cartagena, and Portobelo. These re-exported slaves were probably redistributed in Peru and Honduras, and only 212 were sold on the island of Puerto Rico[19].

Despite these re-exports to other ports and cities in the Americas, the number of slaves brought into Puerto Rico between 1774 and 1807 was 15,000[20] – a 33-year period involving some 545 slaves annually, a significant figure given the limited resources of the island. Sugarcane was the

---

[18] A G I. Santo Domingo 2288. Puerto Rico 7 de agosto de 1776.El gobernador Muesas y el contador Puente Piden a favor de aquellos vecinos las gracias que están expresadas en la representación.

[19] AGI, Santo Domingo, legajo 2516. El apoderado del Asiento de negros, Goycoa 25 de marzo de 1772.

[20] Picó, Fernando. *Historia general de Puerto Rico*. Pag.143. Ediciones Huracán, Rio Piedras, Puerto Rico.2004.

product that triggered the slave trade[21], but in no other case did colonial culture come to have the same importance or productive capacity as Cuba.

Despite the scarcity of capital and labor resources, the island's economic growth contributed to an increasingly heated international context. The depletion of sugar production in some English possessions and the Haitian Revolution led emigrants from Santo Domingo arriving in Puerto Rico. These persons encouraged coffee cultivation in inland areas. Two important elements of the slave population's growth were the Crown's elimination of carimbo and the lowering of tariffs on the entry of slaves to the island, which favored Puerto Rico. As a result, the percentage of slaves among Puerto Rico's inhabitants went from 10.4% to 13.9% over a period of ten years (1784 to 1794). The population increase mainly owed itself to "crecimiento vegetativo"; two-thirds of the population growth came from improved health and the other third came from increased migratory flows from the metropolis and slave trade. Nonetheless, the most significant growth, both economically and demographically, was from the nineteenth century, especially between the years of 1840 to 1860. Since that time though, the slave population declined, and a year before emancipation, slaves represented only 5 percent of the island's population[22].

Graph 1. Evolution of the Puerto Rican Population from 1775-1807[23]

Year	Whites	Free pardos	Free blacks	Aggregated	Slaves	Indians[24]	Total Population
1775[25]	30.383	15.073	2.279	7.660	6.534	-	61.929
1789[26]	46.756	34.867	7.866	-	11.260	2.302	103.051

[21] Moscoso, Francisco. *Agricultura y sociedad en Puerto Rico siglos 16 al 18*. Pags 133-142. Editorial ICP (Instituto de Cultura Puertorriqueña. San Juan 2001. Picó, Fernando. *Historia general de Puerto Rico*. Pags.150-165. Ediciones Huracán, Rio Piedras, Puerto Rico. 2004.

[22] Dietz, James, l. *Historia económica de Puerto Rico*. Pag 53. Ediciones Huracán, Rio Piedras, Puerto Rico 2002.

[23] A.G.I.Santo Domingo legajo 2396. Estado general de la isla de Puerto Rico. El cuadro es de elaboración propia.

[25] A.G.I.Santo Domingo legajo 2396.Estado general de la isla de Puerto Rico.

[26] A.G.I.Santo Domingo legajo 2288.Estado general de la isla de Puerto Rico.

Year	Whites	Free pardos	Free blacks	Aggregated	Slaves	Indians[24]	Total Population
1790[27]	48.293	34.578	8.333	-	13.173	2.302	106.679
1793	50.937	37.490	9.481	-	15.212	2.437	115.557
1794	57.832	39.203	10.136	-	17.822	2.740	127.733
1795	60.785	38.354	9.713	-	18.053	2.853	129.758
1797	57.064	45.903	12.930	-	21.549	1.312	138.758
1799	71.437	44.215	13.053	-	21.219	3.308	153.232
1800	71.406	45.971	12.798	-	21.931	3.320	155.426
1801	70.690	47.254	12.874	-	23.878	3.355	158.051
1802	71.723	50.164	14.414	-	24.591	2.300	163.192
1807	82.832	57.202	18.677	-	24.500	-	183.211

With respect to distribution of the slave population by sex, we find a relative balance in the sex ratio, at least if we compare to the Cuban case.

Graph 2. Distribution of the slave population by sex[28]

Year	Male	Female	Total
1775	3.384	3.150	6.534
1789	6.037	5.233	11.260
1790	6.938	6.235	13.173
1793	8.004	7.208	15.212
1794	9.374	8.448	17.822
1795	9657	8.396	18.053
1797	11.208	10.341	21.549
1799	10.232	10.978	21.219
1800	10.706	10.513	21.931
1801	12.065	11.813	23.878
1802	12.576	12.015	24.591
1807	13.062	11.483	24.500

[27] From 1790 to 1807, the reference is. A.G.I.Santo Domingo legajo 2288. Estado general de la isla de Puerto Rico.

[28] This data is taken from the previous graph.

The sex ratio is relatively balanced between male and female slaves, which facilitated the reproduction of slave labor, despite high infant mortality. These figures show the beginnings of a process of expansion that was maintained during the first half of the nineteenth century. It was not until 1815 that Puerto Rico entered the world of the "segunda esclavitud" and the "atlantización," systems resulting from re-enslavement.

"La segunda esclavitud" in Puerto Rico

We believe that eighteenth-century trade, in the hands of the Arístegui Aguirre Company, was a key element that generated capital accumulation based on the re-export of labor to other colonies, so that Puerto Rico became an intermediate point between Africa and the Americas for at least 20 years. While it is true that the slave trade increased the slave population, the balanced sex ratio facilitated the creation of a relatively important Creole slave population (despite high infant mortality).

Theoretically, an average of 500 slaves per year were introduced to the island, a number never actually reached. The slave trade was, however, maintained, and as mentioned earlier, in 1766, the island received a total of 12,575 slaves from Guinea, though 11,575 were re-exported to other Spanish ports. Hence, the bottom line is that 212 slaves were sold on the island[29]. This view shows the limited capacity of the islanders to operate an economy based on export to Europe, and that in any case, the Aguirre-Arístegui company acquired slaves under contract with the Crown.

Another factor to consider in understanding the lack of contact with the African connection is the abundance of a free black population already engaged in agricultural work and a significant presence of runaway slaves formerly possessed by foreigners, who once relocated in Puerto Rico, could obtain freedom and small plots of land where their population was grouped. The importance of these settlers became apparent in areas like San Mateo de los Cangrejos and Loiza, both of which were used as sources of free labor for sugar plantations and herding in the area.

[29] AGI, Santo Domingo, legajo 2516. El apoderado del Asiento de negros, Goycoa 25 de marzo de 1772.

Change began after 1815 when the Crown decreed free trade. The phenomenon was similar to one occuring in Cuba – a free trade decree followed by the beginning of mass slavery. While Puerto Rico's enslavement did not reach the scale of the Greater Antilles, it was important for the island's dimensions and possibilities and gave way to a second savage slave trade that changed the face of the island's population[30].

The gender proportions of male and female slaves in Puerto Rico were quite balanced compared to the skewed Cuban case[31]. In the Puerto Rican case, although imports of slave labor appeared to lead to development of production in medium and small sugar or coffee farms, Creole slave labor and free labor played equally important roles. With respect to the production on large farms, production was predicated on massive incorporation of slaves[32].

---

30 Cfr. Morales Carrión, Arturo. *Auge y decadencia de la trata negrera en Puerto Rico (1820-1860).* Centro de Estudios Avanzados de Puerto Rico y el Caribe. Instituto de Cultura Puertorriqueña. San Juan, 1978.

31 Para Cuba el desequilibrio entre hombres y mujeres era notable, Moreno Fraginals, Manuel. *El Ingenio. Complejo socioeconómico cubano del azúcar.* Ed. Ciencias Sociales. La Habana 1978. Tomo 2 pág 86. En el cuadro que nos ofrece Moreno, aparece de forma muy clara la africanización del campo entre 1791-1822, en que un 81,76% de los esclavos africanos son varones, frente a un 14,39% de mujeres. Y el total de varones en estos años es del 84,06% de total de los trabajadores esclavos con tan sólo un 15,94% de mujeres. Este desequilibrio sufre una ligera variación entre 1822 a 44 con un 65,85% de hombres y un 34,15% de mujeres. El reequilibrio de la ratio sexo y de la criollización se dio en los años siguientes, con un 55,46% de varones y un 44,54% de mujeres, en estos años la ratio criollo bozal también se reequilibró siendo el total de criollos hombres y mujeres del 47,02% y los africanos el 53, 98%. Cfr. Zeuske, Michael. *Schwarzen Karibik. Sklaven, Sklavereikultur und Emanzipation.* Rotpunkntverlag. Zürich, 2004. Pags 131-156; 191- 246.

32 Scarano, Francisco A. *The Plantation Economy of Ponce 1800-1850.* University of Wisconsin Press, Madisson 1984. San Miguel, Pedro. *El Mundo que creó el azúcar. Las Haciendas en Vega Baja, 1800-1873.* Ediciones Huracán, Río Piedras, Puerto Rico 1989. Dietz, James, l. *Historia económica de Puerto Rico.* Ediciones Huracán, Rio Piedras, Puerto Rico 2002. Picó, Fernando. *Cayeyanos. Familias y solidaridades en la historia de Cayey.* Ediciones Huracán, Rio Piedras, Puerto Rico. 2007. Picó, Fernando. *Cayeyanos. Familias y solidaridades en la historia de Cayey.* Ediciones Huracán, Rio Piedras, Puerto Rico. 2007. Cabrera Salcedo, Lisset. *De los bueyes al vapor: Caminos de la tecnología del azúcar en Puerto Rico y el Caribe.* Universidad dePuerto Rico, Río Piedras, 2010. Scarano, Francisco A. Inmigración y estructura de clases: los hacenda-

Sugar cane cultivation doubled its size in just 18 years, with coffee production following a similar upward tren (also doubling). Snuff, however, after a spectacular rise in 1817, fell in 1824, before rising again in 1827[33]. Puerto Rico became the second largest exporter of sugar in the Caribbean (Jamaica held this position before, according to the trade balance of 1828). However, several factors contributed to the "segunda esclavitud" process that was taking place in Puerto Rico: (1) falling sugar prices motivated by competition from beet sugar and (2) the British monitoring compliance with the abolition of slavery, to which the Spanish Crown had agreed. These two external factors, outside island investors' control, coincided with deforestation in certain areas and consequent drought[34] so that sugar production was reduced, thus slowing down the slave trade. From the second half of the nineteenth century though, commercial activity re-emerged, and with it, so did the slave trade.

Cattle and coffee production depended in large part on free labor, both by family members and those exiled to the interior of the country. From the second half of the nineteenth century, however, slave labor became an important part of production, in part by the presence of "refraccionistas," wholent money to homeowners[35].

---

dos de Ponce, 1815-1845, en Scarano, Francisco A. (ed).*Inmigración y clases sociales en el Puerto Rico del siglo XIX.* Ediciones Huracán, Río Piedras, Puerto Rico, 1981. Pags 21-66.Wesseman, James W.The Demographic Structure of Slavery in Puerto Rico: Some Aspects of Agrarian Capitalism in the Late Nineteenth Century. *Journal of Latin American Studies*.12, 2, 1980.pags. 271-289

33 Cfr. Ramos Mattei, Andrés A (ed). *Azúcar y esclavitud.* Universidad de Puerto Rico. San Juan, Puerto Rico 1982. Pag 15. Cabrera Salcedo, Lisset. *De los bueyes al vapor: Caminos de la tecnología del azúcar en Puerto Rico y el Caribe.* Universidad dePuerto Rico, Río Piedras, 2010.

34 Ramos Mattei, Andrés A (ed). *Azúcar y esclavitud.* Universidad de Puerto Rico. San Juan, Puerto Rico 1982. Pags 20-21.

35 Picó, Fernando. *Amargo café (los pequeños y medianos caficultores de Utuado en la segunda mitad del siglo XIX).* Ediciones Huracán, Río Piedras, Puerto Rico. 1981. Pags. 41-63. Picó, Fernando. *Libertad y servidumbre en el Puerto Rico del siglo XIX.* Ediciones Huracán, Río Piedras, Puerto Rico 1985. Pags. 45 82. Picó, Fernando. *Vivir en Caimito.* Ediciones Huracán, Río Piedras, Puerto Rico, 1989. Pags 35-59. Negrón Portillo, Mariano; Mayo Santana, Raúl. *La esclavitud Menor: La esclavitud en los municipios del interior de Puerto Rico en el siglo XIX.* Centro de Investigaciones sociales Universidad de Puerto Rico, Río Piedras 2007. Pags 7-38.

Another element to consider in the "segunda esclavitud" in Puerto Rico is the phenomenon of urban slavery, which in San Juan's case, was particularly devoted to industry. Productive work outside productive centers was not uncommon among slaves in other parts of America[36]. In fact, slaves were present in all economic activities of both Spanish colonies and other powers. In the case of urban Puerto Rican slavery, San Juan[37] was similar to other cities. Women were employed in domestic service but also served as confectioners, cooks and washers, jobs that allowed a degree of autonomy and savings to buy one's freedom. The economic importance of slavery was undisputed and allowed empires to maintain their control in the New World[38].

Slavery and culture

Certainly, slavery transformed the economy of the West Indies. Wherever there was the introduction of numerous bodies, the ensuing work generated great wealth for both the producers and traders who profited from trade in men and goods. Another important factor that occurred with slavery was massive social change. Large numbers of male and female slaves were transported to the New World and formed a new settlement. Finally, they created a new culture, with common features in all areas but also with differences, depending on the place of origin of the destination's slaves and the circumstances of the place receiving them.

Perhaps the best place for viewing the commonalities and diversities generated is in the Caribbean. The Caribbean region serves as a paradigm of the region as a space alive, changing, and contradicting internal logic, creating its own mentality and force in nature, which marks the daily life of its inhabitants. We can say that the Caribbean shows us a sea of common

---

36 Cfr. Bertran,Carmen. *Negros esclavos y libres en las ciudades hispanoamericanas*. Fundación Históricca Tavera, Fundación Hernando de Larramendi Madrid 2001.

37 Para la esclavitud de San Juan ver el trabajo de Negrón Portillo, Mariano; Mayo Santana, Raúl. *La esclavitud urbana en San Juan*. Ediciones Huracán, centro de investigaciones Sociales, Universidad de Puerto Rico, Río Piedras Puerto Rico 1992. Pags 67-94.

38 Thornton, John. *A África e os africanos na formação do mundo Atlântico*. Elsevier Editora Campus. Rio de Janeiro 2004. Pags 189-204.

cultures, where the key elements are planting and, therefore, mass slavery. The colonial interdependencies, comercial trade, and economic system generated a specific type of settlement in which the percentages of the black population outnumber those that occurred in other areas of the Americas. Agricultural production thus left its mark on social relations and resistances.

Cultural forms were generated that revolve around religious expression, recreation, song, and dance, where prayer is mixed with polyrhythms and dance to form a set of representations of intimate slave resistance. This religion helped solve everyday problems and reinterpeted European beliefs alongside those of Africans and the indigenous.

Caribbean planters and European investors sought to expand the colony's economic base and enjoy greater prestige in the metropolis. Caribbean masons and revolutionaries emigrated in search of a place to establish their utopia. But there was also the Caribbean slaves, which converted the Atlantic shore into a place of death[39], chains, and resistance. Drum rhythms marked the veiled or open fighting that represented not only codes but also communication and collective resistance around the party and freedom fighters who fought and triumphed over their masters. From the collective imaginary, slaves re-created the heat of tropical rains, which eventually prevailed over the religious, moral, and social landlords.

The rural slave world generated an inward-looking culture – inbred and different from the urban culture – that we might call the "cimarrona" resistance, which countered attempts and systems intended to impose dominant culture[40]. Puerto Rico's contemporary culture is largely composed of elements introduced by the "esclavitud segunda." Because the arrival of slaves to the island had not occurred on a large scale, the culture and mixture that

---

39 Price, Richard. Encuentros dialógicos en un espacio de muerte. En Gutierrez Estevez, Manuel; León Portilla, Miguel; Gossen Gar H; Klor de Alva, J. Jorge. *De palabra y Obra en el Nuevo Mundo. 2 Encuentros interétnicos*. Ed. Siglo XXI. Madrid 1992. pags 33-62.

40 Quintero Rivera, Ángel. De ritmos y la etnicidad cimarroneada en la caribena cultura de la contraplantación. *Boletín Americanista*. Nº 42-43. pp 87-106. Universidad de Barcelona. Barcelona 1993.

had begun in the sixteenth century maintained and imprinted itself on the island[41].

This did not result from mixing among the mestizo class, as they instead sought to kept the white elite in place. Rather, the mixture was a phenomenon of high culture and society, one that scandalized the Bishop of Puerto Rico, as in his remark below:

> "Ha llegado el caso que una mujer viuda, noble, con hermanos y parientes honrados con empleos por el estado eclesiástico dio libertad a un moreno su esclavo para casarse con él como con efecto lo ejercitó, que hay vecinos y otros muchos que con desigualdad incomparable han contraído matrimonio de que ha resultado ser tan corto el número de republicanos que apenas hay sujetos en quienes recaigan elecciones de los oficios políticos y muy pocas las familias de blancos y limpios de toda mala raza que puedan ser admitidos a los hábitos eclesiásticos de las religiones.Y no hay negro, grifo o mulato que no se atreva a manchar linajes desdeñándose de casar con sus iguales pretendiendo las de superior calidad…"[42]

The mixture allowed not only for the survival of specific social structures but also stressed the importance of slaves and former slaves in not only San Juan's population, but in and Puerto Rico's as a whole[43].

Besides the folkloric aspects that are recurrent when showing the contributions of the Afro-descendents to the national culture, other elements of no less importance were forged. The religious element built a Caribbean belief system possessing a great amount of common traits, regardless of origin. In the Puerto Rican case, like in many places of the Iberian world, African religions were mixed with popular Catholic beliefs and other practices that were not accepted by the church. In spite of the church's fierce opposition, it was unable to stop these new practices that were created by slaves.

---

41 Knight, Franklin W. Introduction, in. Garrigus, John, Morris Christofer. *Assumed Identities*. Texas A&M University Press. 2010.

42 *AGI* Santo Domingo 576.Puerto Rico 28 de Agosto de 1739 Informe del Obispo de Puerto Rico Francisco Pérez Lozano al rey.

43 Negrón Portillo, Mariano; Mayo Santana, Raúl. *La esclavitud urbana en San Juan*. Ediciones Huracán, centro de investigaciones Sociales, Universidad de Puerto Rico, Río Piedras Puerto Rico 1992. Pags 67-94. Scarano, Francisco A. The Jibaro Masquerade and Subaltern Politics in Puerto Rico, 1745-1823. *American Historical Review.* December 1996, pags 1398-1431.

Catholicism blended to give way to practices that have formed part of the ethnic and national identity process, where it is difficult to distinguish the religious and the profane, the Catholic and the Afro, where religious feelings are mixed with dance beats, and where dance is introduced into churches as a sign of respect and religious practice – previously reviled by the Bishops of the eighteenth century[44].

Among the institutions that more successfully blended in were the brotherhoods that spent their funds on profane dances and, in many cases, grouped members of the same ethnic African origin, thus reinforcing the ethnicity of the members and creating elements of resistance to Christianity and enslavement. The brotherhoods, which were controlled by the Church, built religious systems close to African cults, and in many cases, the Catholic cults were used to disguise African cults that have survived until today. The fusions of different cultural elements and African groups that took place in America resulted in the cultural and social reality created by the slaves and the freedmen[45].

The brotherhoods emerged as religious institutions in which the brothers put themselves under the protection of a patron saint, so celebrating rituals on the days they were entitled. Yet, at the same time, they were working as mutual aid societies and were in charge of assisting the sick brothers, widows and orphans, and celebrating funerals. The black brotherhoods served as institutions where slaves were integrated and, later, the freed black men, into the colonial world.

The brotherhoods were mainly in the cities, where the urban slaves and free black men gathered for their cult celebrations. In spite of the ecclesiastic vigilance and a constant presence of priests during the celebrations, the black brotherhood chapters were very important in the maintenance of costumes and African rituals adapted to the circumstances of the New

44 Quintero Rivera, Ángel G (ed). *Vírgenes, Magos y escapularios. Imaginería, etnicidad y religiosidad popular en Puerto Rico.* Entro de Investigaciones Sociales, Universidad de Puerto Rico, Río Piedras; Centro de Investigaciones Académicas, Universidad Sagrado Corazón; Fundación Puertorriqueña de las Humanidades, San Juan de Puerto Rico 1998. Pags, 83-85. Zayas Micheli, Edgardo. *Catolicismo popular en Puerto Rico. Una explicación sociológica.* Ed. Raices. Ponce, 1990,

45 Vide. Mintz, Sidney; Price, Richard. *The birth of African-American culture: an anthropological perspective.*Boston: Beacon Press, 1992

World[46]. From this point of view and according to several written sources, we may assert that in the colonial period, a number of specific cultural African characteristics adapted to the American context, where a fusion of some indigenous and European elements took place. This led to the formation of an Ethnogenesis process[47], understood as the social construction of a new culture that allowed the collective and individual survival of the slave descendents of the Americas[48].

Funeral rituals were a common and extended practice in both the countryside and the city and empowered group cohesiveness, which were apart from religious structures, with their complex pantheons, that have remained strong in Brazil, Cuba and Haiti, among others. The African groups with their less complex religious structures, had as the centre point, the cult to the forefathers, which is why all rituals about death were so important, because through them, the protection of the forefathers was guaranteed[49].

---

46 Cfr. Friedemann, Nina S. Cabildos de negros refugio de africana en Colombia. *Montalbán* n° 20. Páginas 121-135. Laviña, J. Afroamerikanischen. Feste und Toten Ritual. Páginas, 68-80. *Comparativ*, 13, n° 2. Leipzig, 2003.

47 Entendemos etnogénesis como el conjunto de elementos sociales y culturales que adopta un grupo con la intención de proyectarse hacia el futuro mediante el control del horizonte social, político, cultural y económico. Esta definición va en la línea del planteamiento que hizo Guillermo Bonfil Batalla en su trabajo, La teoría del control cultural en el estudio de procesos étnicos. En *Revista Papeles de la Casa Chata*. Año 2, N° 3 pp 23-43 México 1987.

48 Thorton, John K. *A Cultural History of the Atlantic World, 1250-1820*. Cambridge University Press 2012

49 There is a relatively abundant bibliography that demonstrates, in Spanish America, the perseverance of funeral rituals among Afrodescendants. Vide. Laviña, Javier. Fiesta y ritual afroamericanos. En: Verdú Macía, Vicente; Martín Rodríguez, José Luis; Martínez Gomis, Mario; Andreo García, Juan; Uría , Jorge: *Fiesta Ocio y Juego en la Historia*. pags. 237-251. Ed. Universidad de Salamanca. Salamanca, 2002.Friedemann, Nina; Patiño Roselli, Carlos. *Lengua y sociedad en el Palenque de San Basilio*. Instituto Caro y Cuervo. Bogotá, 1983. Schwegler, Armin. Hacia un arqueología afrocolombiana. Restos de tradiciones religiosas bantúes en una comunidad negrocolombiana. P 48. en *América negra. Expedición humana a la zaga de la América oculta*. Pontificia Universidad Javeriana. N° 4, Diciembre. Pp. 35-82.. Bogotá 1992. Hernández Soto, Carlos. *Morir en Villa Mella. Ritos funerarios afrodominicanos*. CIASCA. Santo Domingo 1998. Pp 27-34. Davis, Martha Ellen, *La otra ciencia. El vudú dominicano como religión y medicinas populares*. Editora Universitaria, Santo Domingo 1987. Pp. 190-203. Rodríguez Vélez, Wendolina. *El turbante blanco*. Ed Museo del hombre

Indeed, in Puerto Rico today, the death of important figures of the popular musical culture, like Cortijo, are filled with rituals of old. His funeral was full of rhythms, rhythms that he interpreted through the years. It was as if the music ghosts were searching for a time and space for which to attach, so as not to abandon this world where they once lived; thereby stillness and the memory of the deceased are achieved[50].

Sources and Bibliography

Archivo General de Indias.

AGI Santo Domingo 576.Puerto Rico 28 de Agosto de 1739 Informe del Obispo de Puerto Rico Francisco Pérez Lozano al rey.

A.G.I. Santo Domingo leg. 2527. Visita pastoral del obispo Pedro Martínez de Onca 14 de abril de 1760.

A G I. Santo Domingo 2288. Puerto Rico 7 de agosto de 1776.El gobernador Muesas y el contador Puente Piden a favor de aquellos vecinos las gracias que están expresadas en la representación.

A.G.I.Santo Domingo legajo 2288. Estado general de la isla de Puerto Rico.

A.G.I.Santo Domingo legajo 2288. Estado general de la isla de Puerto Rico.

A.G.I.Santo Domingo legajo 2396. Estado general de la isla de Puerto Rico.

A.G.I.Santo Domingo legajo 2396. Estado general de la isla de Puerto Rico.

AGI, Santo Domingo, legajo 2516. El apoderado del Asiento de negros, Goycoa 25 de marzo de 1772.

A.G.I. Santo Domingo leg. 2527. Visita pastoral del obispo Pedro Martínez de Onca 14 de abril de 1760.

Abad y la Sierra, Íñigo. *Historia geográfica civil y natural de la isla de Puerto Rico.* Ediciones Doce Calles, Historiador oficial de Puerto Rico. Madrid 2002.

Bertran, Carmen. *Negros esclavos y libres en las ciudades hispanoamericanas.* Fundación Histórica Tavera, Fundación Hernando de Larramendi Madrid 2001.

dominicano, Santo Domingo 1982. Schwegler. Armin. *"Chima ,n "kongo". Lengua y rito ancestral en el Palenque de San Basilio (Colombia).* 2 vols. Ed. Biblioteca iberoamericana. Frankfurt-Madrid 1996.Catáolgo de la exposición. *Velorios y Santos vivos. Comunidades negras, afrocolombianas, raizales y palequeras.* Bogotá 2008.

50 Rodríguez Juliá, Edgardo.*El Entierro de Cortijo.* Ediciones Huracán, San Juan de Puerto Rico 1991.

Bonfil Batalla, Guillermo.La teoría del control cultural en el estudio de procesos étnicos. En *Revista Papeles de la Casa Chata.* Año 2, N° 3 pp 23-43 México 1987.

Cabrera Salcedo, Lisset. *De los bueyes al vapor: Caminos de la tecnología del azúcar en Puerto Rico y el Caribe.* Universidad de Puerto Rico, Río Piedras, 2010.

Cardaillac, Louis. Le problème morisque en Amérique. *Mélanges de la Casa de-Velázquez*.t.12, París, 1976, pp. 283-303.

Catáolgo de la exposición. *Velorios y Santos vivos. Comunidades negras, afrocolombianas, raizales y palequeras*. Bogotá 2008.

Davis, Martha Ellen, *La otra ciencia. El vudú dominicano como religión y medicinas populares*. Editora Universitaria, Santo Domingo 1987. Pp. 190-203.

Dietz, James, l. *Historia económica de Puerto Rico.* Ediciones Huracán, Rio Piedras, Puerto Rico 2002.

Fernández Méndez. Eugenio. *Las encomiendas y la esclavitud de los indios de Puerto Rico. 1508-1550.* Ediciones el Cemí. San Juan Puerto Rico 1995.

Friedemann, Nina S. Cabildos de negros refugio de africana en Colombia. *Montalbán* n° 20. Páginas 121-135.

Friedemann, Nina; Patiño Roselli, Carlos. *Lengua y sociedad en el Palenque de San Basilio*. Instituto Caro y Cuervo. Bogotá, 1983.

Hernández Soto, Carlos. *Morir en Villa Mella. Ritos funerarios afrodominicanos.* CIASCA. Santo Domingo 1998. Pp 27-34.

Kneight, Frankiln W. Introduction, in. Garrigus, John, Morris Christofer. *Assumed Identities*. Texas A&M University Press. 2010.

Laviña, Javier. Afroamerikanischen. Feste und Toten Ritual. *Comparativ*, 13, n° 2. 68-80. Leipzig, 2003.

Laviña, Javier. Fiesta y ritual afroamericanos. En: Verdú Macía, Vicente; Martín Rodríguez, José Luis; Martínez Gomis, Mario; Andreo García, Juan; Uría , Jorge: *Fiesta Ocio y Juego en la Historia*. pags. 237-251. Ed. Universidad de Salamanca. Salamanca, 2002.

López Cantos, Ángel. *Historia de Puerto Rico, 1650-1700*. Escuela de Estudios Hispanoamericanos, Sevilla 1975.

Mintz, Sidney; Price, Richard.*The birth of African-American culture: an anthropological perspective*.Boston: Beacon Press, 1992

Morales Carrión, Arturo. *Auge y decadencia de la trata negrera en Puerto Rico (1820-1860).* Centro de Estudios Avanzados de Puerto Rico y el Caribe. Instituto de Cultura Puertorriqueña. San Juan, 1978.

Moreno Fraginals, Manuel. *El Ingenio. Complejo socioeconómico cubano del azúcar.* Ed. Ciencias Sociales. La Habana 1978. Tomo 2

Moscoso, Francisco. *Agricultura y sociedad en Puerto Rico siglos 16 al 18*. Editorial ICP (Instituto de Cultura Puertorriqueña). San Juan 2001.

Moscoso, Francisco. *Agricultura y sociedad en Puerto Rico siglos 16 al 18*. Pags 133-142. Editorial ICP (Instituto de Cultura Puertorriqueña). San Juan 2001.

Moscoso, Francisco. *Caciques aldeas y población taína de Boriquén, Puerto Rico 1492-1582*. Academia Puertorriqueña de la Historia. San Juan 2008.

Negrón Portillo, Mariano; Mayo Santana, Raúl. *La esclavitud urbana en San Juan*. Ediciones Huracán, centro de investigaciones Sociales, Universidad de Puerto Rico, Río Piedras Puerto Rico 1992.

Negrón Portillo, Mariano; Mayo Santana, Raúl. *La esclavitud Menor: La esclavitud en los municipios del interior de Puerto Rico en el siglo XIX*. Centro de Investigaciones sociales. Universidad de Puerto Rico, Río Piedras 2007.

Picó, Fernando. *Amargo café (los pequeños y medianos caficultores de Utuado en la segunda mitad del siglo XIX)*. Ediciones Huracán, Río Piedras, Puerto Rico. 1981. Picó, Fernando. *Libertad y servidumbre en el Puerto Rico del siglo XIX*. Ediciones Huracán, Río Piedras, Puerto Rico 1985.

Picó, Fernando. *Vivir en Caimito*. Ediciones Huracán, Río Piedras, Puerto Rico, 1989.

Picó, Fernando. *Historia general de Puerto Rico*. Pags.150-165. Ediciones Huracán, Rio Piedras, Puerto Rico. 2004.

Picó, Fernando. *Cayeyanos. Familias y solidaridades en la historia de Cayey*. Ediciones Huracán, Rio Piedras, Puerto Rico. 2007.

Price, Richard. Encuentros dialógicos en un espacio de muerte. En Gutierrez Estevez, Manuel; León Portilla, Miguel; Gossen Gar H; Klor de Alva, J. Jorge. *De palabra y Obra en el Nuevo Mundo. 2 Encuentros interétnicos*. Ed. Siglo XXI. Madrid 1992.

Quintero Rivera, Ángel G (ed). *Vírgenes, Magos y escapularios. Imaginería, etnicidad y religiosidad popular en Puerto Rico*. Centro de Investigaciones Sociales, Universidad de Puerto Rico, Río Piedras; Centro de Investigaciones Académicas, Universidad Sagrado Corazón; Fundación Puertorriqueña de las Humanidades. San Juan de Puerto Rico 1998.

Quintero Rivera, Ángel. De ritmos y la etnicidad cimarroneada en la caribeña cultura de la contraplantación. *Boletín Americanista*. N° 42-43. pp 87-106. Universidad de Barcelona. Barcelona 1993.

Ramos Mattei, Andrés A (ed). *Azúcar y esclavitud*. Universidad de Puerto Rico. San Juan, Puerto Rico 1982.

Rodríguez Juliá, Edgardo.*El Entierro de Cortijo*. Ediciones Huracán, San Juan de Puerto Rico 1983Rodríguez Vélez, Wendolina. *El turbante blanco*. Ed Museo del hombre dominicano, Santo Domingo 1982.

San Miguel, Pedro. *El Mundo que creó el azúcar. Las Haciendas en Vega Baja, 1800-1873*. Ediciones Huracán, Río Piedras, Puerto Rico 1989.

Scarano, Francisco A. *The Plantation Economy of Ponce 1800-1850*. University of Wisconsin Press, Madison 1984.

Scarano, Francisco A. Inmigración y estructura de clases: los hacendados de Ponce, 1815-1845, en Scarano, Francisco A. (ed).*Inmigración y clases sociales en el Puerto Rico del siglo XIX*. Ediciones Huracán, Río Piedras, Puerto Rico, 1981. Pags 21-66.

Scarano, Francisco A. The Jibaro Masquerade and Subaltern Politics in Puerto Rico, 1745-1823. *American Historical Review*. December 1996, pags 1398-1431.

Schwegler, Armin. Hacia un arqueología afrocolombiana. Restos de tradiciones religiosas bantúes en una comunidad negrocolombiana. P 48. en *América negra. Expedición humana a la zaga de la América oculta*. Pontificia Universidad Javeriana. N° 4, Diciembre. Pp. 35-82. Bogotá 1992.

Schwegler. Armin. *"Chima ,n "kongo". Lengua y rito ancestral en el Palenque de San Basilio (Colombia)*. 2 vols. Ed. Biblioteca ibero-americana. Frankfurt-Madrid 1996.

Sued Badillo, Jalil, López Cantos, Angel. *Puerto Rico Negro*. Pags 82-111. Editorial Cultural. Rio Piedras, Puerto Rico 1986.

Torres Ramírez, Bibiano. *La isla de Puerto Rico (1765-1800)*. Instituto de Cultura Puertorriqueña. San Juan 1968.

Thornton, John. *A África e os africanos na formaçao do mundo Atlântico*. Elsevier Editora Campus. Rio de Janeiro 2004.

Thorton, John K. *A Cultural History of the Atlantic World, 1250-1820*. Cambridge University Press 2012.

Vila Vilar, Enriqueta. *Historia de Puerto Rico 1600-1650*. Escuela de Estudios Hispanoamericanos, CSIC, Sevilla 1974.

Wallerstein, Immanuel. *El moderno sistema mundial. La agricultura capitalista y los orígenes de la economía-mundo europea en el siglo XVI*. Ed. Siglo XXI. Madrid 1979

Wesseman, James W.The Demographic Structure of Slavery in Puerto Rico: Some Aspects of Agrarian Capitalism in the Late Nineteenth Century. *Journal of Latin American Studies*.12, 2, 1980. pags. 271-289

Zayas Micheli, Edgardo. *Catolicismo popular en Puerto Rico. Una explicación sociológica*. Ed. Raices. Ponce, 1990.

Zeuske, Michael. *Schwarze Karibik. Sklaven, Sklavereikultur und Emanzipation*. Rotpunktverlag. Zürich, 2004.

The Second Slavery: Modernity, mobility, and identity of captives in Nineteenth-Century Cuba and the Atlantic World

Michael ZEUSKE

University of Cologne (Koeln)

Introduction

There is already a relatively large corpus of excellent literature about the concept of "Second Slavery" and the realities of different types of second slaveries. Dale Tomich wrote the founding essay, *The ‚Second Slavery': Bonded Labor and the Transformations of the Nineteenth-century World Economy,* in 1988.[1] Enrico Dallago uses the concept of second slavery for

[1] Tomich, Dale W. "The ‚Second Slavery': Bonded Labor and the Transformations of the Nineteenth-century World Economy", in: Ramírez, Francisco O. (ed.), Rethinking the Nineteenth Century: Contradictions and Movement, New York: Greenwood Press, 1988, pp. 103-117; Tomich, *Slavery in the Circuit of Sugar: Martinique and the World Economy, 1830-1848*, Baltimore and London: Johns Hopkins University Press, 1990; Tomich, "World Slavery and Caribbean Capitalism: The Cuban Sugar Industry, 1760-1868", in: *Theory and Society* 20 (1991), pp. 297-319; Tomich, "Spaces of Slavery, Times of Freedom: Rethinking Caribbean History in World Perspective", in: *Comparative Studies of South Asia, Africa, and the Middle East* 57 (1997), S. 67-80; Tomich, "The Wealth of the Empire: Francisco de Arango y Parreño, Political Economy, and the Second Slavery in Cuba", in: *Comparative Studies in Society and History*, No. 1 (2003), pp. 4-28; Tomich, *Through the Prism of Slavery. Labor, Capital, and World Economy*, Boulder [etc.]: Rowman & Littlefield Publishers, Inc. 2004; Tomich, "Atlantic History and World Economy: Concepts and Constructions", in: *Proto Sociology. An International Journal of Interdisciplinary Research* Vol. 20 (2004), pp. 102-121 (=World-System Analysis: Contemporary Research and Directions); Tomich; Zeuske, Michael, "The Second Slavery: Mass Slavery, World Economy and Comparative Microhistories", in: *Review*. A Journal of the Fernand Braudel Center, Binghamton University XXXI, no. 3 (2008), pp. 91-100 (=special issue edited by Dale Tomich & Michael Zeuske, eds., *The Second Slavery: Mass Slavery, World-Economy, and Comparative Microhistories*, Part I). An earlier version has been published under the titel: Zeuske, "The

comparisons of slaveries in the Americas, Africa, and forms of forced labor in Southern Europe.[2] Anthony Kaye is using the concept to redefine the slavery of the North-American South (see his chapter).[3] All these works highlight slavery, slave trade, and slaving in general, but above all as mass slavery and mass slave trades, that is, as Second Slaveries in the nineteenth century, which were a "variant of modern capitalism"[4] and a corner stone of modernity. "Second slavery was, in a word, modern"[5]. Slaves, i.e., captive African men, women, and children, were indeed "the first modern commodities"[6] and "mobility would prove the key not only to the survival of slavery but also to its economic dynamism and capitalist character".[7]

In the following essay, I will emphasize mobility as one of the most important dimensions of the Second Slavery in Cuba and of the *atlantization* of that island, not without mentioning, that mobility is still one, if not the defining, dimension of today's globalization. And I will also emphasize the written construction of new identities in the *hidden Atlantic* and *Cuba grande*.

From 1800 onwards, the successful revolution of Saint-Domingue/Haiti (1791-1803) already influenced everything in West Indian and American slavery societies. The revolution changed not only the use of individual names, but also the name and the identity of the land itself: from colonial

---

Names of Slavery and Beyond: the Atlantic, the Americas and Cuba", in: Schmieder, Ulrike; Füllberg-Stolberg, Katja; Zeuske, Michael (eds.), The End of Slavery in Africa and the Americas. A Comparative Approach, Münster-Hamburg-Berlin-Wien-London: LIT-Verlag, 2011 (= Sklaverei und Postemanzipation. Esclavitud y Postemancipación. Slavery and Postemancipation, Vol. 4), S. 51-80.

2 Dal Lago, Enrico; Katsari, Constantina (eds.), *Slave Systems. Ancient and Modern*, Cambridge [etc.]: Cambridge University Press, 2008; Dal Lago, *American Slavery, Atlantic Slavery, and Beyond. The U.S. "Peculiar Institution" in International Perspective*, Boulder; London: Paradigm Publishers, 2012.

3 Kaye, Anthony, "The Second Slavery: Modernity in the Nineteenth-Century South and the Atlantic World" in: *The Journal of Southern History* Vol. LXXV: 3 (Aug. 2009), pp. 627-650.

4 Ibid. p. 628.

5 Ibid, p. 632.

6 Gilroy, Paul, *The Black Atlantic: Modernity and Double Consciousness*, Cambridge: CUP, 1993, p. 55.

7 Kaye, "The Second Slavery: Modernity in the Nineteenth-Century South and the Atlantic World," pp. 627-650, p. 633.

Saint-Domingue to national Haiti.[8] In the twenty years after this revolution, the more or less 15 slave societies in the Americas were reduced to three great and modern societies of second slavery (and some smaller second slaveries, like Spanish Puerto Rico, French Martinique, Cayenne, Guadeloupe, English Demerara (Guiana), Trinidad and Dutch Suriname). After 1820 the great systems of slavery left in the Americas were the U.S. South, the South of Brazil, and, the most modern slave society of the world, Cuba (*Cuba grande*, the Western part of Cuba around Havana, Matanzas and Cienfuegos). Saint-Domingue/Haiti was destroyed by revolution and, beginning with the war against the French intervention in 1802-1803. Then, Jamaica, Barbados, and Bahia entered in crisis.[9]

It was a reduction in numbers, but an explosion in mobility, first of all a mobility of slavers, slaveholders, and their personal property. By 1820, writes Anthony Kaye, the explosive expansion and mobility of second slavery were well underway. "As slaveholders migrated to the Deep South, their peers pushed into the interior of Jamaica and south-central Brazil, swept over Western Cuba [*Cuba grande* – M.Z.] and the Lesser Antilles, and settled onto South American coast in British Guiana".[10]

This type of new mobility also leads to a new and massive mobility of captives, controlled and structured by violence, infrastructures and modern technologies (steamers, railroads, telegraphs, new forms of mass transport and communication, like newspapers). The combination of these types of modern mobility I call *atlantization*, and the space in which it took place, the *hidden Atlantic* and beyond.

---

8 Geggus, David, "The Naming of Haiti", in: *New West Indian Guide/Nieuwe West-Indische Gids* 71 (1997): 43-68; Dubois, Laurent, *Avengers of the New World. The Story of the Haitian Revolution*, Cambridge, Mass.; London, England: The Belknap Press of Harvard University Press, 2004.

9 Tomich; Zeuske, "The Second Slavery: Mass Slavery, World Economy and Comparative Microhistorics", pp. 91-100; Kaye, "The Second Slavery: Modernity in the Nineteenth-Century South and the Atlantic World," pp. 627-650; Dal Lago, American Slavery, Atlantic Slavery, and Beyond …, passim; Zeuske, *Die Monte Christos des verborgenen Atlantik. Ramón Ferrer, das Sklavenschiff Amistad und die Welt der Sklavenhändler* [*The Monte Christos of the Hidden Atlantic. Slave Traders in the 19th-Century*] (forthcoming 2014), passim.

10 Kaye, "The Second Slavery: Modernity in the Nineteenth-Century South and the Atlantic World," pp. 627-650.

I will attempt to analyze what this mobility of Second Slavery did with African captives who were abducted through the infrastructures of violence, which spanned the Atlantic and two continents.

The Cuban second slavery had a special position in the horizon of American second slaveries. *Cuba grande* was special because of its compactness, the high productivity of the slaves, the high profits of the *negreros* (slave traders), their huge investment not only in technologies and industrial machines from other countries, but also in the preparation of new lands and the foundation of their own agro-industrial complexes (industrialized *ingenios* with production of refined white sugar), the uses of science (first of all medicine[11]), natural history, pharmacy, history and literature. Cuba had also the longest time of contraband-atlantization (1820-1880) of all American second slaveries.

The official interfaces between the Atlantic "transport" of slaves as commodities and the regional plantation societies were the American slave ports until 1808 (for the United States and the British West Indies), 1818 (for the French *les Amériques*), 1820 (for Cuba and the Spanish Colonies) and after this latter year – informally (as contraband traffic) – nearly all the coastlines of the Caribbean.[12] In these years, the Atlantic slave trade under British pressure was formally abolished by all "Western" and American nations (including Portugal in Africa (1836), and Brazil in 1831 and 1850) –

[11] Palmer, Steven, "From the Plantation to the Academy. Slavery and Production of Cuban Medicine in the Nineteenth Century", in: Wright, David; De Barros, Juanita; Palmer, Steven (eds.), *Health and Medicine in the Circum-Caribbean, 1800-1968*. New York: Routledge 2009 (Routledge Studies in the Social History of Medicine), pp. 53-75; Palmer,"Beginnings of Cuban Bacteriology: Juan Santos Fernández, Medical Research, and the Search for Scientific Sovereignty", in: *Hispanic American Historical Review* (HAHR) 91:3 (2011), pp. 445-468.

[12] Smallwood, "Turning Atlantic Commodities into American Slaves", in: Smallwood, *Saltwater Slaves …*, pp. 153-181; Sosa Rodríguez, Enrique, *Negreros, catalanes y gaditanos en la trata cubana 1827-1833*, La Habana: Fundación Fernando Ortiz, 1998 (Colección La Fuente Viva; 6); Beckles, Hilary McD., ",An Unfeeling Traffick': The Intercolonial Movement of Slaves in the British Caribbean, 1807-1833", in: Johnson, Walter (ed.), *The Chattel Principle: Internal Slave Trades in the Americas, 1808-1888*, New Haven: Yale University Press, 2004, pp. 256-274; Drescher, Seymour, "The Fragmentation of Atlantic Slavery and the British Intercolonial Slave Trade", in: Ibid., pp. 234-255.

one author speaks about an "abolition rally" from 1803 (Denmark) to 1836 (Portugal).[13] Trading in slaves became contraband that violated all existing discourses, laws and treaties. Some enemies of the contraband trade were willing to declare that slave smuggling was piracy.

The normal trading economy of the West was built on written texts, laws and legal processes; these were framed by the system of international treaties concerning the slave trade that had been signed by Spain, Portugal, Netherlands and Brazil, more or less in order to keep up appearances and extract concessions from Britain.[14] After 1820 the ports continued as administration centers of all kind of trade, including the forbidden and hidden slave trade, but the main points of physical entrance of the captives were now the small islands, hidden coasts and small bays of the Caribbean.

Slave names and "writing the slavery" in Cuban Second Slavery 1820-1886

The coast of the Caribbean, including the south and east coast of the United States, were the US is part of the Caribbean, functioned as indispensable points through which to channel the input of new captives from Africa and the Atlantic (*bozales, bossale, bosal*, *saltwater slaves*, and also *emancipados*) for the maintenance of American slaveries, including, I repeat, the United States.[15]

The first to pay attention to the problem of identity and names was Fernando Ortiz, but without a deep analysis of documents which bear slave designations and names.[16]

---

13 Brown, Christopher Leslie, "Explaining abolition", in: Heuman, Gad; Burnard, Trevor (eds.), *The Routledge History of Slavery*, London and New York, Routledge, 2011, pp. 287-290.

14 Sherwood, Marika, *After Abolition: Britain and the Slave Trade since 1807*, London: I. B. Tauris, 2007, Drescher, Abolition. *A History of Slavery and Antislavery*, Cam bridge: Cambridge University Press, 2009; Linden, Marcel van der (ed.), *Humanitarian Intervention and Changing Labor Relations. The Long-Term Consequences of the Abolition of the Slave Trade*, Leiden/ Boston: Brill, 2011 (Studies in Global History, Vol. 7); Brown, "Explaining abolition", S. 287-290.

15 Obadele-Starks, Ernest, *Freebooters and Smugglers. The Slave Trade in the United States after 1808*, Lafayetteville: The University of Arkansas Press, 2007.

16 Ortiz, Fernando, "El esclavo es herrado. El nombre del esclavo. Los barracones. Venta

From 1808-1820-1831 onwards, the Atlantic trade was transformed into a hidden Atlantic contraband trade. Most of the papers documenting cargoes of slaves in the Atlantic slaving economy disappeared in two major steps: from 1820 onwards in the sector north of the equator (to be replaced by contraband trading to Cuba and the Caribbean islands), and from 1840 onwards south of the equator (with massive contraband trading from Cabinda (Northern Angola), Luanda and Benguela to Brazil and to Cuba[17]). So for the era 1826-1850-1880s, we have only very little evidence of the paper trail that usually accompanied slave economies in Western written cultures.[18]

The main problem now became that of assigning official presence to

---

del los Bozales. Anuncios por la prensa", in: Ortiz, *Los negros esclavos,* La Habana: Ed. deCiencias Sociales, 1975, pp. 163-168 (first editions as: Ortiz, *Los negros brujos (apuntes para un estudio de etnología criminal).* Carta prólogo del Dr. C. Lombroso, Madrid: Librería de Fernando Fe, 1906 (1st edition); Ortiz, *Hampa afro-cubana: Los negros esclavos. Estudio sociológico y de derecho público*, La Habana: *Revista Bimestre Cubana*, 1916 (2nd edition), see also: Cody, Cheryll Ann, "There Was No ‚Absalom' on the Ball Plantations. Slave-naming practices in the South Carolina Low Country, 1720-1865", in: Heuman; Gad; Walvin, James (eds.), *The Slavery Reader*, London and New York: Routledge, 2003, pp. 300-331; Diouf, Sylviane A., *Dreams of Africa in Alabama: The Story of the Clotilda and the Last Enslaved Africans Brought to America*, Oxford: Oxford University Press, 2007 (in the "inner circle" of the "last slaves" the shipmates always used African names; lists of names of shipmates); Eltis, David; Richardson, David (eds.), Extending the Frontiers: Essays on the New Transatlantic Slave Trade Database, New Haven: Yale Unisersity Press, 2008.

17 Ferreira, Roquinaldo, "The Suppression of the Slave Trade and Slave Departures from Angola, 1830s-1860s", in: *História Unisinos* 15:1 (2011), pp. 3-13.

18 Here is an example of search for papers at the slave vessel *Sierra de Pila*, captured June 12, 1839 by H.M. S. *Pickle*. On board the capturers found 173 *negros bozales*, but only few paper work: "On searching the Slave Vessel for papers, none were found except a sort of log book of the Voyage and a number of letters, among which were some addressed to Pedro Martinez & Co appearing to have been written by an Agent of theirs on the [African] coast" (p. 33). The *Sierra de Pila* had loaded her *cargazón de negros* (cargo of captives) in December of 1838 in one of the Cape Verde islands. During the middle passage 176 of the original cargo had died. The judges of the Mixed Commission described the job of the captain of the slave vessel as follows: "to bring the Negroes for those notorious dealers [Martinez & Co.] to the Havana" [p. 34]; see: The National Archive, London (TNA), FO 313/17 (1839-1840), 18/1839, S. Kennedy and C.A. Dalrymple to Palmerston from La Habana, June 25, 1839, pp. 33-34.

a human body/a commodity of the hidden Atlantic contraband-economy within the written and official slave economy in given American territories, under the control of a state. This was the hour of *curas* (priests) and *notarios* (scribes/notaries) in harbor hubs and on the plantations. For example, the "entrance" of new "saltwater" slaves into the Cuban slave society after 1820 was documented in three ways:

a) The new captives from Africa (*bozales*), transported by slave traders (*negreros*) over the Atlantic until 1820, arrived without a name, marked only by body, sex and price (the documents were printed formularies with empty parts for handwritten information, like names and other specific notes).[19]

Se presentará en la administración general, ántes de formar la escritura para tomar la filiacion	Muy señor mio : sírvase Vmd. formar escritura á favor de *la morena M.ª Josefa Zetti* *de una* ...... negr*a* que le he vendido del armazón que ha conducido *de la costa de Africa el Berg.*^tin^ nombrado *Henrrique capt.* .... su maestre *D. Simon Sanets* en el precio *de trescientos cincuenta pesos* con la calidad de bozal, alma en boca, huesos en costal, á uso de feria, sin asegurar de tachas ni enfermedades, mal de corazón , gota coral, de S. Lázaro, ni otra cualquiera que pueda padecer la humana naturaleza; porque todas corren por cuenta del comprador y también la escritura. Nuestro Sr. guarde á Vmd. muchos años. Matanzas y *Mayo 20* .... de 18*20*. B.L.M. de Vmd. S.S.S. *Zacarias Atkins*

By using only the deceptive term *bozal*, these written entries express the Catholic theory of legitimized slavery, that the enslaved person was practically "reborn" in the "civilized" community of the (American) believers. The term *bozal* implied that they had only a "wild, dark, pagan, and uncivilized" past in Africa.

19 Archivo Nacional de Cuba (ANC), La Habana, Escribanía varios, leg. 461, no. 6593 (1827): "Tomas Falguerra contra Ma. Josefa Oseti sobre la venta de una negra", f. 11r . The original is a printed formulary, called *papeleta de venta* (paper of sale). The formulary is in some positions empty; the empty parts were filled with handwritten informations. Other exemplars of the formulary can be found in: Moreno Fraginals, Manuel, El Ingenio. Complejo económico social cubano del azúcar, 3 vols., La Habana: Editorial de Ciencias Sociales, 1978, II, pp. 12-13, see also: Portuondo, Olga, "Un africano recién llegado ... es un negro bozal", in: Portuondo Zúñiga, Entre Esclavos y libres de Cuba colonial, Santiago de Cuba: Editorial Oriente 2003, pp. 113-116; p. 114 (1810).

Now the slave dealers used falsified papers with lists of invented Christian names, which were placed behind the usual numbers. These "names" were "given" without any baptism or even the presence of priests. The *Amistad* captives, who arrived after 1820, give us some insights of this first pragmatic "naming" by the slavers.[20] In the case of the *Amistad*, we are in the happy position of having some of those deemed "voiceless" who – because of the process at Hartford – speak for themselves and their memory of their captivity from Africa to the Americas. Thus the *Amistad* captives represent themselves as African men, women and children with their original names – first of all in the person of Cinque (the spelling and pronouncing in the United States was another problem). While the captives spoke and thought of themselves as having African names, the written system of slave smuggling in the Spanish colonies introduced them, when they had arrived in Cuba in a Portuguese slave schooner, normally mentioned as *Teçora* (really it was the American ship *Hugh Boyle*[21]), as part of a falsified list as "criollo"-slaves (slaves born in Cuba) with Christian names. On June 27, 1839, in Havana, one Martínez, perhaps the notorious slave dealer Pedro Martínez, on behalf of Captain General Ezpeleta, had issued a *licencia*, which the subsequent court papers refer to as a passport, authorizing the passage by sea to Puerto Príncipe of forty-nine *negros ladinos* owned by Don José Ruiz and named Antonio, Simon, Lucas, José, Pedro, Martin, Manuel, Andres, Eduardo, Celedonio, Bartolo, Ramon, Agustin, Evaristo, Casimiro, Melchor, Gabriel, Santorion, Esclastico, Pascual, Estanislao, Desiderio, Nicolas, Esteban, Tomas, Cosme, Luis, Bartolo [sic, there are two] Julian, Federico, Salustiano, Ladislao, Celestino [sic], Epifaneo, Tibureo, Venancio, Felipe, Francisco, Hipolito, Benito, Ysidoro, Vicente, Dionisio, Apoloneo, Esequiel, Leon, Julio, Hipolito [sic], y Zenon[22]

---

20 Zeuske; García Martínez, "*La Amistad* de Cuba. Ramón Ferrer, contrabando de esclavos, captividad y modernidad atlántica", pp. 97-170; Zeuske, "Die Gefangenen der Amistad", in: Zeuske, *Geschichte der Amistad. Sklavenhandel und Menschenschmuggel auf dem Atlantik im 19. Jahrhundert*, Stuttgart: Reclam, 2012, pp. 43-91.

21 Zeuske, "Rethinking the Case of the Schooner *Amistad*. Contraband and Complicity after 1808/1820", in: Slavery and Abolition: A Journal of Slave and Post-Slave Studies (http://dx.doi.org/10.1080/0144039X.2013.798173).

22 The first mention of these *ladino* names from the ship's "passport" is in the diary of Roger Sherman Baldwin, the attorney for the captives. The diary is titled "Slaves case"

A similar document was drawn up listing the *ladino* names (and omitting the African names) of the three African girls owned by Montes.[23]

The slaving captain Ramón (*mongo*) Ferrer, along with José Ruiz and Pedro Montes, had evidently obtained these papers through bribery and corruption (the technical term at the time was *cohecho*), in which those captured in Africa were inscribed as *negros ladinos* – that is to say, Spanish-speaking and born in a territory under Spanish control, or what today would be termed *criollo*.[24] The false papers described them as slaves brought from the interior of the island of Cuba. The captives themselves knew otherwise, using their African names and describing the cruel transatlantic passage lasting "three moons," and ten more days in the outskirts of Havana.[25]

The next step was the above-mentioned baptism, on the American plantations for rural slaves, or in small villages of the Cuban interior, or, for urban slaves, in a church near the houses of the new owners. In this baptismal act for adults, the *bozal*-captives of the Atlantic contraband trade,

---

and is held with Baldwin's personal papers, see Yale University Library, Manuscript Collections, Ms 55, Series VII, Box 135, Folder 1243: Baldwin, Roger Sherman Legal Papers Briefs, 1836-39 (without foliation), see also: Africans Taken in the *Amistad*. Congressional Document, Containing the Correspondence, & c., in Relation to the Captured Africans, New York: For sale at the Anti-Slavery Depository, 1840, pp. 1-48 (Doc. No. 185), p. 29, núm. 4 in: Beinecke, Cb 79110.

23 Ibid., pp. 29-30.

24 These documents were confiscated from the *Amistad*.They are available National Archives de los EE.UU see: Message from the President of the United States to the two Houses of Congress, at the Commencement of the First Session of the Twenty-Sixth Congress, Washington: Blair and Rives, 1839; formerly also available under:see National Archives de los EE.UU www.amistad.org/File://A:/EzpeletaJune251839 (May 18, 2007); see also: Zeuske, *Geschichte der Amistad* . . . ; Theodore Canot refers to such type of falsified "list", see: Canot, "30. Kapitel. Landung der "schwarzen Schüler" auf Cuba. Der Hafenmeister von Havanna. Die unbeschriebene Seite im Hafenregister de rein- und ausfahrenden Schiffe", pp. 257-261, p. 259.

25 See Testimony of Cinque, January 8, 1840, U.S. District Court, Connecticut, in: Message from the President of the United States to the two Houses of Congress [1839] . . . ; formerly also available under:www.amistad.mysticseaport.org/library/court/district/1840.1.8.cinquetest.html (May 18, 2007); see also: Zeuske; García Martínez, Orlando, "The Amistad: Ramón Ferrer, Cuba, and the Transatlantic Dimensions of Slaving and Contraband Trade", in: Schmidt-Nowara, Christopher (eds.), Slavery and Antislavery in Spain's Atlantic empire, New York; Oxford: Berghahn Books, 2013, pp. 200 228.

and also some *emancipados* or, in some cases, free men of colour (robbed from Jamaica or the Bahamas – as newly enslaved named *criollos – creole slaves*), were "written" into the slavery system of Cuba. This means that the first written "hard fact" mention of them did not appear in ships' ledgers, but in baptismal lists in Cuba. Under the term *nación* (nation[26]) the writers of these documents (priests or notaries – *escribanos*) noted places/cultures/ethnic markers, such as "Congo", "Angola", "Arará/Mina [Coromantee]", "Mandinga", "Carabalí" [Igbo], "Lucumí" [Yoruba], or even "Gangá", which was widely used in Cuba in reference to slaves coming from the interior of the Gallinas and Sherbro ports in southern Sierra Leone.[27] As examples of *bozal* slaves entering as *emancipados* after 1820, with no mention of their African names from the lists of the Mixed Commissions, I have chosen some individuals from baptismal lists of the plantation region Sagua la Grande on the north coast of central Cuba:

"No. 468. Pedro. Emancipado

Domingo, 19 de enero de 1868 "bauticé solemnemente y puse por nombre Pedro á un moreno emancipado, no. 5829, de nación congo, de quince años de edad ... Fueron sus padrinos Rafael criollo y Paula lucumí"

No. 469. Pio. Emancipado

Domingo, 19 de enero de 1868 "puse por nombre Pio á un moreno emancipado, no. 5804, de nación congo, de diez y seis años de edad ... Fueron sus padrinos Nicario Gangá y Agustina criolla"

No. 470. Santiago. Emancipado

26 For the real life of "African Nations in the Americas", not the construction of close descriptions of commodities in the notaries records, see: Childs, "Pathways to African Ethnicity in the Americas: African National Associations in Cuba during Slavery", in: Falola, Toyin; Jennings, Christian (eds.), *Sources and methods in African history : spoken, written, unearthed*, Rochester : University of Rochester Press, 2003 (Rochester studies in African history and the diaspora ; [vol. 15]), pp. 118-143.

27 Arnalte, "Cónsules, comerciantes y negreros (españoles en Sierra Leona en el siglo XIX)", pp. 65-79, the best publications about corporal markers of the enslaved in Cuba are: Portuondo, "Marcas para carimbar esclavos en el siglo XVIII", in: Portuondo Zúñiga, Entre Esclavos y libres de Cuba colonial ..., pp. 35-43; La Rosa Corzo, Gabino, *Tatuados. Deformaciones étnicas de los cimarrones en Cuba*, La Habana: Fundación Fernando Ortiz, 2011.

Domingo, 19 de Enero de 1868 "puse por nombre Santiago á un moreno emancipado, no. 5321, de nación congo, de quince años ...Fueron sus padrinos José Eligio criollo y Margarita conga".[28]

The act of baptism has, in its Christian sense, the function of strengthening the relationship between the baptized person, the community and the saint. In a systemic Atlantic sense, it has the function of integrating the slaves into the Catholic American colonies. But on the *ingenios* another systemic aspect of the culture of slavery was even more important: this was the relationship of godparent between newcomers from Africa, many of them young persons or even children, and older slaves from the same cultural area, who had been living for a longer time on the plantation (expressed in the terms *lucumí*, *congo*, *arará*, *mandinga*, *macuá*, *carabalí* (igbo), etc.).[29]

These "ethnic markers" or "ethnic makeups" of the so-called *naciones de Africa* (nations of Africa) were not used in sea-based (or ship-based) records of the nineteenth century after 1820. And we do not know who used them first in massive and oral form: perhaps the captives themselves as a type of cultural distinction and resistance already in the hidden Atlantic (or even in the African *barracoons* of the slave ports?) forming wider networks of *carabelas* (shipmates) among those with the same *nación* or similar languages in resistance to the hostile generalization of the terms slave and *bozal*, and using information that may have been circulated among them and *emancipados* or among them and the African personnel of the slave ports or the Atlantic creoles of the ships? What we know is that they were first of all used in written form in land-based lists of slaves by writers of official records (notary records, baptismal records) and private writers in the *ingenios* (plantation lists, hereditary lists[30]). Either way, "ethnic" terms in Cuba were broadly used in notaries' sales records, which meant the writ-

---

28 Registros parroquiales de bautizo, parroquía Inmaculada Concepción, Sagua la Grande, diocésis Santa Clara (Registros Sagua la Grande); Libro de bautismos de color 3, fs. 64v-66v, nos. 468-473, see also: "Lista de emancipados bautizados en masa en la parroquía de Sagua la Grande", in: Zeuske; García Martínez, "Estado, notarios y esclavos en Cuba", passim.

29 García, "Familia y parentela", in: García Rodríguez, Gloria, La esclavitud desde la esclavitud. La visión de los siervos, México: Centro de Investigación Científica "Ing. Jorge Y. Tamayo", 1996, pp. 36-44.

30 "D.n Walter Balfour, vecino de este puerte ... vende ... á D.n Juan Beronda del mismo

ten notation of a contract of sale or resale of a human body. There they can be found together with slave names taken from the bible (like María, Jesús or Josef), or from local notions of places in Africa. These names of places or peoples in the notaries' documents were almost always written in lower-case.[31] This suggests that these names were understood to convey information about the ascribed "character" of slaves from a given African region.

b) The second way captives, who arrived in Cuba and worked as rural slaves after 1820, were documented pertains to the majority of *emancipados*. After a big sea-based paper work, done by British commanders and captains, it was done with a document, called a *carta de emancipado* (letter of liberated slave); these were captives found on Spanish, Portuguese, or Cuban ships and declared "liberated" by the Mixed Courts. *Emancipados* entered Cuban slave society with this document on which their African name and their Christian name were noted. An example of such a document is the one that identified an *emancipado*-slave who was given the Christian name Sotero. He came

"del bergantin goleta Español Firme, con cargamento de negros bozales ... Y siendo uno de ellos el que en Africa era conocido con el nombre de *Yáo* según su informe dado por medio de *Pedro Betancur libre y Juan Betancur esclavo de D. Jose Fernandes* individuos de su misma Nacion é intérpretes de su idioma, presentes en este acto para ser en todo tiempo testigos de la identidad de su persona; cuya filiacion [[32]] se anota al pié, al cual se le ha puesto ahora por nombre *Sotero* le consignamos la presente [...]

---

vecindario ... las treinta y dos avas [aras ?] partes del ingenio Resulta de que es condueño ... se compone de sesenta caballerías de tierra ... con ciento cuarenta y cuatro esclavos [all with names] ... en cantidad de cuatro mil quinientos treinta y siete pesos ...": AHPVC, Santa Clara, Protocolos Notariales de Manuel Lino Surí, Tomo I 1854, f. 125r-v, No. 161 "Venta de ingenio", en el puerto de Sagua la Grande á veinteidos de marzo de 1854. More than a half were slaves from Mozambique (*macuás*).

31 For the use of these place/caracter-concepts in Cuba, see: Zeuske, "Nach der Sklaverei: Sklavennamen und Kultur des Vergessens" [After Slavery: Slave Names and a Culture of Forgetting], in: Zeuske, *Schwarze Karibik. Sklaven, Sklavereikulturen und Emanzipation,* Zürich: Rotpunktverlag, 2004 [Black Caribbean. Slaves, Cultures of Slavery and Emancipation], pp. 465-502.

32 The term *filiación* refers to corporal markers, for example a scar (also ritual scars), but also for brand marks.

Nacion *Mina*

Edad *trece años*

Estatura *Cuatro pies y una pulgada*

Señales *Cuatro cicatrices en la pierna derecha y otra al lado de la rodilla izquierda".*[33]

But there is an astonishing aspect of the official treatment of *emancipados* in bureaucratic documents of the colonial state. The colonial officials fairly often do not use the *emancipado's* names but only their numbers from the Mixed-Court-lists (I do not know if this can signify that the numbers were tattooed in some place of the body of the *emancipados*).[34]

c) The third way that slaves' arrival, not only in Cuba, but in the whole Catholic Slave Americas, was documented, pertains to *Creole* (American-born) slaves and involves formal baptismal acts in this cases not for adults (sometimes robbed from other Caribbean territories, as mentioned under a)), but for newborn children of slaves (despite the fact that it was written down sometimes a year or more later). For this symbolic entrance of a Creole slave, in this case of the famous "*cimarrón*" Estebán Montejo[35], we have his baptismal record:

---

[33] AHN Madrid, Estado, Trata de negros, leg. 8024/14, no. 3: "Expediente de Emancipado No 97" [print], given in the name of Claudio Martínez de Pinillos by the "Comisión Mixta" (Mixed Commission), La Habana, December 18, 1828. In this case, the document was also a printed formulary with empty parts for handwritten information, like names and other specific notes).

[34] Archivo Histórico Provincial de Matanaz (AHPM), Fondo Negociado de Emancipados, No. 11330, leg. 108: "Comunicaciones relativas a reclamaciones de emancipados", 27 de Marzo-28 de Septiembre de 1844, f. 2r-v.; letter by Captain General Leopoldo O'Donnell Havana, June 3, 1844, ibid., f. 12r; another letter written by O'Donnell from Havana to the governor of Matanzas, september 26, 1844, in: AHPM, Fondo Negociado de Emancipados, No. 11330, leg. 108: " Comunicaciones relativas a reclamaciones de emancipados", 27 de Marzo-28 de Septiembre de 1844, f. 23r-24r.

[35] See my articles: Zeuske, "The Cimarrón in the Archives: A Re-Reading of Miguel Barnet's Biography of Esteban Montejo", in: *New West Indian Guide/Nieuwe West-Indische Gids*, vol. 71, no. 3 & 4 (1997), pp. 265-279; Zeuske, "Más novedades de Esteban Montejo", in: *Del Caribe*, Santiago de Cuba, Núm. 38 (2002), pp. 95-101; Zeuske, "Hidden Markers, Open Secrets. On Naming, Race Marking and Race Making in Cuba", in: *New West Indian Guide / Nieuwe West-Indische Gids* vol. 76, no. 3 & 4 (2002), pp. 235-266.

"N°. 188
Estéban Santa Teresa
M^{o}.E^{o}.
Libre por beneficio de la Ley de 23 de Junio de 1870
Por autorización de S.S.I.

Jueves cinco de Agosto de mil ochocientos sesenta y nueve años:
Yo D. Franc^{o}. Sirola, Cura Beneficiado de la Iglesia Parroquial de ascenso de la Purísima Concepción de Sagua la Grande y Vicario Fóraneo de ella y su jurisdicción, bauticé solemnemente y puse por nombre Estéban[36] a un niño que nació el día veinte y seis de Diciembre del año próximo pasado [1868 - M.Z.], hijo de la morena Dionisia conga, perteneciente al Ingenio Santa Teresa, de D. Tomas Ribalta. Fué su padrino Quintín criollo, á quien advertí el parentesco espiritual y obligaciones que contrajo; y lo firmé = Franc^{o}. Sirola"[37]

A fundamental difference between the naming patterns I have labeled under a) (adult "bozal"-slaves) lies in the fact that groups of adult *bozales* were listed with place/people/character-labels, like "congo" or "lucumí". Under c) (new born "creole"-slaves), in contrast, these slaves were given the surname of their owner (Ribalta, in the example presented) or the name of the plantation where they were born.

The examples represent different acts of taking possession by naming. The newcomer captives, adult *bozales* or *saltwater slaves*, entered as new property of the extended family of their new owner and at the same time were part of the "congo-section of the slave roll of a plantation" (*dotación*). In later acts of possible selling, the adult slave Estéban Santa Teresa or Estéban Ribalta would appear as "Estéban congo". The Creole child Estéban, in contrast, was regarded as part of the family of his owner, but for the owner and the writing priest, it was more important to fix the place (the plantation, the *ingenio*) where he was born. So he was marked with the name of the *ingenio*, Santa Teresa.

We can also observe that in the act of baptism, the little baptized child was rendered fatherless. The slave owner gave him or her fictive kin. We also observe that Estéban was assigned only a godfather and not, as was the usual practice for free persons, a godmother. Estéban's owner or the priest gave him the godfather Quintín criollo.[38]

[38] Morrison, Karen Y., "Creating an Alternative Kinship: Slavery, Freedom, and Nineteenth-Century Afro-Cuban *Hijos Naturales*", in: *Journal of Social History* (fall 2007), pp. 55-80.

The business of *curas* and notaries: writing second slavery and writing freedom before emancipation (manumission)

Curas (priests), and, for the most part notaries, were the agents of this system of "writing slavery".[39] With their writing they maintained the control of slaves as private property in "roman" tradition within a slave society. In the hundreds of thousands of notaries' protocols of slave sales and purchases, the vast majority of slave women and men appear with slave names from the biblical canon of "Maria, Josef and Jesus", like María, Antonio, María del Rosario, Luis, María del Carmen, Manuel, Jesús, Ramona, Bárbara, Francisco, Dolores, Estéban – biblical names, common Spanish names, or Catholic saints' names – followed by a term that refers to a constructed place/culture/ethnic group in Africa, like "María del Carmen lucumí", and makes reference to invented and constructed innate characteristics of the "African" group, as explained above.[40]

---

[39] Zeuske; García Martínez, Orlando, "Notarios y esclavos en Cuba, siglo XIX, in: Fuente, Alejandro de la (coord.), *Su "único derecho": los esclavos y la ley*, Madrid: Fundación Mapfre | Tavera, 2004 (=Debate y perspectivas. *Cuadernos de Historia y Ciencias Sociales*, No. 4 (Diciembre 2004)), pp. 127-170; Zeuske; García Martínez, "Estado, notarios y esclavos en Cuba. Aspectos de una genealogía legal de la ciudadanía en sociedades esclavistas", passim.

[40] Classifications, also classifications of names or parts of names, are always problematical. There are many efforts to realize that the naming patterns of place/culture/capacity-concept, constructed by slave traders: López Valdés, Rafael L., "La Sociedad Secreta ‚Abakuá' en un grupo de obreros portuarios", in: *Etnología y Folklore* 2, La Habana (Julio-Dic. 1966), pp. 5-26; López Valdés, *Componentes africanos en el etnos cubano*, La Habana: Ed. de Ciencias Sociales, 1985; López Valdés, "Notas para el estudio etnohistórico de los esclavos lucumí de Cuba", in: Menéndez, Lázara, *Estudios Afrocubanos*, 4 vols., La Habana: Universidad de la Habana, 1998,Vol. II, pp. 311-347; Guanche Pérez, Jesús, "Contribución al estudio del poblamiento africano en Cuba", in: *África: Revista do Centro de Estudos Africanos*. USP, São Paulo, 18-19/1 (1995-1996), pp. 119-138; see also: Morgan, Philip D., "The Cultural Implications of the Atlantic Slave Trade: African Regional Origins, American Destinations and New World Developments", in: *Slavery & Abolition* 18,1 (1997), pp. 122-145; the perspective of Africanists is in: Lovejoy, Paul E. (ed.), "Identifying Enslaved Africans in the African Diaspora", in: Lovejoy (ed.), *Identity in the Shadow of Slavery*, London; New York: Continuum, 2000, pp. 1-29 and passim; see also: Oriji, John N., "The Slave Trade, Warfare and Aro Expansion in the Igbo Hinterland", in: *Transafrican Journal of History* 16 (1987), pp. 151-166; Chambers, Douglas B., "'My own nation': Igbo Exiles in the Diaspora", in: Eltis, David;

Thus denominated, slaves were, for the notaries and for their records, a "person with a price"[41] who must be described in words understandable to the buyer. The place/people/character-concept was part of the marketing process. This means, first of all, that slaves had to bear a "Christian name" and a description of their presumed characteristics.

From the sixteenth century to the nineteenth century, the most common denomination that appeared as the second part of captives' names was "congo" (Bantu, Loango, Libolo, Benguela); in Eastern Cuba the term "casta Congo" also frequently appeared, as in the following protocol: "un negro de mi propiedad nombrado Manuel de Jesus, casta Congo".[42] The great change under the criterion of more mobility during the atlantiza-

---

Richardson, David (eds.), *Routes to Slavery. Direction, Ethnicity and Mortality in the Atlantic Slave Trade*, London: Frank Cass, 1997, pp. 72-97; Chambers, "Tracing Igbo into the African Diaspora" in: Lovejoy (ed.), *Identity in the Shadow of Slavery*, London; New York: Continuum, 2000, pp. 55-71; Northrup, "Igbo and Myth Igbo: Culture and Ethnicity in the Atlantic World, 1600-1850", in: *Slavery and Abolition* 21:3 (2000), pp. 1-20; Miller, Joseph C., "Retention, Reinvention, and Remembering. Restoring Identities through Enslavement in Africa and under Slavery in Brazil", Curto, José C.; Lovejoy (eds.), *Enslaving Connections. Changing Cultures of Africa and Brazil during the Era of Slavery*, New York: Humanity Books, 2004, pp. 81-121; in reference to "Gangá": Basso Ortiz, Alessandra, *Los gangá en cuba. La comunidad de Matanzas*, La Habana: Fundación Fernando Ortiz, 2005 (La Fuente Viva; 25); see also: Childs, "Pathways to African Ethnicity in the Americas: African National Associations in Cuba during Slavery", pp. 118-143 and: Lohse, Russell, "Slave Trade Nomenclature and African Ethnicities in the Americas: Evidence from Early Eighteen-Century Costa Rica", in: ibid., pp. 145-154. The fundamental base of all Cuban classifications is the scheme made by Henri Dumont in the 1870s; see: Dumont, Henri, *Antropología y patología comparada de los negros esclavos* [1876] (Traducción por el Prof. L. Castellanos), Habana: Calle L, 1922 (Colección Cubana de Libros y Documentos Inéditos o Raros, dirigida por Fernando Ortiz; Vol. 2); see also: La Rosa Corzo, "Orígenes de los cimarrones africanos capturados entre 1830 y 1857 en le región occidental de la Isla", in: La Rosa Corzo, *Tatuados ...*, pp. 9-30, p. 11.

41 Johnson, Walter, "Introduction: A Person with a Price", in: Johnson, *Soul by Soul. Life Inside the Antebellum Slave Market*, Cambridge, Mass.; London: Harvard University Press, 2000, pp. 1-18.

42 Archivo Histórico Provincial de Santiago de Cuba (hereafter AHPStC), Fondo Protocolos, Escribanía Real de Manuel Caminero Ferrer, Bd. 85 (1835), f. 24r/v: "Venta de esclavo" D. Gaspar Hechavarria á D. Pedro Cupull, Santiago de Cuba, 10 de febrero de 1835.

tion of the second slavery was that more and more children were abducted. Other common denominations, beginning in the nineteenth century, were "lucumí" (Yoruba, Nago), and, even earlier, "arará" (Aja-Fon, Gbe, Ewe-Fon, Ashante, Ewé, Ga-Adagme, Cormartinos/Coromantee[43]), "mina" (Ewe, Fanti, Akan-nations), as in the following protocol: "*una negra de mi propiedad nombrada Iris, casta Acanda*" (Akan).[44] In Eastern Cuba the reference to the Mina-group also is documented as "casta Mina": "*un negro de mi propiedad nombrado José Dolores, casta Mina*".[45] The majority of slaves from West Africa until the first years of the nineteenth century were Minas. This group included various peoples, but generally Gbe-Speakers.[46] The "mandinga" (also: Malinke) in the early years of the slave trade could comprise also "jolof" (wolof), "fulbe" (*poules* in French) "astute traders and merchants", many of them literate, or their captives.[47] Paul Lovejoy has argued that a man captured in war from Timbuctu in the powerful Songhay empire, transported westward to Senegal and sold to European slavers would became a slave in the Americas called a *mandingo* (or *mandinga*).[48] In Eastern Cuba such a slave could be described as "*una negra de mi propiedad nombrada Candelaria, casta Mandinga*".[49] The "carabalí"

43 Thornton, "The Coromantees: An African Cultural Group in Colonial North America and the Caribbean", pp. 161-178; Brice Sogbossi, Hippolyte, *La tradición ewé-fon en Cuba. Contribución al estudio de la tradición ewé-fon (arará) en los pueblos de Jovellanos, Perico y Agramonte, Cuba*, La Habana : Fundación Fernando Ortiz, 1998 (Colección Africanía); Jones, Adam; Sebald, Peter, *An African Family Archive: The Lawsons of Little Popo / Aneho (Togo) 1841-1938,* Oxford: Oxford University Press, 2005 (British Academy Fontes Historiae Africanae, New Series 7).

44 AHPStC, Fondo Protocolos, Escribanía Real de Manuel Caminero Ferrer, Bd. 85 (1835), f. 319r/v: "Venta de esclava", D. Juan Silvestre Fourir al Cap.n Cayetano Cabrera [without numbering the escrituras], Santiago de Cuba, December 12, 1835.

45 AHPStC, Fondo Protocolos, Escribanía Real de Manuel Caminero Ferrer, Bd. 85 (1835), f. 36v/37r: "Venta de esclavo", D. Juan Bautista de la Torre á D. Gregorio Reito, Santiago de Cuba, March 2, 1835

46 Lovejoy, "The context of Enslavement in West Africa", in: Landers, Jane G.; Robinson, Barry M. (eds.), *Slaves, Subjects, and Subversives. Blacks in Colonial Latin America*, Albuquerque: University of New Mexico Press, pp. 9-38.

47 Guitar, Lynne, "Boiling It Down. Slavery on the First Commercial Sugarcane Ingenios in the Americas (Hispaniola, 1530-45)", in: Ibid., pp. 39-82, here p. 50.

48 Lovejoy, "The context of Enslavement in West Africa", pp. 9-38, here p. 9.

49 AHPStC, Fondo Protocolos, Escribanía Real de Manuel Caminero Ferrer, Bd. 85

(Efik, Ekoi, Ibibo and Igbo[50]), in the Trinidad region of Central-south Cuba were labelled also "casta Ybo"[51]; in Eastern Cuba "casta Carbaly", "Carbalí" or "Carabaly".[52]

There were also references to the "bibis" or "viví" ("casta Viví"[53]) as parts of slave's names or "gangás" (in Eastern Cuba also: "casta Cangá"[54]), as mentioned in the following protocol of Santiago de Cuba "*Isabel (á) Zabek, casta cangá*" [Isabel (a[lias]) Zabek][55], the nation-term written with a lower-case initial letter. Because of the alias-addendum "Zabek", we have here one of the few cases of an original African name or a nick-name, chosen by herself or other slaves and written down in an official document of sale, of the woman with the slave name Isabel. The terms "monjolo" or "monzolo" (from the Congo/Angola regions), as well as "macúa" (from Mozambique) also appear, but they are less frequent in Cuban sources.[56]

These denominations as parts of slave names were used in Cuba during the boom period of the second slavery, the illegal slave trade, and *atlanti-*

(1835), f. 24v/25r: "Venta de esclava", D. Desiderio de Vera á D. M.a Antonia Sanchez de Ruiz , Santiago de Cuba, 11 de febrero de 1835.

50 Afigbo, Adiele, "Through a Glass Darkly: Eighteenth-Century Igbo Society through Equiano's Narrative", in: Afigbo, *Ropes of Sand: Studies in Igbo History and Culture*, Ibadan: University Press Ltd., 1981, pp. 145-168; Northrup, David, "Igbo: Culture and Ethnicity in the Atlantic World", in: *Slavery and Abolition* 21 (2000), pp. 1-20; Kolapo, Femi J., "The Igbo and Their Neighbours During the Era of the Atlantic Slave-Trade", in: *Slavery and Abolition* 25 (2004), pp. 114-133.

51 Archivo Histórico Municipal de Trinidad (AHMT), Fondo Escribanía José Mariano Piedra, legajo 17 (1808), "V.ta R.l", f. 213v-214r, Trinidad, 6 de septiembre de 1808.

52 AHPStC, Fondo Protocolos, Escribanía Real de Manuel Caminero Ferrer, Bd. 85 (1835), f. 15r: "Venta de esclavo" D. Gaspar Hechavarria á D. Pedro Cupull , Santiago de Cuba, 29 de enero de 1835.

53 AHPStC, Fondo Protocolos, Escribanía Real de Manuel Caminero Ferrer, Bd. 85 (1835), f. 216r/216v: "Venta de esclava", D. Antonio Pesent á D. Victor Ssansouber , Santiago de Cuba, 9 de septiembre de 1835.

54 AHPStC, Fondo Protocolos, Escribanía Real de Manuel Caminero Ferrer, Bd. 85 (1835), f. 4r/v: "Venta de esclavo" D.a María Dolores Mustelier a D.n Demetrio del Castillo, Santiago de Cuba, 5 de enero de 1835.

55 Ibid., f. 12v: "Venta de esclava", Mr. Carlos Drago á Mm.e Eleonora P. Feriel [ohne Nummerierung der Escrituras], Santiago de Cuba, 22 of January 1835.

56 Thornton, "Cannibals, Witches, and Slave Traders in the Atlantic World", in: *William and Mary Quarterly* 3d series, Vol. LX, Nr. 2 (April 2002), pp. 273-294, p. 273, FN 1.

zation, from 1790 to the 1880s. I repeat that their main formal function was marketing and commodification. The hidden function was establishing the identity of the enslaved and their descendants (as a diasporic ethnicity). As late as 1874 the "names" of slaves in a notary's record could appear in this way: "*los esclavos, animales utiles y labranzas siguientes: Son los primeros Manuel criollo, Ramos id, Jose id, Eligio id, Ignacio id, Manuel pardo, Jose Manacas congo, Urbano de nacion y Miguel id, estos dos últimos ancianos*" [the slaves, livestock, and fields as follows: the first are Manuel criollo, Ramos id [the same], José id, Eligio id, Ignacio id, Manuel pardo [mulato], José Manacas congo, Urbano de nación [from Africa] and Miguel id, the last ones older people]".[57] Simple names like "Alejandro de Africa" were also possible.[58]

Only in very few cases were the men and women who were bought and sold and documented in notaries' protocols during this half century named with a "civil" surname, such as, María González. When this occurred, they were, in the huge majority, slaves of well-known owners in urban spaces. In these cases, the owner's surname or last name was the first *apellido*. "*Apellido*" is a *paternal surname* in the Iberian naming culture. There is also a *second surname*, a *maternal surname*. Normally, the first (paternal) *apellido* is used in the oral culture.

Only children of a legitimate marriage could bear the double last name of the two *apellidos*. Children of unmarried women – most slave mothers were formally unmarried – bore the maternal last name as sole last name. So the majority of urban house slaves bore only the first *apellido* of one of their owners, because the two *apellidos* were only allowed for persons born to parents who were officially and ecclesiastically married. So, a former slave woman could appear with various forms of her name: "Maria de Leon Nacion conga" (in the *carta de libertad*)[59], "la morena libre M.a del Car-

[57] Archivo Provincial de Cienfuegos (hereafter: APC) , Protocolos José Rafael de Villafuerte y Castellanos, Cienfuegos, 1874, (Enero - Dic.), vol. II, 1874, Escritura No. 60 "Arrendamiento", f. 138r.-141r.

[58] APC, Protocolos José Rafael de Villafuerte y Castellanos, 1877 (Enero - Dic.), fols. 211r.-214r., escritura no. 81 "Venta de esclavos ...", Cienfuegos, 17 de Mayo de 1877.

[59] "Carta de libertad", written by the owner Andres de Leon, "then.te coronel del Regim.to de matanzas comand.te de armas del partido de yomuri y su Jurisdiccion", Cafetal La Soledad, Octubre 16, 1831, in: ANC, Escribanía de Barreto, leg. 98, no. 34, 1840, Maria

men Conga" (as a liberated ex-slave, a *liberta*)[60], in the description of her properties (*manifestacion de los bienes*) appears the old form of her slave name, the "cadaver muerta del colera M.a del Carmen Nacion conga"[61] and, finally, in the receipt of the priest, "Carmen conga, morena libre".[62]

Cuban society at the end of second slavery and during the period of post emancipation, seen through the official documentation, appears as a "fatherless society".[63] In legal documents, too, slaves, who represented a large part of the Cuban social world in the nineteenth century, appear basically as a "fatherless" group.

Beginning at the end of the *Isabellian* era in Spain and Cuba (1834-1838), more and more slaves appeared in manumission protocols and in protocols, which bore the title *libertad* (liberty)[64], which signified protocols by which slaves were emancipated as individuals by their owners. This process was accelerated as a result of the legal efforts of slaves, ex-slaves, and their allies, and of revolutions in Spain (1868-1874: "La Gloriosa") and Cuba (1868-1878: "Ten Years War").[65]

---

del Carmen: "Intestado de la morena Maria del Carmen Conga", f. 7r.

60 Ibid., f. 4r.

61 "Tasación", in: Ibid., f. 4v-5r, here f. 4v, Francisco Peraza, Capitán Juez Pedaneo, Pueblo de Gibacoa, april 23, 1833.

62 "Derechos de parroquía del entierro", in: Ibid., f. 8r, Josef Ramón Dávila, Gibacoa, Junio 29 de 1833.

63 Méndez Ródenas, Adriana, "Identity and Incest in Cecilia Valdés: Villaverde and the Origin(s) of the Text". In: *Cuban Studies* 24 (1994), pp. 83-104.

64 The only book about manumission during the existence of second slavery is: Meriño Fuentes, María de los Ángeles; Perera Díaz, Aisnara, *Para librarse de lazos, antes buena familia que buenos brazos. Apuntes sobre la manumisión en Cuba*, La Habana, Santiago de Cuba: Editorial Oriente, 2009.

65 The classical study of Abolition and Emancipation for Cuba is: Scott, Rebecca J., *Slave Emancipation in Cuba. The Transition to Free Labor, 1860-1899*, Princeton, N.Y.: Princeton University Press, 1985 (Reprint: Pittsburgh: The University of Pittsburgh Press, 2000); see also: Schmidt-Nowara, Christopher, "National Economy and Atlantic Slavery: Protectionism and Resistance to Abolitionism in Spain and the Antilles, 1854-1874", in: HAHR 78, 4 (1998), pp. 603-629; Schmidt-Nowara, *Empire and Antislavery: Spain, Cuba, and Puerto Rico, 1833-1874*, Pittsburgh, Pa.: Pittsburgh University Press, 1999; Schmidt-Nowara, "The End of Slavery and the End of Empire: Slave Emancipation in Cuba and Puerto Rico", in: *Slavery & Abolition. A Journal of Slave and Post-Slave Studies*, vol. 21, Num. 2 (August 2000), Special Issue: After Slav-

In these documented acts of the emancipation era (1868-1886), the last decades before the final abolition of slavery, and then afterwards, the written representation of the men and women who were emerging from slavery, increasingly took the form of a "civil" name, like the above mentioned forms "María González" or "María del Carmen Conga".

Notaries also began this process of "writing freedom," for the most part as a reflection of the social process of emancipation between 1868 and 1886, although in some cases they did so earlier than 1868. This means that they began to write more and more notaries' protocols with the title *libertad* (freedom) or recorded other arrangements under which slaves got freedom (for example *manumisón* and, through self-purchase (*coartación*)).[66] They also began to write down notaries' records for ex-slaves as mandates. Then they would have to use a new written "civil" name of the ex-slaves.

Rebellions, resistance, African names, nick names, and informal kin-ties

At this point we should make a break and have a look at slave rebellions as well as cultural resistance (William Norman names it "cultural change"[67]), and the connections to names and identities. At the time of a rebellion or a heavy conflict (first of all between slave traders (*negreros*), in Cuba first of all documented in the *Tribunal de Comercio* in Havana), the boundaries between the hidden cultures of the Atlantic worlds, also called *diaspora*,

ery. Emancipation and its Discontents, ed. Temperley, Howard, pp. 188-207.

66 Zeuske; García Martínez, "Estado, notarios y esclavos en Cuba. Aspectos de una genealogía legal de la ciudadanía en sociedades esclavistas", passim; Fuente, Alejandro de la, "Slaves and the Creation of Legal Rights in Cuba : Coartación and Papel", in: *Hispanic American Historical Review* 87:4 (November 2007), pp. 659-692; Varella, Claudia, "La Coartación: ¿Coartada de un falso abolicionismo?", in: *Ibero-Americana Pragensia – Supplementum* 19 (2007), pp. 285-292 (=Opatrný (ed.), *Pensamiento caribeño. Siglos XIX y XX*); Brana-Shute, Rosemary; Sparks, Randy J. (eds.), *Paths to Freedom. Manumission in the Atlantic World*, Columbia: University of South Carolina Press, 2009; Varella Fernández, "El canal administrativo de los conflictos entre esclavos y amos. Causas de manumisión decididas ante síndicos en Cuba", in: *Revista de Indias* 251 (2011), pp. 109-136.

67 Norman Jr., William C. Van, "The Process of Cultural Change among Cuban Bozales during the 19th Century", in: *The Americas* (TAm) 62,2 (2005), S. 177-207.

and the process known as *writing the slavery* were broken for a moment. The *long black veil* of silence was tattered – but only, as it has been said, for a moment. So rebellions or conflicts were snapshots into the deep and hidden culture of spoken African names, identities, meanings, and other Lacanian elements beyond the written culture of slavery. African names and nicknames can be found almost exclusively in police files and other sources about rebellions (including shipboard rebellions[68]). One of the rare examples is the list of personal slaves of the American slave trader and *mongo* (factor in Africa) Jacob Faber: "Serah an prime girl/ Fárra an prime boy/ Sabu an prime boy/ Yattá an prime boy/ Yorrá an prime boy/ Sabudie an prime boy/ Culipa an prime boy ... in all seven"[69] Faber used for the "prime" children only African names, may be because they still were not baptized. The writers of policy files explicitly mention "African names" in addition to Christian ones: "*Ayusó en su tierra, aqui Guillermo*", "*Eguiyove en su tierra, Matías aqui*", "*nombrados en su tierra Ayai, Churipe, Bale y Agó*", "*Fanguá en su tierra, Prudencio aqui*".[70] Fermín lucumí, a slave

68 Taylor, Eric Robert, If We Must Die. Shipboard Insurrections in the Era of the Atlantic Slave Trade, Baton Rouge: Louisiana State University Press, 2006; Eltis, David; Engerman, Stanley L., "Shipboard Revolts and Abolition", in: Drescher; Emmer, Pieter C. (eds.), Who Abolished Slavery? Slave Revolts and Abolitionism. A debate with João Pedro Marques, New York/Oxford: Berghahn Books, 2010 (European Expansion & Global Interaction; Vol. 8), S. 145-155;for (the first) examples of rebellions on Spanish-Cuban slave ships, see: ANC, Tribunal de Comercio (TC), leg. 240, no. 14 (1820). Hernandez (Gaspar). "Varios de la Tripulación del Bergantin Negrero "Solicito" contra D.n Gaspar Hernandez su armador sobre soldadas"; Ibid., leg. 504, no. 32 (1815). Escoto (Antonio). "D.n Antonio Escoto, sobre justificar el numero de negros con que arribo a Rio Pongo en el Africa, la goleta de su propiedad titulada "Isabel".

69 List (original), written August, 21, 1815 Rio Pongo (in English), in: ANC, TC, leg. 184, no. 13 (1815). Faber (Jacobo): "Jacobo Faber, contra Juan Madrazo, sobre pesos de ciertas cuentas de negros bozales", f. 4r. The term "prime" means best price; the Spanish term for prime girl was *muleca* and for prime boy *muleco*.

70 ANC, Fondo Miscelanea de Expedientes [Comisión Militar] (FM), leg. 540, Exp. B (1833): "Contra los autores y complices principales de la sublevación de negros del Cafetal Salvador de D. Francisco Santiago de Aguirre ubicado en Banes ocurrida la noche del 13. de Agosto por cuyo delito se juzgan á Pedro el Carretero, Gonzalo mandinga, Eusebio gangá, Luis idem, Pascual Lucumí, Romualdo id., Antonio lucumí, Agustin id., Hilario id., Juan id., Hermenegildo id.": "La Guerra en tierra de Mariel", Banes, 13 de agosto de 1833.

on the ingenio *Balear* in Rancho Veloz in middle Cuba, took revenge for continuous harassment by killing the *mayoral* (white slave driver) of the plantation with a *machete*. During the investigation he said, with the help of a translator because he did not speak Spanish: "*que en su tierra se llamaba Malade, que aquí su señor le puso Fermín*" [That in his land he is called Malade, and here his master put him Fermin].[71]

On the night of August 13, 1833 a rebellion broke out in the *cafetal* (coffee plantation) *Aguirre* in the West of Havana.[72] The leader of the conspiracy of the rebellion was a man with the slave name Joaquín lucumí. He had convinced other *contramayorales ladinos* (Spanish speaking slave drivers), Luis lucumí and Gonzálo mandinga, enslaved drivers who already spoke Spanish, to take part in the rebellion. Other *cabezas* ("heads" or leaders) were men of different African backgrounds who are listed in the files as "Alejo lucumí (NN [73] Aquivare)", "Perico [or Pedro] lucumí (NN Abunó (a) El Carretero)", "Carlos gangá" and "Eusebio gangá".[74] The leader, Joaquin lucumí, also succeeded in convincing the *contramayoral* of the *bozales* – the enslaved driver of new captives who did not speak Spanish, nicknamed "(a [lias]) Fierabrás also (a) El Labrao" – to take part together with the *ladinos*. This man "Fierabrás or El Labrao, lucumí (NN

---

71 ANC, Fondo Miscelánea de Expedientes, 235/E: "Fermín lucumí, jefe en su tierra, da muerte a su mayoral en el ingenio Balear", Rancho Veloz, 31 de julio de 1840, see also García Rodríguez, La esclavitud desde la esclavitud ..., pp. 139-141.

72 Zeuske, "Saint-Domingue auf Kuba: Der Aufstand in Banes, 13. und 14. August 1833 [Saint-Domingue in Cuba: the Uprising in Banes, August 13 and 14, 1833]", in: Zeuske, Cuba grande ..., pp. 693-723.

73 NN signifies "nombre de nación [name of nation]"=African name. The investigators of the Comisión Militar [Military Commission, a institution for repression] noted very fast, that the majority of the rebellious slaves were using the "lucumí"-language (or "Yoruba") for communication. They compiled a list of "Christian names" of the rebels with their respective African names and their "nation"; see: ANC, La Habana, FM, leg. 540, no. B (1833): "Contra los autores y complices principales de la sublevación de negros del Cafetal Salvador de D. Francisco Santiago de Aguirre ubicado en Banes ocurrida la noche del 13. de Agosto por cuyo delito se juzgan á Pedro el Carretero, Gonzalo mandinga, Eusebio gangá, Luis idem, Pascual Lucumí, Romualdo id., Antonio lucumí, Agustin id., Hilario id., Juan id., Hermenegildo id.", f. 173r-177v.

74 Iduarte, "Noticias sobre sublevaciones y conspiraciones de esclavos: Cafetal Salvador. 1833", in: *Revista de la Biblioteca Nacional José Martí* 24 (1-2) (1982), pp. 117-153, here p. 122.

Edú)" does not have a Christian name in any of the documents pertaining to the case.[75] Perhaps Edú belonged to the category of slaves with military training in Africa. Because of his physical strength, his wildness, and his tirelessness, he could avoid being named with a Christian name (or the *cura* had simply not yet passed through this plantation). It is clear that his owner and the white slave drivers in some way respected him.

The following example of cultural resistance in the form of recognition of paternity by an ex-slave shows us that even they, ex-slaves, could overcome the distance between the written culture of the slavery society and the hidden cultures of the Atlantic and the cultures of slaves. Here we have the use of a written "civil name", and of the Spanish laws by an ex-slave, and, as an interesting exception, one of the few attempts to introduce memorized African genealogical lines in written Spanish-Cuban documents. The ex-slave with the "civil name" Antonio Pérez declared in 1885 that the child Julio Domingo was his *hijo natural* (natural son):

"The moreno Antonio Pérez, without a second surname, native of the town of Yisá, of the Lucumí nation in Africa, single, fifty-one years of age, field worker and from this place, [...] the neighborhood Pueblo Nuevo [...] says: in consequence of the relationship which he had with one of his class, morena libre [free brown woman] Regina Pared, native and citizen of this city, single, adult and already deceased, the latter gave birth the twentieth of December in eighteen-hundred seventy-eight [1878] to a child that is her son and that of an unknown father and was baptized [...] with the name of Julio Domingo the thirtieth of the following month of January [1879] specifying that his grandmother was Ascensión Pared of the same origin [...] Concerning this child, the moreno Antonio Pérez [...] arranges [for it]: that he declares and acknowledges as his illegitimate son the named Julio Domingo [...] who therefore gains the right to child support and education and to follow him as his lawful heir [...] empowering him to use his surname [the boy could use two apellido-surnames, the paternal and the maternal, thus Julio Domingo Pérez Pared]; wishing to record for opportune purposes that the grandparents of the acknowledged child were Yícocun Hova and Fá Chipe, both native of the aforementioned town of Yisá

[75] The other slaves were calling to this man "Fierabrás" (verbatim: "arm of fury").

and already deceased, and that the person appearing was baptized about the year eighteen-hundred and fifty [at the age of 16] in the parish church of the hamlet of Guaracabuya, as belonging to the *dotación* of the cattle pen [*portrero*] called ‚El Platanal'".[76]

In this case we also have kin or even a family beyond formal family and household – a fact that contradicts the two popular assumptions that there were no "slave families" or those slaves did not have "normal families" (also in rural areas). As emerges from this document, informal families and kinships were built with the participation of slaves or ex-slaves and even the formally "absent" fathers.[77]

Outcomes of the Second Slavery: Writing the Nation – Writing Race?

A great process of "Writing the Nation" began after the end of the Ten Years War (1878), the first great anticolonial uprising of Cuban nationalists and insurgents, as Ada Ferrer has argued in her book *Insurgent Cuba*.[78] After the war, the final phase of slave emancipation in Cuba began, with the two main steps of *patronato*, a kind of apprenticeship (1880-1886), and final abolition (1886), followed by a new anticolonial war (1895-1898),

---

[76] Normally I quote the documents in Spanish. In this case the document has been already translated into English; the document comes from: APC, Protocolos José Rafael de Villafuerte y Castellanos, 1885, t. 1 (Enero – Abril), fols. 164r-166v, escritura no. 27 "Acta de reconocimiento de hijo natural por el Meno [Moreno] Antonio Pérez", Cienfuegos, February 28, 1885.

[77] Barcia Zequeira, María del Carmen, *La otra familia. Parientes, redes y descendencia de los esclavos en Cuba*, La Habana: Casa de las Américas/Colombia: Ministerio de Cultura, 2003 (Ensayo Histórico-Social); Meriño Fuentes, María de los Ángeles; Perera Díaz, Aisnara, "Matrimonio y familia en el ingenio, una utopia posible. Cuba (1825 1886)", in: *Caribbean Studies* Vol. 34, No. 1 (January-June 2006), S. 201-237; Morrison, "Creating an alternative kinship: Slavery, Freedom and the nineteenth-century Afro-cuban hijos naturales", pp. 55-80.

[78] Robert, Karen, "Slavery and Freedom in the Ten Years' War, Cuba, 1868-1878", in: *Slavery & Abolition* Vol. 13, Number 3 (December 1992), pp. 181-200; Ferrer, Ada, "Writing the Nation. Race, War, and Redemption in the Prose of Independence, 1886-1895", in: Ferrer, *Insurgent Cuba. Race, Nation, and Revolution, 1868-1898*, Chapel Hill & London. The University of North Carolina Press, 1999, pp. 112-139.

which led to the Spanish-American War of 1898.[79] Just as happened after the Ten Years War, again a process of "writing race without race" began, together with the process of enrolment of the ex-slaves in lists that stated their new civil status and the territories where they lived or where they were going to live after abolition.[80] With masses of new citizens in the final phase of emancipation, the civil registry offices, *registros civiles* created on January 1, 1885, more or less one year before final abolition, began their work. They registered, together with those who were ex-slaves, all the nation's inhabitants (*vecinos*) as citizens. The documentation of enrolment was the duty of official notaries and scribes in the city and town councils. There they registered the ex-slaves as new citizens with their new "civil names". The naming of the ex-slaves followed the model of former house slaves. Slaves, in this process,[81] received the first surname of their last (or in some cases, next-to-last) owner as their own civil surname. So ex-slaves in some regions, for example in Cienfuegos and Sagua la Grande, bore the first surnames of the wealthiest and most powerful owners. I have described these surnames of the great planters as first surname (*apellido*) of many ex-slaves as *grandes apellidos esclavos* – major slave surnames, that is, the surnames of large-scale slave-owners used by persons other than these owners.[82]

79 Scott, *Slave Emancipation in Cuba. The Transition to Free Labor* ..., passim.

80 Scott; Zeuske, "Property in Writing, Property on the Ground: Pigs, Horses, Land, and Citizenship in the Aftermath of Slavery, Cuba, 1880-1909", in: *Comparative Studies in Society and History. An International Quarterly* 44, No. 4, Ann Arbor (October 2002), pp. 669-699; Scott; Zeuske, "Le ‚droit d'avoir des droits': l'oral et l'écrit dans les revendications legales des anciens esclaves à Cuba, 1872-1909", in : *Annales HSS*, No. 3 (mai-juin 2004), pp. 521-545.

81 With very few exceptions, like the Atkins slaves; see: Atkins, Edwin F., *Sixty Years in Cuba*, New York: Arno Press, 1980 [1. Ed. 1926: *Sixty Years in Cuba. Reminiscences of Edwin A. Atkins*. Cambridge: At the Riverside Press.]

82 Zeuske, ‚Los negros hicimos la independencia': Aspectos de la movilización afrocubana en un hinterland cubano. Cienfuegos entre colonia y república", in: Fernando Martínez / Rebecca J. Scott / Orlando García Martínez (eds.), *Espacios, silencios y los sentidos de la libertad: Cuba 1898-1912*, La Habana: Ediciones Unión, 2001, pp. 193-234; Zeuske, "Hidden Markers, Open Secrets. On Naming, Race Marking and Race Making in Cuba", pp. 235-266. I am unable to exclude what might be termed the "slaves-in-the-family-problem" (see: Ball, Edward, *Slaves in Family*, New York: Ballantine Books, 1999). That is, how can one distinguish between those who take the master's name as a sign

But there was, as mentioned briefly above, a new job for notaries. In the final phase of slavery and emancipation (1880-1886) more and more ex-slaves began to buy or sell small properties, first of all, small gardens and huts in the small rural towns of the sugar zones or in the now fast growing "black" quarters (*barrios*) of port cities. And they appear as buyers and sellers in the offices of the notaries, which means no longer as objects, but now as judicial subjects, as actors by law.

The majority of notaries' records in which former slaves, men and many women, appear as actors by law (mandates), are, however, those dealing with the purchase of land plots (*fincas rústicas*, *terrenos*, *sitios de labor*) for urban houses, or for the houses themselves (*fincas urbanas*), with the latter representing the largest number. Other records deal with testaments, the recognition of *hijos naturales* (natural children), or giving *poder* (power of attorney) to lawyers.[83]

In these documents, the phenomenon of marking through naming appears in all the forms described above: the use of one sole surname, the use of major slave surnames, and, until the 1890s, with a direct marker of constructed color, *moreno* or *morena* (Brown man or Brown woman as euphemism for *negro* or *negra*) and *pardo* or *parda* (as euphemism for the insulting *mulato* or *mulata*).[84] But, in nearly all these cases, and primarily in the records dealing with property or financial transactions, a written addendum *sin segundo apellido* or *sin otro apellido* (abbreviation: "s.s.a" or "s.o.a.") appears in the formularies of the notaries' records from the early

of previous ownership and those who may take it as a result of unofficial recognition of parentage? This problem can best be addressed in micro-regional studies, like that of Ball.

83 Scott; Zeuske, "Le ‚droit d'avoir des droits': l'oral et l'écrit dans les revendications legales des anciens esclaves à Cuba, 1872-1909", pp. 521-545; Zeuske, "Two stories of Gender and Slave Emancipation in Cienfuegos and Santa Clara, Central Cuba – Micro-historical Approaches to the Atlantic World", in: Scully, Pamela; Paton, Diana (eds.), *Gender and Slave Emancipation in the Atlantic World*, Durham: Duke University Press, 2005, pp. 181-198.

84 Since 1893 the Spanish (Colonial) State no longer allowed the use of "moreno" or "pardo" because of the fight for civil rights of the "Directorio Central de las Sociedades Negras de Cuba" (Central Directory of the Negro Societies of Cuba); see: Scott, Slave *Emancipation in Cuba* ..., pp. 274-78; Hevia Lanier, Oilda, *El directorio central de las sociedades negras de Cuba, 1886-1894*, La Habana: Ed. de Ciencias Sociales, 1996.

1880s. At a specific moment, notaries began to write in the empty place of the absent second surname in their formularies, explicitly the words "without other surname" (*sin otro apellido*) or "without second surname" (*sin segundo apellido*). The notaries quickly began to use only the abbreviation "s.s.a." (sin segundo apellido) or, mostly, "s.o.a." (sin otro apellido). The explicit notation of "s.o.a." seems mostly to be linked to individuals who appear to have one of the "big" or major slave surnames of their respective region as a single surname.[85] And for reasons of chronological correspondence it seems also that, with this little word, the notaries, who belonged to the group of ex-slave owners, chose to record not only the single surname (which could also be borne by children of poor white unmarried women) and the slave surnames, but the explicitly written addendum "s.a.o" in order to link the former slaves to their previous state of possession, of being owned, ex-slave and Black or Coloured. For me, this explicit written "s.o.a." is thus a hidden marker, but nevertheless a race marker, and suggests that "s.o.a." is a point of entry in the search for the open secrets of race in Cuba. We cannot catch the spoken words of the contemporaries, but, in written records, notaries had begun "writing race", just as they did in the last years before the abolition. This means that we do not know whether notaries were only the ones divulging this new form of control of the now former slaves, but it forms a powerful tool to support the concept of "race-blindness" and "silence about race" (both developed by Ada Ferrer), which formed the core of a Cuban racism without mentioning race.[86]

Conclusion

The first time I came across "s.o.a.", after having copied thousands of names from records without understanding what importance this addendum might

85 For Cienfuegos: Acea, Tellería, Sarría; for Lajas: Moré, Terry, Apezteguía; for Sagua: Ribalta, Moré, Beronda; etc.

86 Ferrer, "The Silence of Patriots: Race and Nationalism in Martí's Cuba", in *José Martí's ‚Our America': From National to Hemispheric Cultural Studies*, Jeffrey Belnap; Raúl Fernández (eds.), Durham, N.C.: Duke University Press 1998, pp. 228-249; Ferrer, *Insurgent Cuba ...*, passim; Fuente, *A Nation for All": Race, Inequality, and Politics in Twentieth-Century Cuba*, Chapel Hill & London: The University of North Carolina Press, 2001.

have, it was linked to the "apellido" Fortún, in a record of the purchase of land in the country town of Lajas located in the Cienfuegos hinterland, the most modern province during the last stages of Cuban second slavery: "the *morenos libres* León and Natalia Fortún, without second surnames, who are from Africa".[87] This mention of "s.o.a." appears six years after 1878, when purchases by former slaves of small houses in Lajas, had become common.[88] Later, I found many records of sales of this type in Sagua la Grande, Cienfuegos, Santiago de Cuba, and Remedios.

But what exactly was the sense and the function of this tag or marker, "s.o.a.", from 1878 onward and continuing into the early years of the Cuban republic? Cuba's ex-slaves became citizens very quickly, in the sixteen years between 1886 and 1902, but many of them were citizens "without another surname", meaning that they remained stigmatized citizens. In fact, the long tradition of using this addendum even yielded a rare second surname in Cuba, borne by individuals such as Julio González Soa.[89]

Thus, the lack of a normal civil name of two apellidos and especially of a father's name was usual not only for the times of the middle passage and for the moment of entry into the Cuban society of the Second Slavery, but also for the end of the emancipation process and as a legacy of Second Slavery.[90] The great majority of ex-slaves passed the gates to "freedom" without proper names but with imposed names, which linked them

---

87 APC Protocolos D. José Rafael Villafuerte y Castellanos 1883 (Enero – Dic.), fols. 418r-421r, escritura no. 98 "Venta de solares yermos",, Cienfuegos, June 14, 1883.

88 APC Protocolos D. José Rafael Villafuerte y Castellanos 1878 (Enero – Dic.), fols. 387r-388v, escritura no. 149 "Venta de solares", Cienfuegos , Julio 13, 1878.

89 After half-a-century of silence, the marker "s.o.a". appeared in the national discourse of writers and artists as a cultural problem of under classes; see: Vallhonrat Villalonga, Francisco (1948): S.O.A. "Drama". En prosa, con un prólogo y 3 actas,Manzanillo: Editorial El Arte, 1948. In 1951, a film with the title "Sin otro apellido",was produced in Santiago de Cuba; see also: Sommer, Doris (ed.), *The Places of History. Regionalism Revisited in Latin America*. Durham & London: Duke University Press, 1999. The problem of illegitimate birth plays also a role in the biographies of Fulgencio Batista or even Fidel Castro; see Zeuske, "Hidden Markers, Open Secrets. On Naming, Race Marking and Race Making in Cuba", pp. 235-266.

90 Zeuske, "Legados de la esclavitud en Cuba", in: Rodrigo y Alharilla, Martín (ed.), *Cuba: De colonia a repúblic*a, Madrid: Editorial Biblioteca Nueva, S.L., 2006 (Colección Historia Biblioteca nueva, dir. por Juan Pablo Fusi), pp. 99-116.

continuously to their former status. But, the Second Slavery in Cuba was not a "fatherless society" for the enslaved and their descendants.[91] Fathers and informal families tried to oppose these developments by strengthening their informal family and kin ties, as we can deduce from the increasing *declaratorias de paternidad* (as in the case of Antonio Pérez); the sources of these *declaratorias* in the notaries' archives are directly linked to land buying.[92]

So the end of second slavery in Cuba (1886) or Brazil (1888) was by no means marked by a "ground zero" culturally and in relation to identity-politics or status struggles, as well as real struggles. The problems symbolized by the lack of proper "father"-names (and the resistance against the racial marking), many nicknames, formal alterations of surnames, as in the case of *Reyita*, and many names in different social milieus, characterized the post emancipation period.[93] Fully legal changes in relation to the status of *hijos naturales*, for example, were only achieved after the Cuban revolution of 1959, when the revolutionary elite also began to use only one surname.[94]

---

91 Perera Díaz; Meriño Fuentes, *Nombrar las cosas: aproximación a la onomástica de la familia negra en Cuba*, Guantánamo : Editorial El Mar y la Montaña, 2006.

92 Scott; Zeuske, "Property in Writing, Property on the Ground: Pigs, Horses, Land, and Citizenship in the Aftermath of Slavery, Cuba, 1880-1909", pp. 669-699 ; Scott; Zeuske, "Le ‚droit d'avoir des droits': l'oral et l'écrit dans les revendications legales des anciens esclaves à Cuba, 1872-1909", pp. 521-545; Morrison, "Creating an alternative kinship: Slavery, Freedom and the nineteenth-century Afro-cuban hijos naturales", pp. 55-80.

93 Rubiera Castillo, Daisy, *Ich, Reyita. Ein kubanisches Leben*. Aus dem Spanischen von Max Zeuske, mit einem Nachwort von Michael Zeuske [*Me, Reyita. A Cuban Life*. Translation from Spanish by Max Zeuske, with an afterword by Michael Zeuske], Zürich: Rotpunktverlag, 2000.

94 Zeuske, "Hidden Markers, Open Secrets. On Naming, Race Marking and Race Making in Cuba", pp. 235-266.

Commodity Frontiers, Conjuncture and Crisis: The Remaking of the Caribbean Sugar Industry, 1783-1866.

Dale TOMICH

Fernand Braudel Center
Binghamton University

Introduction

The British West Indies have, in many respects, been at the focus of the historiography of Caribbean slavery. They are generally regarded as classic sugar plantation colonies and through their direct relation with British industrialization and abolitionism, they are commonly treated as the paradigmatic case of the incompatibility of slavery with a modern liberal industrial capitalist order. Within this framework, scholars have debated whether humanitarian or economic forces were responsible for the destruction of slavery. In his classic work, *Capitalism and Slavery*, Eric Williams[1] forcefully made the case for the primacy of economic forces. In his view, industrial capitalism, not humanitarian concerns, destroyed West Indian slavery. He argued that slavery, the colonial system, and mercantilist monopoly were inextricably linked. With the breakup of the colonial system after the American War of Independence, the West Indian slave colonies represented an obstacle to expanding industrial capitalism in Britain. In Williams' words: *"When British capitalism found the West Indian monopoly a nuisance, they destroyed West Indian slavery as the first step in the destruction of the West Indian monopoly"*[2].

1 Williams, Eric. (1944, repr. 1994). *Capitalism & Slavery*. Chapel Hill: University of North Carolina Press.

2 Williams, Eric.(1944, repr. 1994). *Capitalism & Slavery*. Chapel Hill: University of North Carolina Press. Page 169.

The "Williams thesis" has engendered more than fifty years of scholarly debate. Since the 1960s, it has become fertile ground for the criticism by the New Economic History. Their challenge has, in large measure, set the parameters of the "Williams Debate"[3]. New economic historians have generally accepted Williams' analytical framework, but they have submitted his claims to quantitative scrutiny based on neo-classical economic theory. With few exceptions, they feel that they have disproved his claims on empirical grounds. Most prominently, Seymour Drescher[4] contends that the British West Indies were not in decline at the time of the abolition of the slave trade in 1807, and that abolition was the cause of the economic crisis, not the other way round. Others concur and find no other impediment to what they view as the prospect for continued West Indian prosperity[5]. Thus, in their view, there was no economic decline that led to abolition of the slave trade and slave emancipation in the British West Indies. Having disqualified the economic motive for abolition and emancipation, they have turned to political and ideological explanations.

The new economic historians present a positive assessment of the British West Indian sugar industry after abolition of the slave trade, especially with the acquisition of Trinidad, Guyana, and the other ceded islands after 1815. They emphasize increasing imports, favorable prices, and

---

3 Williams, Eric. (1944, repr. 1994). *Capitalism & Slavery*. Chapel Hill: University of North Carolina Press.

Eltis, David. (1987). *Economic Growth and the Ending of the Transatlantic Slave Trade*. New York: Oxford University Press.

Drescher, Seymour M. (1977). *Econocide: British Slavery in the Era of Abolition*. Pittsburgh: University of Pittsburgh Press.

Solow, Barbara L. (1985). "Caribbean Slavery and British Economic Growth: The Eric Williams Hypothesis." *Journal of Development Economics*: 99-115.

Solow, Barbara L. (1987a). "Capitalism and Slavery in the Exceedingly Long Run." *British Capitalism & Caribbean Slavery: The Legacy of Eric Williams*. Barbara L. Solow and Stanley L. Engerman. Cambridge, Cambridge University Press: Pages 51-77.

Barbara L. Solow and Stanley L. Engerman. (1988). *British Capitalism & Caribbean Slavery: The Legacy of Eric Williams*. Cambridge: Cambridge University Press.

4 Drescher, Seymour M. (1977). *Econocide: British Slavery in the Era of Abolition*. Pittsburgh: University of Pittsburgh Press.

5 Eltis, David. (1987). *Economic Growth and the Ending of the Transatlantic Slave Trade*. New York: Oxford University Press. Page 5.

a growing share of British trade immediately after abolition. According to David Eltis, war and revolution put a greater share of the world's plantation produce in Britain's hands than ever before. Seymour Drescher differentiates between the British West Indies, which declined slightly in both value and tonnage after 1807, and imports from conquered and occupied territories, which increased by 86 percent in value and nearly 150 percent by weight. The aggregate figure, he argues, disguised the decline of the older British sugar colonies in the Caribbean. The real situation in the British West Indies only became apparent with the end of the conflict in 1814. Nonetheless, even with the return of some of the occupied territories at the end of hostilities, slave produced sugar from the British colonies still accounted for over half of world supply[6].

For both Drescher and Eltis, the acquisition of Guyana and Trinidad were essential to the increase of British West Indian production after 1814. Together they brought more cultivated land into the empire than all of the cultivated land in the existing West Indian colonies[7]. According to Drescher, the British slave colonies were "still capable of vigorous growth and expansion"[8], while Eltis emphasizes that "the long-run economic data testify to the continuing vitality of the British West Indies well into the nineteenth century"[9]. However, in their view there was only one factor that prevented the British colonies from taking full advantage of the post-war boom — labor. Abolition of the slave trade undercut the potential prosperity of the British West Indian sugar colonies. In Drescher's well-known formulation, abolition of the slave trade was an act of *econocide* provoked by abolitionism in the form of a mass movement and a new liberal sensi-

---

6 Eltis, David. (1987). *Economic Growth and the Ending of the Transatlantic Slave Trade.* New York: Oxford University Press. Pages: 5-6. Drescher, Seymour M. (1977). *Econocide: British Slavery in the Era of Abolition.* Pittsburgh: University of Pittsburgh Press. Pages: 147-148.

7 Eltis, David. (1987). *Economic Growth and the Ending of the Transatlantic Slave Trade.* New York: Oxford University Press. Pages: 5-6.

8 Drescher, Seymour M. (1977). *Econocide: British Slavery in the Era of Abolition.* Pittsburgh: University of Pittsburgh Press. Page 160.

9 Eltis, David. (1987). *Economic Growth and the Ending of the Transatlantic Slave Trade.* New York: Oxford University Press. Page 5.

bility. It was the first step in an inevitable chain of events that dismantled slavery and culminated in slave emancipation.

This assessment of the long-term prospects of the British West Indian sugar industry is, in my view, overly optimistic. The quantitative economic historians show that there was considerable room to reorganize and expand productive activities in the British West Indies, since the colonies remained productive and could return a reasonable rate of profit.However, these findings are not incompatible with decline. By focusing on market and price competition between national units, their approach underestimates, if it does not ignore, the changing structure of the Atlantic economy. Foreign competitors only enter this analysis insofar as they affect conditions for British producers. Further, by treating land, labor, and capital as independent factors of production, it disaggregates the historical relations through which production is organized. The result is an abstract and one-sided economic interpretation that juxtaposes economic to non-economic factors. Historical processes operating at the level of the world and Atlantic economies, — the expansion and reorganization of production, restructuring of markets, and the creation of a new division of labor, — are eliminated from consideration. Similarly, the ways that particular ecologies, material processes of production, technologies, and forms and scales of collective labor are combined in specific historical circumstances are not regarded as analytically significant. Instead, it is as if the single act of the abolition of the slave trade is grantedcausal primacy for the subsequent historical transformations of the British West Indies, of the Caribbean, and, ultimately, of the entire Atlantic world.

What is missing from the neo-classical account is the historical and material geography of capital. The vitality of capitalism as an historical relation has less to do with profitability in an accounting sense than with its capacity to create new productive spaces on an expanding scale. From such a perspective, the US South (cotton), Cuba (sugar), and Brazil (coffee) appear not as external factors that act upon the British West Indies from the outside, but rather as new slave commodity frontiers that formed as part of the same world-economic processes that resulted in the crisis of mercantilism and slavery in the British Empire. These new productive zones entailed the massive redeployment of slave labor under new conditions and the creation of new commodity circuits linking the Atlantic world. Slavery itself was reconfigured with increasing scales of production, growing pressure to increase the productivity of labor, new technologies of production and transport, and new modes of labor discipline and social control. The traffic in slaves, — legal and illegal, or international and internal, — was the motor of these developments, even as slave trading operated under new conditions in the face of British abolitionism. The economic and material expansion of the world-economy and the formation of these new slave commodity frontiers created the crisis of the old colonial spaces that were no longer able to compete under the new conditions even though they remained substantial producers and brought profitable returns.

The World Sugar Market, 1815-1866.

World sugar production and consumption expanded dramatically between 1815 and 1866. Old producing regions increased their output and new regions emerged. British West Indian sugar production also expanded during this period, but it was unable to keep pace with the changing conditions of world production. From 1791 to 1815, British West Indian sugar production increased more rapidly than at any other time in its history. Peace in 1814 brought about a boom in sugar production as pent-up demand was released and planters throughout the Americas rushed to fill the void left by the revolution in Saint Domingue[10]. The British colonies were best positioned to take advantage of this situation. They had been least disrupted by war and revolution, had regular access to shipping, and benefitted from the acquisition of new territories, particularly Guiana. Their output fell below that of the previous period but between 1815 and 1819 they still accounted for nearly half of world supply, which had risen by 38 percent despite the destruction of Saint Domingue [11].

---

[10] Marrero, Levi. (1985). *Cuba: Economia y Sociedad.* Vol. 12. *Azúcar, Ilustración y Con ciencia 1763-1868* (IV). Madrid: Editorial Playor, S.A. Vol 12, Cap IV, Page: 108.

[11] Tomich, Dale. 1990. *Slavery in the Circuit of Sugar: Martinique in the World Economy, 1830 1848*. Baltimore: The Johns Hopkins University Press. Page: 23.

By 1820 the post-war boom ended and prices fell. Markets became more stable and increasingly synchronized with one another. Competition between producing regions became more acute. This economic contraction disclosed considerable geographical differentiation among the British West Indian colonies. After 1814-1818, sugar production ceased to expand in the small islands, and they accounted for a progressively smaller share of British output. Jamaica remained an important center of production, although it no longer attained pre-1807 levels. In 1820, it still produced nearly 98,000 metric tons of sugar. Afterwards production gradually declined, and it was replaced by Cuba as the world's largest single supplier during the decade of the 1820s. Led by Demerara, British Guiana became a valuable addition to the Empire and grew rapidly. Its production increased nearly fivefold between 1814-1818 and 1829-1833 and reached a pre-emancipation high of nearly 60,000 metric tons in 1830. By the late 1820s and early 1830s, sugar production stagnated and declined in the Lesser Antilles and Jamaica The losses in these old colonies were offset by increases in Guiana, Mauritius, and Trinidad, but the British colonies' share of world production fell from nearly 50% in 1815-1819 to just under 25% in 1838-1842. During the same period, sugar production also fell in the French West Indian colonies and in the Brazilian Northeast where the slave trade remained active.[12] It would appear, then, that the crucial distinction to be drawn is not between zones in which the slave trade was active and those in which it had been suppressed, but between mature production zones and new sugar frontiers.

Changes in sugar markets and sugar consumption also undermined the British West Indian colonies. British West Indian producers continued to enjoy a protected position in the British national market as long as the Navigation Acts remained in effect. However, British territorial expansion in the Caribbean ended in 1815 and planters there were faced with rising costs. With the end of the Napoleonic Wars Britain gained command of the Con-

---

[12] Deerr, N. (1949). *The History of Sugar*. 2 vols. London: Chapman and Hall. Vol I. Pages :193-201.

Moreno Fraginals, Manuel. 1978. *El ingenio. Complejo económico social cubano del azúcar*. 3 vols. Havana: Editorial de ciencias sociales. Vol I: 40-42. Vol II:173.

tinental market. British refiners, shippers, warehousemen, and commercial and financial interests were becoming involved in trading large quantities of both British and foreign sugar in Europe. As cheaper Cuban and Brazilian sugar found markets in Europe, British West Indian sugar was excluded. Re-exports of British West Indian sugar had to be subsidized by government drawbacks and bounties in order for British West Indian planters to be competitive with countries that were customers for British manufactures. At the same time, Britain either warehoused cheap foreign sugar for re-sale on the Continent of British merchants or carried it directly to Europe for sale in "spot markets." British West Indian re-exports dropped from about 100,000 tons in 1802 to 27,000 tons in 1827. As British sugar producers became increasingly dependent on preferential duties and the home market, British domestic consumption doubled between 1815 and 1840. By the 1830s, the West Indian colonies were no longer able to supply British demand. If mercantilism had been intended to secure sources of overseas production and trade for the metropolis, here it had become the means for West Indian planters to protect themselves from competition. Britain continued to pay higher prices for sugar without the benefits that mercantilism had provided for the national economy. This problem was especially acute in the re-export market [13].

Scholars have perhaps been too attentive to industrialization as the cause of slave emancipation and free trade and to the bilateral relation between Britain and its West Indian colonies. Williams' teleological association of industrial capital and the free market and the more general preoccupation with the relation between West Indian production and the British home market obscures the financial and commercial motives for removing

[13] Marrero, Levi. (1985) *Cuba: Economía y Sociedad.* Vol. 12. *Azúcar, Ilustración y Conciencia 1763-1868* (IV). Madrid: Editorial Playor, S.A. Page: 108.

Tomich, Dale. 1990. *Slavery in the Circuit of Sugar: Martinique in the World Economy, 1830-1848.* Baltimore: The Johns Hopkins University Press. Page: 28.

Drescher, Seymour M. (1977). *Econocide: British Slavery in the Era of Abolition.* Pittsburgh: University of Pittsburgh Press. Pages: 155-157.

Moreno Fraginals, Manuel. 1978. *El ingenio. Complejo económico social cubano del azúcar.* 3 vols. Havana: Editorial de ciencias sociales. Vol II. Pages: 157-161.

Ragatz, Lowell. 1971. *The Fall of the Planter Class in the British West Indies, 1763-1833.* New York: Octagon Books. Pages: 434-435.

the restrictions on trade. There are significant commercial, financial and political reasons for the British state to end the favored position of British West Indian sugar in the British market. With the end of the Napoleonic Wars, Britain dominated Atlantic trade. The export of British goods depended upon commercial linkages with the newly independent states of the Americas. The sale of American produce to the Continent was not only good business; it was also good politics. Britain's strategy for maintaining the Balance of Power on the Continent rested upon control of the sea and controlling the supply of overseas goods[14]. The key to the economic fate of the British West Indian colonies is not Britain's domestic market, but the changing world market and Britain's position within in it. Huskisson wanted to make London the "depot of the merchandise passing between the two worlds." In 1823 his Warehousing Bill allowed foreign goods, including sugar, to be re-exported free of duty. This policy was based on notions of "comparative advantage" and the allocative efficiency of the market system[15]. Nonetheless, until the Corn Laws were repealed, Britain had a dual market system: one that subsidized colonial producers and kept domestic prices high, and another that attempted to control Continental markets by controlling the unrestricted flow of produce from American producers. The West Indian monopoly was an obstacle to Britain's economic and *political* interests. Britain's abolition of slavery and opposition to the international slave trade needs to be interpreted in relation to the economic and political processes that were restructuring the Atlantic economy during the first half of the nineteenth century.

New Commodity Frontiers and the Crisis of the British West Indian Sugar Colonies.

If the British West Indies remained significant centers of sugar production and continued to yield profits to those who invested in them into the 1830s

---

14 Dehio, Ludwig. (1962). *The Precarious Balance: Four Centuries of the European Power Struggle*. New
York: Vintage.

15 Ingham, G. (1984). *Capitalism Divided? The City and Industry in British Social Development*. New York,:Schocken Books. Pages: 113-115

and beyond, that does not mean that they did not decline. The condition of a capitalist market economy is not simply to make profit. Rather, it is to make profits on an ever renewed and ever increasing scale. This process of capital accumulation continually establishes new material and social conditions of production.

The decline of the British West Indian sugar industry is apparent if we look beyond the British colonial economy to the dramatic rise of new producing zones, especially Cuba, and the restructuring of the Atlantic division of labor as a whole. While Jamaica was a mature production zone where efforts to restructure sugar production were constrained by geography, environment, and the existing organization of the plantation system. In contrast, Guyana and Cuba were commodity frontiers, that is, they were territories at the margin of the Atlantic economy where further expansion was possible[16]. Each in its own way presented ideal conditions for sugar production that could be exploited under the emergent conditions of the first half of the nineteenth century. At the same time, the open character of the frontier meant that the relation of land, labor, and technology could be restructured in radically new ways. Nonetheless, geographical and environmental conditions in Guyana were such that the potential for the development of sugar production there was much more limited than in Cuba.

Sugar production in Jamaica and Guyana, the two most important British West Indian sugar colonies, was eclipsed by Cuba (Figure One). Jamaican production declined gradually after the post-war boom, while Guyana's output increased sharply between 1807 and about 1827. Its production remained relatively stable until the abolition of slavery, when it declined slowly until the 1840s, when indenture resolved the labor question, and climbed to a bit beyond its previous high levels after that. Cuban sugar production, in contrast, climbed steadily and sharply upward. It surpassed both Jamaica and Guyana in the early1820s to become the world's leading producer and increased nearly eightfold between 1820 and

---

[16] Moore, J. W. (2000). "Sugar and the Expansion of the Early-Modern World Economy: Commodity Frontiers, Ecological Transformation, and Industrialization." *Review* XXIII(3): 409-433.

1860 to dominate world sugar production.

Figure 1

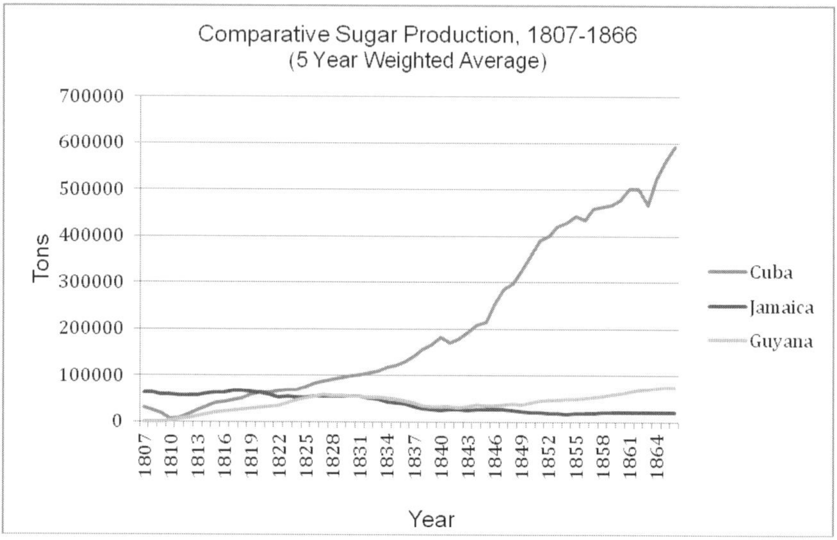

Source: Noel Deerr, A History of Sugar, I, 126,131,193-204.

Jamaica

Jamaica was a settled plantation zone in which the size and geography of the island, as well as the existing pattern of land tenure and cultivation, restricted possibilities for expansion and greater productivity. It had been the leading sugar producer in the British West Indies during the eighteenth century. The plantation zone was concentrated on the prime sugar lands in the southern coastal lowlands, across the north coast, and into the Westmoreland plain. At the time of the Haitian Revolution, there was still room for new investment and territorial expansion. Jamaican sugar production nearly doubled between 1792 and 1805, and surpassed the output of Saint Domingue at its peak. New plantations were constructed, but these were often located in regions with less favorable soil and climatic conditions or in the interior of the island, where transportation costs here higher. Eighty-four new sugar estates were established between 1792 and 1799, over half of them in the northern districts of St. Ann, St. James, and Trelawny. James Robertson's map, drawn in 1804 at the highpoint of Jamaican sugar production, documents 830 sugar estates for the entire island. These were densely concentrated on the northern and western coastal plains as well as the southern coastal lowlands. However, after the downturn of the sugar market in 1806, a quarter of Jamaica's new plantations were abandoned. By 1832, the number of estates had dropped to about 670. This contraction of productive land was especially pronounced in Portland, where climatic conditions were unfavorable, and among those estates that had been opened up in the interior of the island. Those parishes that were affected least by emancipation were those that had been occupied longest[17].

Within the core plantation zone, the built environment itself was an obstacle to the amelioration of production. The dense occupation of the soil and the existence of contiguous properties made it difficult for estates to expand or to establish new properties. Production was organized on a scale adequate to eighteenth-century technical conditions, that is, to wind, water, or animal powered mills. However, expansion might be possible within individual properties, as planters often occupied more land than they could cultivate in order to limit competition. In such instances it could be difficult to maintain the optimal proportions between the capacity of the slave gangs, the size of the cane fields and the factory. Further, planters with capital already sunk in slaves and equipment might be reluctant to invest in

[17] Deerr, N. (1949). *The History of Sugar*. 2 vols. London: Chapman and Hall. Vol I. Pages: 193-202.

Drescher, Seymour M. (1977). *Econocide: British Slavery in the Era of Abolition*. Pittsburgh: University of Pittsburgh Press. Pages. 93-103.

Moreno Fraginals, Manuel. 1978. *El ingenio. Complejo económico social cubano del azúcar*. 3 vols. Havana: Editorial de ciencias sociales. Vol II. Páages: 106-130, 156-165.

Higman, Barry W. 1976. *Slave Population and Economy in Jamaica, 1801-1834*. Cambridge: Cambridge University Press. Page: 14.

Higman, Barry W. 1988. *Jamaica Surveyed*. Kingston: Institute of Jamaica Publications, Ltd. Pages: 10-11.

Satchell, Veront. (2010). *Sugar, Slavery, and Technical Change: Jamaica, 1760-1830*. Saarbrücken: VDM Verlag Dr. Müller GmbH & Co. KG. Pages: 102,166.

a new plant that could offer only marginal increases in output. Nonetheless, Jamaica possessed large sugar estates that were capable of technical improvement. In 1830, 36% of the slaves lived on units of over 200 slaves[18].

Jamaican planters were actively concerned with increasing their efficiency and with technological improvement of their operations. Beginning around 1800, they were quick to take advantage of new industrial technologies, including the horizontal three-roller mill and the steam engine. Before 1815 the majority of steam engines purchased in Jamaica were low-pressure engines of 10 horsepower or less. Afterwards, Jamaican planters preferred to buy more powerful and efficient high-power engines of American manufacture. These ameliorations allowed Jamaican planters to maintain high levels of production and productivity. New steam-powered milling technologies could process more cane, and extract more juice from a given quantity of cane. However, they could only reach their full potential if the area under cultivation could be increased and more cane could be supplied to the mill. The possibilities for the extension of cane cultivation in Jamaica were limited. After the 1820s, productivity, like production, declined gradually from the high levels attained between 1796 and 1805, but remained above the pre-1796 levels[19]. However much the planters of Jamaica exhibited entrepreneurial behavior and sought to maximize their opportunities, they could not go beyond the constraints of the physical environment.

Guyana

Guyana was the most important addition to Britain‘s West Indian colonies after the Napoleonic Wars. Attracted by the rich soil and favorable climatic conditions, English planters began moving to the Dutch colonies of Berbice, Demerara, and Essequibo as early as the 1760s. By 1813, 95% of the European settlers were British. Guyana was late in developing, compared to the rest of the Caribbean, and at the beginning of the nineteenth

[18] Higman, Barry W. 1976. *Slave Population and Economy in Jamaica, 1801-1834*. Cambridge: Cambridge University Press. Page: 14.

[19] Satchell, Veront. (2010). *Sugar, Slavery, and Technical Change: Jamaica, 1760-1830*. Saarbrücken: VDM Verlag Dr. Müller GmbH & Co. KG.

century was still a new commodity frontier. It possessed large tracts of virgin land and excellent conditions for cotton, coffee and sugar cultivation. However, the colony's unusual ecology imposed distinctive conditions on the development of the plantation system there. The Guyanese plantation belt was restricted to the coastal plane, an area of 1,750 square miles. This land was at or below sea level and subject to alternating periods of heavy erosion and substantial accretion. The plantations were constructed on land reclaimed from the sea using Dutch techniques of polder construction. Plantation agriculture in Guyana depended on an elaborate system of dams, canals, and sluices for drainage, irrigation, and transportation. The construction and maintenance of this infrastructure required an enormous amount of labor and capital. Walter Rodney estimates that the original construction of this hydraulic system required moving at least 100 million tons of soil by hand[20]. Hence a heavy capital investment was required even before sugar production was undertaken.

Poldering and the need to control the movement of both water and land created a particular agricultural landscape. Plantations in Guyana were large, contiguous, and relatively uniform in their internal organization. Flood and water control was centralized on each estate. Collectively they safeguarded the plantation zone from the sea and backland flooding and controlled the water supply. They were connected with one another through the network of canals and waterways and the coastal road connecting them with Georgetown[21]. Although sugar was grown under the Dutch, cotton and coffee predominated and much land remained uncultivated. Plantations

---

[20] Rodney, Walter. (1981). *A History of the Guyanese Working People, 1881-1905*. Baltimore: The Johns Hopkins University Press. Pages: 2-3.

Costa, Emilia Viotti da. (1994). *Crowns of Glory, Tears of Blood: The Demerara Slave Rebellion of 1823*. New York: Oxford University Press. Page 9.

Mohamed, Wazir. (2008). Frustrated Peasants, Marginalized Workers: Free African Villages in Guyana, 1838-1885. Ph.D. dissertation. Department of Sociology. Binghamton University, Binghamton, NY. Pages: 93-110.

[21] Mohamed, Wazir. (2008). Frustrated Peasants, Marginalized Workers: Free African Villages in Guyana, 1838-1885. Ph.D. dissertation. Department of Sociology. Binghamton University, Binghamton, NY. Page: 99.

Costa, Emilia Viotti da. (1994). *Crowns of Glory, Tears of Blood: The Demerara Slave Rebellion of 1823*. New York: Oxford University Press. Page: 44.

were already large. Initial allotments along the coast were 250 acres, and planters had the right to a second grant extending into the interior. A limit of 1000 acres was established for sugar plantations and 500 acres for coffee[22].

British re-conquest of Guyana in 1796 initiated a massive shift of British capital and slaves to the colony. The slave population doubled from 1792 to 1802, and between 1803 and 1805 twenty thousand slaves were imported from Africa[23] . Cotton, sugar, and coffee exports increased dramatically between 1789 and 1802 [24]. After 1810, cotton and coffee, faced with foreign competition, began to gradually decline while sugar production rose, particularly during the boom period between 1815 and the early 1820s. Many planters planted all three crops and shifted gradually to sugar. However by the 1820s, the decline of cotton and coffee became more pronounced, while sugar production continued to increase. The need to invest in land, new steam technology, and slaves made Guyanese sugar planters vulnerable to falling prices after 1820. Land was gradually concentrated in the hands of British merchants with enough capital to maintain production, and planters grew more cane and produced more sugar in order to offset falling prices. By 1830 most East Coast Demerara plantations had converted to sugar. Steam mills replaced the wind- and cattle-driven mills. Several plantations had merged, and many passed into the hands of British corporations[25].

While land was abundant and there was room for expansion of the area under cultivation, Guyana was chronically short of labor[26]. Guyanese

---

22 Costa, Emilia Viotti da. (1994). *Crowns of Glory, Tears of Blood: The Demerara Slave Rebellion of 1823*. New York: Oxford University Press. Page: 44.
Mohamed, Wazir. (2008). Frustrated Peasants, Marginalized Workers: Free African Villages in Guyana, 1838-1885. Ph.D. dissertation. Department of Sociology. Binghamton University, Binghamton, NY. Pages: 93-110.

23 Costa, Emilia Viotti da. (1994). *Crowns of Glory, Tears of Blood: The Demerara Slave Rebellion of 1823*. New York: Oxford University Press. Page: 46.

24 Costa, Emilia Viotti da. (1994). *Crowns of Glory, Tears of Blood: The Demerara Slave Rebellion of 1823*. New York: Oxford University Press. Pages: 46-47.
Adamson, Alan H. (1972). *Sugar Without Slaves: The Political Economy of British Guiana, 1838-1904*. New Haven: Yale University Press. Page: 24.

25 Costa, Emilia Viotti da. (1994). *Crowns of Glory, Tears of Blood: The Demerara Slave Rebellion of 1823*. New York: Oxford University Press. Pages: 46-47.

26 Mohamed, Wazir. (2008). Frustrated Peasants, Marginalized Workers: Free African Vil-

plantations were already big in 1815, with 8% having more than 300 slaves, and 40%, between 200 and 300, while 46% had between 100 and 200[27].However, the expansion of sugar production and increased demand for labor coincided with the end of slave trade. High productivity of the soil, economies of scale, and technological innovation compensated for the relative shortage of labor. The size of plantations, the amount of capital required to make them profitable, and the shortage of labor all encouraged technological improvement. At the same time, the size of the estates and the scale of operations meant that planters could take full advantage of the increased capacity of new machinery. That estates were contiguous to one another and relatively uniform in their layout meant that consolidation of estates was a possibility, as new refining technologies required increased area under cultivation in order to achieve their maximum efficiency.

Guyanese planters innovated in both agricultural and manufacturing aspects of sugar production, and they invested heavily in machinery[28]. The firm of Bolton & Watt sold 114 steam engines to Guyanese planters between 1803 and 1820. The number fell to 32 between 1820 and 1852, but by 1830 most estates had steam-power. It is likely that after 1820 these were higher capacity and more efficient high-pressure engines, and not the Bolton & Watt engines. The other major innovation was the vacuum pan, which revolutionized sugar boiling. Various historians have complained that that the vacuum pan was invented in 1813 but only deployed in the

---

lages in Guyana, 1838-1885. Ph.D. dissertation. Department of Sociology. Binghamton University, Binghamton, NY. Page: 133.

Adamson, Alan H. (1972). *Sugar Without Slaves: The Political Economy of British Guiana, 1838-1904*. New Haven: Yale University Press. Page: 24.

27 Costa, Emilia Viotti da. (1994). *Crowns of Glory, Tears of Blood: The Demerara Slave Rebellion of 1823*. New York: Oxford University Press. Page: 47.

Adamson, Alan H. (1972). *Sugar Without Slaves: The Political Economy of British Guiana, 1838-1904*. New Haven: Yale University Press. Pages: 24-25.

28 Stoll, Allyson. (2011a). *NotFor "Want of Go-Aheadism in Field and Factory: The Technological Trajectory of the Guyana (British Guyana) Sugar Industry from 1800 to the 1930s*. PhD dissertation. Cornell University, Ithaca, NY.

Stoll, Allyson. (2011b). "Thoroughly Tested and Tried: Cane Culture, Technology, and Environmental Change in Nineteenth Century Guyana," *Journal of Caribbean History*, 45, 1: 92-127.

Caribbean decades later[29]. However, there is a great difference between the early models and the vacuum pans and multiple effect boilers that appeared in the 1830s-1840s. The latter devices were extremely expensive. They could cost between £40,000-£50,000. They increased both the quantity and quality of the sugar obtained from a given amount of syrup, but they required a far more extensive area of cane to be cultivated than was necessary for non-mechanized mills in order to make full use of their capacity and to compensate for the costs of purchase and maintenance. The first vacuum pans were successfully tried out in Guyana in 1830, sixteen years before they were first installed in Jamaica. By 1832 vacuum pans were operating on six estates in Guyana [30]. Shortage of skilled "pan boilers" slowed their adoption in the 1830s and early 1840s, but they became more common afterwards[31].

Guyanese sugar plantations were larger and more capital intensive than those the rest of the British West Indies. The largest plantations had 400-700 slaves. John Gladstone had 2,000 slaves on several plantations at the time of emancipation[32]. Production more than tripled between 1814-1818 and

---

[29] Adamson, Alan H. (1972). *Sugar Without Slaves: The Political Economy of British Guiana, 1838-1904*. New Haven: Yale University Press. Pages: 26-27.

Satchell, Veront. (2010). *Sugar, Slavery, and Technical Change: Jamaica, 1760-1830*. Saarbrücken: VDM Verlag Dr. Müller GmbH & Co. KG.

[30] Stoll, Allyson. (2011a). *NotFor "Want of Go-Aheadism in Field and Factory: The Technological Trajectory of the Guyana (British Guyana) Sugar Industry from 1800 to the 1930s*. PhD dissertation. Cornell University, Ithaca, NY. Page: 164.

Mohamed, Wazir. (2008). Frustrated Peasants, Marginalized Workers: Free African Villages in Guyana, 1838-1885. Ph.D. dissertation. Department of Sociology. Binghamton University, Binghamton, NY. Pages: 127 -133.

Satchell, Veront. (2010). *Sugar, Slavery, and Technical Change: Jamaica, 1760-1830*. Saarbrücken: VDM Verlag Dr. Müller GmbH & Co. KG. Page: 99.

[31] Tomich, Dale. 1990. *Slavery in the Circuit of Sugar: Martinique in the World Economy, 1830-1848*. Baltimore: The Johns Hopkins University Press. Pages: 195-197.

Stoll, Allyson. (2011a). *NotFor "Want of Go-Aheadism in Field and Factory: The Technological Trajectory of the Guyana (British Guyana) Sugar Industry from 1800 to the 1930s*. PhD dissertation. Cornell University, Ithaca, NY. Page: 162 ff.

[32] Costa, Emilia Viotti da. (1994). *Crowns of Glory, Tears of Blood: The Demerara Slave Rebellion of 1823*. New York: Oxford University Press. Pages: 9, 47-48.

Mohamed, Wazir. (2008). Frustrated Peasants, Marginalized Workers: Free African Villages in Guyana, 1838-1885. Ph.D. dissertation. Department of Sociology. Bingham-

1829-1833[33]. The trend toward consolidation of estates and corporate ownership continued after emancipation, when Asian contract labor replaced slave labor[34]. In 1841, 239 plantations produced about 33,00 hogsheads of sugar. Of these only 31 produced more than 250 hogsheads. Ten years later, 170 plantations produced a total of 460,000 hogsheads of sugar. Eighty-six of these plantations produced more than 250 hogsheads, of which 23 employed the vacuum pan[35].

Cuba

In contrast to Jamaica and Guyana, Cuba offered exceptional conditions for the development of sugar production from the 1790s onward. The Cuban sugar frontier encompassed approximately 30,000 square miles. This zone was virgin prairie, with ideal soils and climate for sugar production. But I am not making the case for geographical determinism. Rather, my concern is with the historical conditions under which land, labor, and technology are combined in order to transform natural environments in accordance with the requirements of sugar production. Indeed, the extent of the Cuban frontier was an obstacle to its development until the problem of overland transportation was solved by the development of the railroad network beginning in 1837.

Slavery and sugar production expanded slowly in the region around Havana from the time of the English occupation in 1763 until 1792. The outbreak of the Haitian Revolution and the destruction of the Saint Domingue sugar industry provided the Havana planters with their great opportunity, and they took full advantage of it. Between 1792 and 1818 the Havana

---

ton University, Binghamton, NY. Pages: 116,127-133.

33 Deerr, N. (1949). *The History of Sugar*. 2 vols. London: Chapman and Hall. Vol I. Pages: 193-201.

Moreno Fraginals, Manuel. 1978. *El ingenio. Complejo económico social cubano del azúcar*. 3 vols. Havana: Editorial de ciencias sociales, Vol II. Pages: 106, 156-165.

34 Stoll, Allyson. (2011a). *NotFor "Want of Go-Aheadism in Field and Factory: The Technological Trajectory of the Guyana (British Guyana) Sugar Industry from 1800 to the 1930s*. PhD dissertation. Cornell University, Ithaca, NY. Page: 21.

35 Adamson, Alan H. (1972). *Sugar Without Slaves: The Political Economy of British Guiana, 1838-1904*. New Haven: Yale University Press. Page: 175.

planters established the conditions necessary to develop the Cuban sugar industry. First, they freed themselves from the restraints of Spanish mercantilism and secured the right to free trade in sugar and the right to import slaves without restriction. They enjoyed exceptional access to the rapidly expanding US consumer market and to US goods and capital. The sugar boom also signaled an unprecedented expansion of the slave trade to Cuba. David Eltis estimates that over 780,000 slaves were imported to Cuba between 1791 and 1867[36]. Cuban planters were competing with protected sugars, especially in European markets. They were constantly concerned with the scale and productivity of production, and sought to systematically promote technological innovation and the application of scientific methods to production. Finally, in 1818 they won the right to absolute private property in land, including the right to clear the forest, which had been the preserve of the Royal Navy[37].

Between 1792 and 1800 the number of sugar mills increased from 237 to 350, with another fifty under construction in the regions around the ports of Havana and Matanzas. Total production increased from 14,500 tons in 1791 to 41,000 tons in 1807, while average production per mill rose from 60 tons in 1791 to 136 tons in 1804. There were no signification technological innovations during this period, but the first giant mills with over 300 slave and producing over 300 tons of sugar each made their appearance. By 1820, there were 625 plantations throughout the entire province of Havana, predominantly located near the coast to facilitate transport, and total production climbed to 55,000 tons. The 1827 census registered 1000 sugar mills in Cuba. Only 2.5% of these had steam power. Nonetheless, Cuba produced nearly 77,000 tons of sugar and surpassed Jamaica‘s peak year. Three years later, its output reached 105,000 tons, and it became the world‘s leading producer[38].

---

36 Eltis, David. (1987). *Economic Growth and the Ending of the Transatlantic Slave Trade*. New York: Oxford University Press. Page: 245.

37 Funes Monzote, R. (2008). *From Rainforest to Cane Field in Cuba: An Environmental History since 1492*. Chapel Hill: University of North Carolina Press.

38 Moreno Fraginals, Manuel. 1978. *El ingenio. Complejo económico social cubano del azúcar*. 3 vols. Havana: Editorial de ciencias sociales. Vol I. Pages: 67-71.

Funes Monzote, Reinaldo and Dale Tomich. (2009). "Naturaleza, Tecnología y Esclavitud en Cuba. Frontera Azucarera y Revolución Industrial," in *Trabajo Libre y Coac-*

Increased production owed more to the multiplication of sugar mills than to technological transformation. The majority of Cuban mills were still clustered around the ports of Havana and Matanzas. Transportation was the key obstacle to the full exploitation of Cuba's sugar frontier, particularly as the volume of sugar to be moved increased so dramatically. Havana's planter elite was increasingly concerned with road construction and developed a plan to build a canal from Havana to Güines. The key breakthrough was the construction of the Havana-Güines railroad in 1837. Rail transport provided cheap and efficient transportation that opened up Cuba's interior to sugar cultivation. As the rail network extended into the interior, the number of sugar mills multiplied[39]. More importantly perhaps, the creation of the railroad coincided with a cycle of technological innovation in sugar manufacture. The steam engine, all metal horizontal grinding mills, the vacuum pan, and the centrifuge were introduced during the 1830s and 1840s, and each of these implements underwent improvement. After the establishment of the railroad, Cuban planters were able to extend the sugar frontier and to establish new plantations on a scale that made optimal use of each new technological innovation. By 1840, Cuba produced over 160,000 tons of sugar (more than 19% of the world sugar market). Ten years later its output reached nearly 295,000 metric tons or one-quarter of the world's supply, and by 1868, Cuban production climbed to 720,000 tons or 30% of a growing world market[40].

Carlos Rebello's 1860 enumeration of sugar production shows both the increasing scale of production and technological innovation on Cuba's sugar mills, and the shift of the center of production toward the interior of the island. There were 359 animal-powered mills with an average capacity

tivo en Sociedades de Plantación, José Antonio Piqueras, ed. México: Siglo XXI.

Knight, Franklin W. 1970. *Slave Society in Cuba During the Nineteenth Century* Madison: University of Wisconsin Press. Pages: 30-31.

39 Zanetti, Oscar and Alejandro García. (1998). *Sugar and Railroads: A Cuban History, 1837-1959*. Chapel Hill. University of North Carolina Press.

40 Moreno Fraginals, Manuel. 1978. *El ingenio. Complejo económico social cubano del azúcar*. 3 vols. Havana: Editorial de ciencias sociales. Vol. I:Pages. 46-47, 67-71, 95-102,167- 255. Vol II: 93-97, 106-174. Vol. III: 35-36.

Knight, Franklin W. 1970. *Slave Society in Cuba During the Nineteenth Century*. Madison: University of Wisconsin Press. Pages: 14-18,40-41.

of 113 tons; 889 semi-mechanized mills with an average output of 411 tons; and 64 fully mechanized mills with and average production capacity of 1,176 tons. (The latter accounted for 5% of the plantations but 15% production.) The average size of an estate was 1,432 acres. The semi-mechanized mills, which combined steam power — frequently high-pressure engines of 100 horsepower or higher — iron horizontal grinding mills, and multiple trains of open kettle boilers and the fully mechanized mills, which integrated the most advanced milling technology with multiple effect vacuum pans, were concentrated in the new zones of the sugar frontier — Colón, and the current provinces of Villa Clara, Cienfuegos, and Sancti Spíritus [41]. Cuba's domination of the world sugar market was achieved through the extensive development of its sugar frontier and significant increases in the productivity of individual plantations.

Conclusion: Redefining the Atlantic Division of Labor

Jamaica, Guyana, and Cuba represent three different trajectories of sugar plantation economies worked by slave labor. In each instance, the local ecology was transformed in strikingly different ways by the material and social requirements of slave sugar plantation production. At the same time, developments in each zone became increasingly interdependent through the expansion of the world-economy, the restructuring of markets, and the reorganization of the Atlantic division of labor between 1783 and 1866. Each zone was capable of responding to the transformations of the world sugar market in different ways. While a more complete account of sugar and slavery during this period would necessarily address many other factors, these material conditions set the parameters of the history of the sugar economy. From this perspective, the "decline" of the British West Indian sugar industry is apparent. In both Jamaica and Guyana, individual estates could adjust to market conditions and remain productive and profitable. Nonetheless, each colony and the British West Indies, as

---

[41] Moreno Fraginals, Manuel. 1978. *El ingenio. Complejo económico social cubano del azúcar*. 3 vols. Havana: Editorial de ciencias sociales. Vol. I. Pages: 170-173.
Funes Monzote, R. (2008). *From Rainforest to Cane Field in Cuba: An Environmental History since 1492*. Chapel Hill: University of North Carolina Press. Pages.: 129-131.

a whole were eclipsed by the unprecedented growth of the slave sugar complex in Cuba. This "decline" is inseparable from restructuring of the Atlantic division of labor, and the increasing scale and productivity of world production. It is not reducible to a single event or series of events. Rather, it is a unified and long-term structural shift, like the movement of tectonic plates against one another. It is within this long-term movement that the social history, politics, and ideology of slavery and emancipation need to be reinterpreted and reassessed.

References

Adamson, Alan H. (1972). *Sugar Without Slaves: The Political Economy of British Guiana, 1838-1904*. New Haven: Yale University Press.

Costa, Emilia Viotti da. (1994). *Crowns of Glory, Tears of Blood: The Demerara Slave Rebellion of 1823*. New York: Oxford University Press.

Deerr, N. (1949). *The History of Sugar*. 2 vols. London: Chapman and Hall.

Dehio, Ludwig. (1962). *The Precarious Balance: Four Centuries of the European Power Struggle*. New York: Vintage.

Drescher, Seymour M. (1977). *Econocide: British Slavery in the Era of Abolition*. Pittsburgh: University of Pittsburgh Press.

Eltis, David. (1987). *Economic Growth and the Ending of the Transatlantic Slave Trade*. New York: Oxford University Press.

Funes Monzote, R. (2008). *From Rainforest to Cane Field in Cuba: An Environmental History since 1492*. Chapel Hill: University of North Carolina Press.

Funes Monzote, Reinaldo and Dale Tomich. (2009). "Naturaleza, Tecnología y Esclavitud en Cuba. Frontera Azucarera y Revolución Industrial," in *Trabajo Libre y Coactivo en Sociedades de Plantación*, José Antonio Piqueras, ed. México: Siglo XXI.

Higman, Barry W. 1976. *Slave Population and Economy in Jamaica, 1801-1834*. Cambridge: Cambridge University Press.

Higman, Barry W. 1988. *Jamaica Surveyed*. Kingston: Institute of Jamaica Publications, Ltd.

Ingham, G. (1984) *Capitalism Divided? The City and Industry in British Social Development*. New York: Schocken Books.

Knight, Franklin W. 1970. *Slave Society in Cuba During the Nineteenth Century*. Madison: University of Wisconsin Press.

Marrero, Levi. (1985). *Cuba: Economía y Sociedad.* Vol. 12. *Azucar, Ilustracion y Conciencia 1763-1868* (IV). Madrid: Editorial Playor, S.A.

Mohamed, Wazir. (2008). Frustrated Peasants, Marginalized Workers: Free African Villages in Guyana, 1838-1885. Ph.D. dissertation. Department of Sociology. Binghamton University, Binghamton, NY.

Moore, J. W. (2000). "Sugar and the Expansion of the Early-Modern World Economy: Commodity Frontiers, Ecological Transformation, and Industrialization." *Review* XXIII(3): 409-433.

Moreno Fraginals, Manuel. 1978. *El ingenio. Complejo económico social cubano del azúcar.* 3 vols. Havana: Editorial de ciencias sociales.

Ragatz, Lowell. 1971. *The Fall of the Planter Class in the British West Indies, 1763-1833.* New York: Octagon Books.

Rodney, Walter. (1981). *A History of the Guyanese Working People, 1881-1905.* Baltimore: The Johns Hopkins University Press.

Satchell, Veront. (2010). *Sugar, Slavery, and Technical Change: Jamaica, 1760-1830.* Saarbrücken: VDM Verlag Dr. Müller GmbH & Co. KG.

Solow, Barbara L. (1985). "Caribbean Slavery and British Economic Growth: The Eric Williams Hypothesis." *Journal of Development Economics*: 99-115.

Solow, Barbara L. (1987a). "Capitalism and Slavery in the Exceedingly Long Run." *British Capitalism & Caribbean Slavery: The Legacy of Eric Williams.* Barbara L. Solow and Stanley L. Engerman. Cambridge, Cambridge University Press: 51-77.

Barbara L. Solow and Stanley L. Engerman. (1987). *British Capitalism & Caribbean Slavery: The Legacy of Eric Williams.* Cambridge, Cambridge University Press.

Stoll, Allyson. (2011a). *NotFor "Want of Go-Aheadism in Field and Factory: The Technological Trajectory of the Guyana (British Guyana) Sugar Industry from 1800 to the 1930s.* PhD dissertation. Cornell University, Ithaca, NY.

Stoll, Allyson. (2011b). "Thoroughly Tested and Tried: Cane Culture, Technology, and Environmental Change in Nineteenth Century Guyana," *Journal of Caribbean History*, 45, 1: 92-127.

Tomich, Dale. 1990. *Slavery in the Circuit of Sugar: Martinique in the World Economy, 1830-1848.* Baltimore: The Johns Hopkins University Press.

Williams, Eric (1944, repr. 1994). *Capitalism & Slavery.* Chapel Hill: University of North Carolina Press.

Zanetti, Oscar and Alejandro García. (1998). *Sugar and Railroads: A Cuban History, 1837-1959.* Chapel Hill: University of North Carolina Press.

The aftermath of Abolition: Distortions of the Historical Record in Machado de Assis' *Counselor Aires' Memorial.*

Luiza Franco MOREIRA

Binghamton University

The great 19th century Brazilian writer, Machado de Assis (1839-1908) published his last novel, *Memorial de Aires*, in 1908, a few months before his death on September 29, 1908. The story is set 20 years earlier, within a few months of 1888 and 1889, during the period that saw the end of slavery in Brazil and nearly saw, and the end of the Empire as well. *Memorial de Aires* is not a universally admired novel. In many ways, it is an atypical novel for Machado. It reaches the conventional happy ending of sentimental stories by making a match between Fidélia and Tristão, two attractive, talented, wealthy, loving, and entirely eligible young people; yet most readers find Machado's novels remarkable precisely because they take liberties with literary convention. Beyond that, *Memorial de Aires* is an unwieldy novel, which tells at least three stories at the same time. It focuses on two generations of characters and calls attention, painfully, to the contrasts between what lies ahead for each group. Fidélia and Tristão are young, find happiness together, and have their whole lives ahead of them; they leave Brazil for Portugal shortly after their marriage, because a brilliant career in politics awaits the young man on the other side of the Atlantic. But the older generation mostly have death and loneliness to look forward to. The narrator, Aires, is deceased; he has left the narrative among his papers, in one of his diaries. Dona Carmo and Aguiar, a childless couple but very attached to Fidélia and Tristão, are left behind in Rio de Janeiro when the young couple leaves. Several critics, most notably, José Paulo Paes, have approached *Memorial de Aires*, as a novel concerned with preparation for death, or "a severe fable about mortality" (35).

In addition to the stories of the young and the old, and pushed into the background of the novel, we find a third story as well, that of the Abolition of slavery in Brazil, the crisis of production in the old coffee area of the valley of the Paraíba River, and the imminent end of the Brazilian Empire. [I‘m afraid the edits change the meaning of the sentence. Please use the original version.] Those familiar with Brazilian history will quickly notice that the dates of the entries in Aires‘ diary are quite significant: the story of the *Memorial* starts on January 9, 1888 and ends on August 30, 1889. The law abolishing slavery was signed on May 13, 1888 – right in the middle of the novel – while the period of republican government started only a few months after the story ends, when the Emperor was overthrown on November 15, 1889. This is a period of quick social and political change in Brazil, yet, for the most part, the polished surface of Machado‘s novel shows, simply, the life of elegance and privilege led by the wealthy in the cosmopolitan city of Rio de Janeiro. Yet, although it is easy to see that the dates of Aires‘ diary must matter, it is not so easy to see in what ways exactly they are significant for this novel in particular. José Paulo Paes has asked, pointedly, what the history of Abolition has to do with *Memorial de Aires*. I propose to address this critic‘s question, but in a roundabout way. Let me start by calling attention to the way that this novel reworks this crucial period of Brazilian history which, when it came to be published, was already 20 years in the past.

One of the secondary characters of the novel is a planter and slave owner. The Barão de Santa Pia (literally, Baron of the Holy Font) is the father of the heroine, Fidélia. Through this character, in a brief but memorable episode, Machado de Assis examines a planter‘s response to Abolition. Readers of *Memorial de Aires* will remember that the Baron decided to make a mass manumission of his slaves shortly before Abolition. Rather than wait for the new law to be signed, he preferred to inflict on himself *o desfalque inevitável* – the unavoidable shortage. As the character explains it, he frees his slaves in April 1888 with the intention to protest the government‘s interference in "a right that belongs only to the owner, and which I exercise to my own loss, because I want to and can" (§221, p. 93). The absurd, self-defeating way that the Baron found to assert his right of property was, precisely, to let go of the slaves as property. Ironically enough, by the time Emancipation was imminent, the only way for Santa Pia to remain a slave owner was to choose not to own slaves. Machado's narrator makes fun of the *grande novidade* – amazing news – that the planter has decided to shoot himself in the foot. The cutting irony that the Counselor Aires is at times capable of comes to the surface here. He can't tell, he writes, if the Baron's idea is "subtle," if it is "profound," or if it is "both things or, again, nothing" (§ 222, p. 93).

Two texts that were published in the newspapers of Rio de Janeiro around the time of Abolition, and so 20 years before *Memorial de Aires*, shed light on this episode of the novel. The first text is a journalistic piece, a *crônica*, which appeared two days before the law was signed, on May 11, 1888. This *crônica* was anonymously published, but John Gledson has convincingly argued that the author was, in fact, Machado de Assis. The second text is a letter by the planter and politician, Paula Souza, published in several Rio de Janeiro newspapers a few months before Abolition, in March or April of 1888. Ana Maria Rios and Hebe Santos discuss this letter in an article reconstructing the post-Emancipation period in the Valley of the Paraíba. Both Machado's unsigned crônica and the planter's letter discuss mass manumission as a strategy for planters to respond to Abolition – by trying somehow to pre-empt it, once it had become inevitable.

Machado's *crônica* is openly satirical. Whereas the irony of the narrator of *Memorial de Aires* is ambiguous and, at times, easy to miss, this *crônica* is direct. Machado takes on here the voice of a dim-witted but extremely self-importat *eiron*:

Não foi o ato das alforrias em massa dos últimos dias, essas alforrias *incondicionais,* que vêm cair como estrelas no meio da discussão da lei da abolição. Não foi; porque esses atos são de pura vontade, sem a menor explicação. Lá que eu gosto da liberdade, é certo; mas o princípio da propriedade não é menos legítimo. Qual deles escolheria? Vivia assim, como uma peteca (salvo seja), entre as duas opiniões, até que a sagacidade e a profundeza de espírito com que Deus quis compensar a minha humildade, me indicou a opinião racional e seus fundamentos. (*Ficção e história* 122)

It is not just the massive instances of manumission (*alforrias*) in the past few days, these *unconditional alforrias*, which have fallen like stars over discussions of the law of Emancipation. It is not that, since these acts are purely voluntary, without any explanation. Well, there is no doubt I like liberty; yet the principle of property is not any less legitimate. Which of the two was I to choose? I spent my days like that, like a shuttlecock (mercy!) between these two opinions, until the cleverness and profundity with which God has wanted to compensate for my humility suggested to me the rational opinion and its ground.

This passage neatly formulates the intractable problem that the Baron of Santa Pia tries to solve with the manumission of his slaves. Liberty and property, the journalist tells us, are incompatible principles: "Qual deles escolheria?" – "Which should I choose?" In this throwaway remark of Machado's *cronista,* we recognize, in hindsight, a concise and lucid formulation of the contradictions of liberalism.

Brazilian historians have turned their attention to the aftermath of Abolition in recent years, devoting their efforts to reconstructing the trajectories of the former slaves once they had become free. Their work proves helpful for reading Machado's last novel. As we will see, *Memorial de Aires* often refers to facts of the past, recognizably and precisely. Yet the reference is seldom accurate. At times the novel distorts events by enlarging the scope of the action, and at times by drastically reducing it, so that a single, apparently idiosyncratic character refers us to a broad historical phenomenon.

If we now turn to the historical document analyzed by Rios and Mattos, we will be able to see this episode of the novel from new angles. The idea that mass manumissions could somehow pre-empt Abolition seems absurd when it is presented by Machado de Assis, either in his unsigned *crônica* or in the novel that was published 20 years afterwards. It seems *um disparate*, to use a word that Roberto Schwarz has made a definitive part of our understanding of Machado's work. Yet this is not an idea dreamed up by a novelist with a great imagination and a talent for satire. It really happened. Rios and Santos report that in March and April of 1888 – and so a few months before Machado's unsigned *crônica* – the planter and politician Paula Souza had published a letter in several Brazilian newspapers , among them the two most important ones in Rio de Janeiro. The historians report that Paula Souza called for unconditional mass manumissions, arguing that this was the only way to keep the former slaves from leaving the plantations and to keep order in the slave quarters.[1]

Both Paula Souza‘s letter and Machado‘s unsigned *crônica* are part of the public dialogue about Abolition conducted in the Rio de Janeiro newspapers in 1888. It is reasonable to assume that the readership of these publications would recognize that the unsigned *crônica,* which we now believe was written by Machado, was a satire of the letter. On the other hand, when the novel, *Memorial de Aires,* came to be published in 1908, the reference to the planter‘s letter was probably all but lost. Yet the text of the novel gives us a clue to the historical referent of this episode. The name of Machado‘s character and that of the historical planter are similar: on the one hand, Santa Pia, on the other, Paula Souza or, if we take their initials only, SP and PS. When we read Machado‘s 1908 novel in the context of the two texts printed in 1888 newspapers, it becomes clear that the Santa Pia episode comments on one of the responses of Brazilian planters to Abolition. It is also clear that Machado kept thinking, for 20 years at least, about how absurd this planter strategy was.

Let me note, finally, that in this instance Machado‘s novel proceeds by drastically reducing the scale of something that had happened historically. Paula Souza‘ letter was published in several newspapers, and enjoyed fairly wide public circulation. In contrast, in *Memorial de Aires,* the Baron of Santa Pia acts alone, discusses his decision only with a small circle of family and friends, and is, moreover, ridiculed by the narrator.

There are further intriguing parallels between the fictional and the historical planter. Rios and Santos report that Paula Souza‘ letter defends mass manumissions on the grounds that these measures serve to keep the former slaves from leaving the plantations and help keep order in slave quarters. The Baron of Santa Pia offers a similar explanation for his decision in a

[1] Rios and Mattos specify that Paula Souza‘s letter was published in the newspapers *Gazeta Sul-Mineira*, on April 19, 1888, and *Monitor Campista*, on April 5, 1888, “after it had been published, in March, in *Jornal do Commercio*, and *O Paiz*, newspapers from the Court [Rio de Janeiro]” (56, ftn. 2). Robert Conrad has published an English translation of a letter on the *same* topic by Paula Souza, dated March 19, 1888; Conrad notes that the source of this document was a major newspaper from São Paulo, *A Províníca de São Paulo*, April 8, 1888 (476-480).

conversation with his brother, a lawyer. The judge wants to protect the inheritance of his niece, Fidélia, the heroine. He doesn‘t want her to lose the capital invested in the slaves and for that reason tries to talk his brother out of the decision to free them. Santa Pia‘s answer echoes the letter circulated by Paula Souza, but with shocking candor:

– Estou certo que poucos [dos antigos escravos] deixarão a fazenda; a maior parte ficará comigo, ganhando o salário que lhes vou marcar, e alguns até sem nada, – pelo gosto de morrer onde nasceram. (§ 227, p. 94).

I am sure that few (of my former slaves) will leave the plantation; most of them will stay with me, accepting the salary I choose to give them, and some even for nothing – for the simple pleasure of dying at the place where they were born.

Machado‘s character expresses himself with brutal clarity. Santa Pia counts on being able to use the former slaves as cheap and perhaps free labor, even after Abolition. He is betting that they will have no other alternative but to stay at the plantation.

At this point, it is useful to return, again, to the historical reconstruction of the aftermath of Abolition by Rios and Mattos. The historians show that the Baron guessed wrong. Contrary to the expectations of Machado‘s fictional planter, and contrary to the wishes of the historical Paula Souza, there was considerable mobility among the former slaves in valley of the Paraíba River, as soon as they were free to leave the old plantations.

The Baron of Santa Pia dies around the time of Abolition, fittingly. The heroine, Fidélia, inherits his plantation (which is no longer profitable) along with the rest of the Baron‘s considerable patrimony, and no debts at all. Now a woman of independent means, Fidélia still has to deal with the problem of what to do with the old plantation and the former slaves, who are still living there. In the end, she decides to donate all of her lands to those who live in them, so that they can work it for themselves. In two passages of the novel, the story of Fidélia‘s decision recalls events that took place historically. However, before focusing on these two passages, let me take a moment to comment on the function that Fidélia‘s choice to donate her lands serves in Machado‘s novel.

At first, it may seem that the heroine‘s decision amounts to a happy ending, parallel to her marriage to the extremely eligible bachelor, Tristão.

Just as the sentimental storyline reaches the end required by convention, Fidélia's gift to her former slaves brings closure to the less evident plotline of *Memorial de Aires*, the one concerned with the public events of the Abolition of slavery and the end of the monarchy. The ends of the two stories seem to be analogous. However, despite the evident parallelism, the novel carefully – and ironically – shows that the two denouements are far from equivalent. John Gledson has already stressed that the new owners of the Santa Pia estate lack the contacts, and above all, the credit that would enable them to cultivate their land for profit. Beyond that, as we know today and as Machado's characters also knew quite well, by the late 1880s, in the valley of the Paraíba, with or without slavery, "*a lavoura decai*" the exploitation of the land for coffee production was no longer commercially viable. In contrast, when the newly married Tristão and Fidélia leave for Portugal, they take with them a fortune that had its origins in coffee production but no longer depends on it. As we have seen, the heroine inherits a patrimony that, although amassed by a planter, could easily absorb the loss of slaves and lands. The man she marries, for his part, was the child of a *comissário de café*.[2] Tristão's father had liquidated his business in Brazil before the novel started, and had gone back to Portugal with the fortune that he had made from coffee intact and safe from the crisis that was to grip production in the old areas. Meanwhile, even though the workers that are given the old Santa Pia estate are free and own the land they work on, all that they have to look forward to is, at best, a life of subsistence agriculture in the poverty of the Brazilian countryside. In the structure of Machado's novel, the financially well-balanced match between Tristão and Fidélia is the other side of the destitution of the former slaves in the abandoned old plantation.

The story of the heiress who gives all of her lands to her former slaves might seem yet another instance of the novelist's imagination running wild. The narrator of *Memorial de Aires* is indeed very moved by the heroine's decision and calls it "romantic." Yet there is a recognizable historical model

2 See Maria Sylvia de Carvalho Franco's *Homens livres na order escravocrata* for the classic account of the key, yet contradictory, role played by the *comissário de café* in articulating the rapid movement of capital, in the sphere of exportation to the world market, and the slow movement of capital, in the sphere of agricultural production.

for Fidélia's character. In 1882, the Condessa do Rio Novo, a widow who owned and managed a plantation in Paraíba do Sul, freed all her slaves in her testament and left them a portion of her lands. Joaquim Nabuco, the influential Brazilian Abolitionist and a personal friend of Machado's, mentions this historical episode in his classic, *O abolicionismo*, and praises the Condessa do Rio Novo as a model of generosity.[3] Two details of Machado's novel serve as clues that Fidélia's character and her actions may be taken as an allusion to the historical Condessa do Rio Novo: when the novel starts, Fidélia is a widow; in addition, the text specifies, more than once, that her plantation is in "Paraíba do Sul". At the same time, although Fidélia is recognizably modeled after the Condessa do Rio Novo, the novel again distorts the events that it refers to. Machado expands the scope of the actions of his fictional heroine. While the historical Condessa left only a portion of her lands to slaves she freed – the area where they already gardened – Fidélia donates all her property to the former slaves.

Let me offer one further example of distorted historical reference in *Memorial de Aires* before concluding. While Fidélia was trying to decide what to do with the plantation, she considered selling it. Her former slaves heard of it and did not like the idea. They went to see her as a group and asked her not sell it, but asked also that she bring all of them to the city with her – "que não a vendesse, que os trouxesse a todos consigo para o Rio de Janeiro" (§448 p. 126). Ana Maria Rios and Hebe Santos report that, in fact, after Abolition, the former slaves, at times, organized themselves in groups in order to negotiate with the planters the conditions under which they would stay in the land and work it. Yet the historians do not report that the former slaves ever asked a landowner to take them away from the countryside and bring them to live in the capital.

In this discussion of *Memorial de Aires*, I have sought to call attention to a pattern of reference to historical events that took place around the time of Abolition in Brazil. For literary purposes – for the sake of telling a good story – the novel considerably distorts the events that it alludes to. A literary scholar might reasonably ask, at this point, what this discussion of histori-

3 I owe to Rafael Marquese the reference to Nabuco's discussion of the Condessa do Rio Novo in *O abolicionismo*, and several other references, too.

cal reference adds to a reading of *Memorial de Aires*. I want to suggest, in closing, that this discussion serves to direct our attention to the irony that underlies Machado's portrayal of the elegant but small world of the elite in Rio de Janeiro. This irony is very evident in the satirical tale of a planter's wrong-headed attempt to pre-empt Abolition. Yet Machado's irony is apparent also in the contrast that this novel establishes between the happy ending of the story of a wealthy widow who finds love and remarries, and the quite unequal happy ending of the story of her former slaves, who end up free and owners of a vast expanse of barely productive land. Machado's ironic use of historical reference serves to interrupt the smooth surface of the story and allows us a glimpse beyond the world of the elite, and into the very different world of slaves and former slaves – whose labors have made possible the elegance of the wealthy, but who generally escape their attention. Once we notice Machado's satirical distortions of events that, in effect, took place in Brazil around the time of Abolition, it is difficult to read *Memorial de Aires* as a nostalgic and unproblematic recovery through fiction of the charmed days of the Brazilian Empire.

Works Cited

ASSIS, Machado de. *Memorial de Aires*. Rio de Janeiro; Brasília: Civilização Brasileira; INL, 1975. Edições críticas das obras de Machado de Assis, v. 10. Parenthetical references in the body of the text refer to this edition. See also: *Counselor Ayres Memorial*, trans. Helen Cauldwell (Berkeley: University of California Press, 1972); *The Wager: Ayres' Journal* (London: Peter Owen, 1990), and *Memorial de Aires*, trans. Antelma Cisneros (Mexico: UNAM, 2001).

CONRAD, Robert Edgard. *Children's of God's Fire: A Documentary History of Black Slavery in Brazil*. Princeton: Princeton University Press, 1994.

FRANCO, Maria Sylvia de Carvalho. *Homens livres na ordem escravocrata*. São Paulo: Ática, 1974.

GLEDSON, John. *Machado de Assis: ficção e história*. Rio de Janeiro: Paz e Terra, 1986.

NABUCO, Joaquim. *O abolicionismo*. São Paulo: Editora Nova Fronteira.

PAES, José Paulo. "Um aprendiz de morto," in: ______. *Gregos e baianos*. São Paulo: Brasiliense, 1985.

RIOS, Ana Maria and Hebe Mattos, "Para além das senzalas: campesinato, política e trabalho rural no Rio de Janeiro pós-abolição," in *Quase cidadão*, Flávio dos Santos Gomes and Olívia Maria Gomes da Cunha, eds. Rio de Janeiro: Fundação Getúlio Vargas, 2007.

The Second Slavery: Modernity in the 19th-Century South and the Atlantic World

Anthony E. KAYE

During the nineteenth century, the South underwent an expansion of slavery that was also transforming political economies across the Americas, a historic departure that Dale Tomich calls "the second slavery." It was distinguished from colonial slavery by new commodities, produced in unprecedented quantities, and in regions formally marginal to the Atlantic economy, which were reconfigured polities. After 1790, slavery expanded onto new ground; slaves tended new crops and new machinery, while planter classes gained dominance in new world markets and acquired new powers from reconstituted states in Cuba, Brazil and the South. Profits reaped from sugar, coffee, and cotton derived, in part, from burgeoning industrial production in two ways. First, upturns in output met increased demand from growing populations of industrial workers. The transition of tropical commodities from elite luxuries to common necessities reached midcourse around 1800 and was completed during the nineteenth century. Second, planters integrated industrial machines with slave labor to market its products. In the new techniques and increased scale of production, with the sheer mobility and adaptability of slave labor, the second slavery was, in a word, modern.[1]

Although southern historians have yet to write in terms of the second slavery, we could begin by building on connections in several directions already made in recent work. This project requires breaking out of the con-

[1] Dale Tomich, *Through the Prism of Slavery: Labor, Capital, and World Economy* (Lanham, Md, 2004), esp. 56-71;Tomich and Michael Zeuske, "The Second Slavery: Mass Slavery, World Economy, and Comparative Microhistories," *Review: A Journal of the Fernand Braudel Center* 31:2 (2008): 91-100. See also Tomich, *Slavery in the Circuit of Sugar: Martinique and the World Economy, 1830-1848* (Baltimore, 1990). This essay is much improved thanks to generous readings and helpful suggestions by Matthew Restall, Adam Rothman.

fines of "antebellum slavery," which point the field headlong toward the Civil War, draw its parameters along the Mason-Dixon line, and cast the history of the Old South as a nation-building project. Since the 1970s, historians have crossed the temporal boundaries in studies of slave kinship, labor, property, and politics encompassing the antebellum and postbellum periods. Explaining the second slavery in the South requires crossing the divide on the earlier side to connect the antebellum period to the early republic. Scholars of slavery in colonial North America have sallied forth into the Atlantic world, but historians of the nineteenth-century South have some catching up to do.[2] Fortunately two related themes prominent in recent historiography on antebellum slavery have lessened the conceptual gap with historiography on the Atlantic world. The long debate about whether the Old South was an anachronistic, seigneurial society or a variant on modern capitalism is approaching a consensus around the latter.[3] This is a revealing

---

2 Ira Berlin, *Generations of Captivity: A History of African-American Slaves* (Cambridge, Mass., 2003); Herbert G. Gutman, *The Black Family in Slavery and Freedom, 1750-1925* (New York, 1976); Barbara J. Fields, *Slavery and Freedom on the Middle Ground: Maryland during the Nineteenth*-Century (New Haven, 1985); Julie Saville, *The Work of Reconstruction: From Slave to Wage Laborer in South Carolina, 1860-1870* (New York, 1994); Dylan C. Penningroth, *Claims of Kinfolk: African American Property and Community in the Nineteenth-Century South* (Chapel Hill, 2003); Steven Hahn, *A Nation under Our Feet: Black Political Struggles in the Rural South from Slavery to the Great Migration* (Cambridge, Mass., 2003): Wilma A. Dunaway, *The African American Family in Slavery and Emancipation* (New York, 2003); Thavolia Glymph, *Out of the House of Bondage: The Transformation of the Plantation Household* (New York, 2008); Philip D. Morgan and Jack P. Greene, "Introduction: The Present State of Atlantic History," in Greene and Morgan, eds., *Atlantic History: A Critical Appraisal* (New York, 2009), 21.

3 Joyce E. Chaplin, *An Anxious Pursuit: Agricultural Innovation and Modernity in the Lower South, 1730-1815* (Chapel Hill, 1993); Mark M. Smith, "Time, Slavery and Plantation Capitalism in the Ante-Bellum South," *Past & Present* 150 (February 1996), 142-68; William Dusinberre, *Them Dark Days: Slavery in the American Rice Swamps* (New York, 1996); Walter Johnson, *Soul by Soul: Life Inside the Antebellum Slave Market* (Cambridge, Mass., 1999); Jeffrey R. Young, *Domesticating Slavery: The Master Class in Georgia and South Carolina, 1670-1837* (Chapel Hill, 1999); Edward E. Baptist, *Creating an Old South: Middle Florida's Plantation Frontier before the Civil War* (Chapel Hill, 2002); David L. Carlton and Peter A. Coclanis, *The South, the Nation, and the World: Perspectives on Southern Economic Development* (Charlottesville, 2003);Wilma A. Dunaway, *Slavery in the American Mountain South* (New York, 2003); William

outlook on Southern slavery with bracing implications. Yet this work wants perspective. It has gone rather far without due attention to such elementary matters as exactly what was capitalist and modern about slavery. This essay aims to move this literature forward by clarifying its terms and placing the South in the context of the second slavery. A comparative perspective sharpens our understanding of modern slavery in the South yet makes it less peculiarly Southern. Like Cuba and Brazil, the South was a modern slave society in many ways, but not necessarily the most modern.

Although Southern historians have said little about just what they mean by *modern*, two distinct tones are discernible. Neither has much truck with the iron triangle of capitalism, democracy, and progress that undergirded modernization theory after World War II. Yet for some historians, modernity still has its virtues, which cast a positive light on the antebellum South and lend an admiring tone to many recent accounts, especially of technol ogy and intellectual history. By contrast, historians of slavery also write of modernity in a discordantly major key, in sharp, sometimes harrowing tones. In *The Black Atlantic*, Paul Gilroy argued that racism, violence, and slavery, long consigned to the annals of the pre-modern, were constitutive of modernity. Black intellectuals, he pointed out, began this counterhistory of modernity in brilliant studies of the formative relationship between slavery and capitalism, the appropriation of French revolutionary ideals by Black Jacobins in the Haitian Revolution, and the part black folks played in the Reconstruction of democracy in the United States. What was required from a new generation of scholars, Gilroy urged, was "a primal history of modernity." During the 1990s historians began writing a history of slavery that was primal indeed. More immediately influential among Southern historians than Gilroy's were Nell Irvin Painter's calls for a full account of the sexual exploitation of slaves. Slave trading, rape, and violence, long

---

K. Scarborough, *Masters of the Big House: Elite Slaveholders of the Mid-Nineteenth-Century South* (Baton Rouge, 2003); David Walker Howe, *What Hath God Wrought: The Transformation of America, 1815-1848* (New York, 2007), 60-61; Tom Downey, *Planting a Capitalist South: Masters, Merchants, and Manufacturers in the Southern Interior, 1790-1860* (Baton Rouge, 2006). For a cogent discussion of debates over slavery and capitalism in the South, see Mark M. Smith, *Debating Slavery: Economy and Society in the Antebellum American South* (New York, 1998), 12-14, 87-94

consigned to the underside of slavery, are increasingly treated as intrinsic to it. Although Painter did not frame this research agenda in terms of modernity, others have. In a disturbing account of the systematic rape of enslaved women by operators of the largest slave-trading firm in the South, Edward E. Baptist suggests slaves were "people converted into symbols and objects of economic power, social status, and psychosexual fulfillment." Slaves were, in short, "the first modern commodities."[4] One can find some of the best work in the field in either register, yet much is written more or less in both. Many historians describe the South as modern because it was progressive despite slavery; others argue that slavery was an extreme form of domination, and this is what modernity is about. That these two accounts are difficult to square only underscores the need for definitions.

To see what was modern about the South from an Atlantic perspective, consider Robin Blackburn's magisterial survey, *The Making of New World Slavery.* The development of slavery in the Americas, he writes, "was associated with several of those processes which have been held to define modernity." In 1800 this tendency was still emergent, yet many elements were already present: the application of instrumental reason, "racialized perceptions of identity," the beginnings of consumer societies, "the spread of market relations," sophisticated methods of commerce and means of transportation, "administrative bureaucracies and modern tax systems," and "the rise of national sentiment and the nation-state." Previous generations of historians were much preoccupied, of course, with the rise of national sentiment in the antebellum South. Recent work has unraveled the recipro-

---

4 Gilroy, *The Black Atlantic: Modernity and Double Consciousness* (Cambridge, Mass., 1994), 55 (first quotation), 221; Painter, *Southern History across the Color Line* (Chapel Hill, 2002); Baptist, ",Cuffy,' ,Fancy Maids,' and ,One-Eyed Men:' Rape, Commodification, and the Domestic Slave Trade in the United States," *American Historical Review* 106 (2001): 1619-50 second and third quotation on 1650. See also Saidiya V. Hartman, *Scenes of Subjection: Terror, Slavery, and Self-Making in Nineteenth-Century America* (New York, 1997); Darlene Clark Hine, "Rape and the Inner Lives of Black Women: Thoughts on the Culture of Dissemblance," in *Hine Sight: Black Women and the Re-Construction of American History* (Bloomington, 1997), 37-47; Alex Bontemps, *The Punished Self: Surviving Slavery in the Colonial South* (Ithaca, 2001); Norrece T. Jones Jr., "Rape in Black and White: Sexual Violence in the Testimony of Enslaved and Free African Americans," in Winthrop D. Jordan, ed., *Slavery and the American South*, (Jackson, Miss., 2003), 93-108.

cal relationship between the modern state, including the federal tax system, and the expansion of slavery. "The dynamic of the Atlantic economy was sustained by new webs of social trust, and gave birth to new social identities," adds Blackburn. The cultural transformations of enslaved people that defined the African diaspora from the outset of colonial slavery persisted in different forms under new conditions through the nineteenth century. This essay cannot address all the aspects of modernity identified by Blackburn but will focus on new social identities forged in African American culture, the expansion of slavery, and its capitalist character.[5]

At the outset of the Haitian Revolution in 1791, Saint Domingue was the leading producer of coffee as well as sugar, the most valuable tropical commodity in the Atlantic world. The fledgling United States, like Cuba and Brazil, were still marginal players in the market for American staples. The South was, at best, a primary producer of secondary staples. The Chesapeake was, since 1710, the largest exporter of tobacco, while the Lowcountry exported rice to England and to the British West Indies to feed slaves on sugar plantations. Planters entered the cotton market during the 1770s, but North American exports to England in 1790 were but a fraction of those from the British Caribbean. Brazil, the leading producer of sugar from about 1580 to 1640, had stagnated during the eighteenth century. In Cuba planters began a shift from sugar production for local markets to a staple crop during the Seven Years' War, but tobacco remained the mainstay.

The juggernaut of the Cuban sugar economy gained much of its impetus from a restructured relationship between metropole and colony in the Spanish empire. During the 1790s a coterie of ambitious creole planters and colonial officials, most notably Francisco de Arango y Parreño and Luis de las Casas, began to look forward to what Cuba would require to capture the world market in sugar. First and foremost, the planters needed slaves, and this required greater access to the trans-Atlantic slave trade. To

[5] Blackburn, *The Making of New World Slavery: From the Baroque to the Modern, 1492-1800* (London, 1997), quotation on 4. For an authoritative survey of North American slavery in an Atlantic context, focusing on the master-slave relation, doctrines of race, and abolitionism, see David Brion Davis, *Inhuman Bondage. The Rise and Fall of Slavery in the New World* (Oxford, 2006).

acquire the best slaves in the greatest number, Arango argued, Cuba needed to encourage all carriers to compete for its market, and for this Spain had to enact a permanent policy of free trade in African slaves. The planters spoke boldly to metropolitan authorities and condemned Spain for an economic and cultural backwardness that impeded the advanced technology and expansive market Cuba required. By 1819 reformers in the Bourbon monarchy had dismantled the most heavily regulated colonial system in the Americas and opened Cuba as well as Puerto Rico to trade with all nations. Planters from Havana used their control over boards of inspection in the marketing of staple crops to drive tobacco farmers off their land and appropriate it for sugar plantations. The new balance of power in the empire enabled Cuba planters to obtain African slaves from British, then Portuguese traders, steam engines from England and the United States, processing equipment from France, and preeminence in the world market for sugar.[6]

Recent work has deeply implicated the national state in the expansion of slavery in the South. The federal system of taxation, for example, protected both wealth and rights in slave property. As Robin L. Einhorn has shown, the Founders joined the controversies over slavery and revenue via the three-fifths ratio. The method devised by the Continental Congress to distribute the burden of provisioning the Revolutionary army was adopted in the Constitution to apportion representatives to the House and the Electoral College. States' reluctance to sustain the army and South Carolina's manifest determination to defend slavery at the Constitutional Convention

---

6 Dale Tomich, "The Wealth of Empire: Francisco Arango y Parreño, Political Economy, and the Second Slavery in Cuba," *Comparative Studies in Society and History* 45 (2003): 4-28; Tomich, *Prism of Slavery*, 82; Michael Zeuske, "Comparing or Interlinking? Economic Comparisons of Early Nineteenth-Century Slave Systems in the Americas in Historical Perspective," in Enrico Dal Lago and Constantina Katsari, eds., *Slave Systems: Ancient and Modern* (New York, 2008), 148-93, esp. 156-69; Antón L. Allahar, "The Cuban Sugar Planters (1790-1820): ,The Most Solid and Brilliant Bourgeoisie Class in all of Latin America,'" *Americas* 41 (July 1984): 37-57; Manuel Moreno Fraginals, *The Sugar Mill: The Socioeconomic Complex of Sugar in Cuba, 1760-1860*, translated by Cedric Belfrage (New York, 1976), 20-25, 47-51; Sherry Johnson, *The Social Transformation of Eighteenth-Century Cuba* (Gainesville, 2001), 7, 124; J. H. Elliott, *Empires of the Atlantic World: Britain and Spain America* (New Haven, 2006), chs. 10.

prompted the U.S. Congress to find a formula for taxation that avoided any valuation of slaves. The tariff relied entirely on foreign trade to provide the government with revenue. This was a novel expedient for a nation-state endeavoring to establish its independence. The tariff also protected slaveholders from the merest possibility of abolition by tax levies that would make slaves prohibitively expensive. In foreign relations federal authorities protected property in slaves wherever they roamed. The U.S. State Department remonstrated with England to return slaves who were confiscated or had absconded during the Revolution and the War of 1812. The government sent federal troops to recover runaways in Spanish Florida and attack the Seminoles and the Creeks, then removed these people from their land and surveyed it for sale. High federal prices conspicuously favored slaveholders in the settlement of Alabama, Mississippi, and Louisiana. Stout federal resistance to the British policy of boarding American ships extended a protective mantle over the African slave trade after the United States withdrew in 1808. Slavers of all nations sailing under the American flag carried over 85,000 Africans to the Americas after 1821. U.S. nationals from the North and the South were active conduits in the slave trade to Brazil. The federal defense of bondage has increasingly convinced scholars that the United States was a "slaveholding republic"—that slavery was not a Southern but a national institution.[7]

By 1820 the expansion of slavery was well underway. As slaveholders migrated to the Deep South, their peers pushed into the interior of Jamaica and south-central Brazil, swept over western Cuba, the Lesser Antilles, and settled on the South American coast in British Guyana. In the South farmers and planters from the Chesapeake, the Lowcountry, the Virginia Piedmont, and the Carolina backcountry migrated to Kentucky and Tennessee

[7] Robin L. Einhorn, *American Taxation, American Slavery* (Chicago, 2006), esp. 113-56; Adam Rothman, *Slave Country: American Expansion and the Origins of the Deep South* (Cambridge, 2005), esp. 123-45, 167-73; Don E. Fehrenbacher, *The Slaveholding Republic: An Account of the United States Government's Relations to Slavery*, edited by Ward M. McAffee (Oxford, 2001); David Eltis, "The U.S. Transatlantic Slave Trade, 1644-1867: An Assessment," *Civil War History* 54 (December 2008), 347-78, 371; Gerald Horne, *The Deepest South: The United States, Brazil, and the African Slave Trade* (New York, 2007). For another approach to the national character of slavery, see Steven Hahn, *The Political Worlds of Slavery and Freedom* (Cambridge, Mass., 2001), ch. 1.

during the 1790s; to lands along the Mississippi River in Louisiana and Mississippi during the 1800s; into the interior of southern Mississippi and along the rivers in western Alabama and Missouri during the 1810s. Sugar planters in the West Indies sought new fields in colonies captured during the Age of Revolution, despite the British abolition of the African slave trade in 1807. Between 1815 and 1825, slaveholders from older colonies producing cotton, coffee, and provisions transferred over 20,000 slaves to new sugar colonies, like Demerara-Essequibo. Between 1790 and 1820 Cuba imported over 300,000 slaves from Africa, a threefold increase over the total number imported during the previous three centuries. Sugar planters poured into the Güines Valley south of Havana to begin production on the lands appropriated from tobacco farmers. As Cuban planters aimed to replace St. Domingue in the sugar market, Brazilians made a foray into coffee. From north of Rio de Janeiro, planters cut a swathe down the Paraíba Valley into western São Paulo.[8] Mobility would prove the key not only to the survival of slavery but its economic dynamism and capitalist character.

Ramping up production in the second slavery required technological innovations to break through bottlenecks in processing staple crops. Slaves had to pick cotton, cut and grind sugarcane before rains, frost, or rot set in. Cotton production, of course, was constrained by the difficulty of breaking the tenacious grip of seeds without tearing the fiber. Until the 1790s slaves could cultivate far more cotton than could be cleaned by the venerable roller gin, which had been in use for centuries in India and pinched seeds from the fiber, gently but all too slowly.

The saw gin exemplifies the collective process of technological invention in the Atlantic basin. Innovation, recent scholarship stresses, owed less to the genius of individual inventors than to the modification of existing

---

8 Matt D. Childs, *The 1812 Aponte Rebellion in Cuba and the Struggle against Atlantic Slavery* (Chapel Hill, 2006), 49-50; Francisco Vidal Luna and Herbert S. Klein, *Slavery and the Economy of São Paulo, 1750-1850* (Stanford, 2003), 53-78; Kenneth Morgan, *Slavery and the British Empire: From Africa to America* (New York, 2007), 10, 48, 169; B. W. Higman, *Slave Populations of the British Caribbean, 1807-1834* (Baltimore, 1984), 55-85, 417-18. On the British political context of migration, see Hilary McD. Beckles, "‚An Unfeeling Traffick‘: The Intercolonial Movement of Slaves in the British Caribbean, 1807-1833," in Walter Johnson, ed., *The Chattel Principle: Internal Slave Trades in the Americas,* (New Haven, 2004), 256-74.

technologies in communities of knowledge and skill. Networks of mechanics borrowed machinery from elsewhere and adapted it to new purposes and conditions. Angela Lakwete has debunked the myth that the cotton gin was Eli Whitney's invention. He was one of many mechanics around Augusta, Georgia, experimenting on roller gins to increase output. Manufacturers complained his wire-toothed gin tore and tangled the fiber and impeded textile production down the line. The saw gin that he is remembered for was actually another mechanic's handiwork and appropriated to Whitney in court. Only after a long transition lasting until 1830 did the saw gin become ubiquitous. The cotton gin was thus the work of many hands—mechanics, free and enslaved, who modified and made gins with rollers and saws; forward-looking planters and skilled slaves who adopted the saw gin; "an industrializing, modernizing, and slave labor-based South."[9]

A skein of biological innovations, long obscured by historians' traditional focus on machinery, was also critical to the expansion of slavery. While machines enabled planters to put more land into cultivation and work more slaves, manipulating the natural properties of cotton and sugar increased the crops that slaves produced per acre. With little knowledge of genetics, a rudimentary understanding of plant breeding, and dogged empiricism, agriculturalists in Mississippi, Tennessee, and Georgia molded short-staple cottons for varied environments, from the interior of the seaboard states to the lower Mississippi Valley. By 1800 farmers in the Cumberland Valley had developed Tennessee Green Seed, which purportedly yielded up its fleece more readily and could be picked faster than the old Georgia Green Seed. In 1806 and 1807 planters around Natchez experimented on seeds of Mexican cottons, which opened their bolls when nights got longer and cooler. To make Mexican varieties ripen earlier than they were inclined to at relatively high latitudes of the U.S. South, planters crossed these cottons with Tennessee and Georgia Green Seed to produce a hybrid for alluvial bottomlands. Contrary to a reputation for a "lack of indigenous

9 Lakwete, *Inventing the Cotton Gin: Machine and Myth in Antebellum America* (Baltimore, 2003), ix (quotation), 47-71; Michele Gillespie, "Building Networks of Knowledge: Henry Merrell and Textile Manufacturing in the Antebellum South," in Susanna Delfino and Michele Gillsepie, ed., *Technology, Innovation, and Southern Industrialization: From the Antebellum Era to the Computer Age* (Columbia, Mo., 2008), 97-124.

technological advances," Alan L. Olmstead and Paul Rhode point out that the South "was the undisputed world leader in the creation and diffusion of superior cotton varieties."[10]

Biological and mechanical innovation, notwithstanding scholarly distinctions between the two, were inseparable on sugar plantations. The rapid deterioration of cane juice obliged planters to integrate agriculture and manufacturing. Moreover, the fifteen months required for Otaheite canes to mature in the tropical Caribbean had to be compressed into eight months before the first frost in Louisiana. Louisiana planters added a month to the growing season when they switched to ribbon cane. Yet its thick bark resisted not only frost but grinding in conventional animal-powered mills, so biological innovation required the mechanical version, too. Louisiana sugar planters converted to steam-powered mills starting in 1822, adopted a retooled grinder with three cylinders, and tightened the space between them. The new mills enabled slaves to extract a higher proportion of juice from each cane than animal-driven grinders yielded; planters were able to increase the acreage under crop and work more slaves. Planters employed more sophisticated technology in sugar than in cotton or coffee because economies of scale offered returns on investments in new machinery.[11]

No fundamental incompatibility existed between slavery and technology. Southern historians have long argued this case in regard to manufacturing and thus mainly the late antebellum decades. Yet it was already apparent by 1830 in the integration of machinery and steam power in staple production and transportation. Everywhere along the Black Belt, slaves cultivated and harvested crops to the rhythms of machines, gins on cotton plantations and grinders in the sugar mills. The steamboat, the most ubiquitous symbol of modern times in the South, was yet another technology borrowed from elsewhere and adapted to Southern uses and conditions. The first boats were

---

10 Olmstead and Rhode, *Creating Abundance: Biological Innovation and American Agricultural Development* (New York, 2008), 98-133 (quotation on 99-100).

11 Richard Follett, *The Sugar Masters: Planters and Slaves in Louisiana's Cane World, 1820-1860* (Baton Rouge, 2005), 22-24; Follett, "Slavery and Technology in Louisiana's Sugar Bowl," in Delfino and Gillespie, eds., *Technology, Innovation, and Southern Industrialization,* 68-96, esp. 71; Morgan, *Slavery and the British Empire,* 107; Tomich, *Prism of Slavery*, 120-36.

engineered by Yankees. During the 1810s Southerners in a dozen towns, especially in Kentucky, built boats with ten-foot hulls to navigate shallow drafts on western rivers. Steamboats were quickly integrated into the staple economy and became the primary means of transporting crops in the Old Southwest. Steam power telescoped the distance between plantations and markets and aligned the price of transporting goods upstream and down during the 1820s and 1830s.On the Mississippi River planters sent their cotton down to New Orleans, while sugar masters shipped muscovado and molasses up as far as St. Paul, Minnesota. Slaves loaded the boats with hogsheads and bales as well as kegs of nails and other goods, stoked the engines, and formed solidarities that ran deep on the "Father of Waters." Perhaps what Dale Tomich has written about technology and slave labor in the Cuban sugar industry——is true of the South as well: "capitalist modernity and slave labor are constitutive of one another."[12]

Though slavery and technology proved compatible, the South was not the most technically sophisticated slave society in the Atlantic world. To be sure, Louisiana had a larger proportion of steam-powered mills than Cuba from the late 1820s. By 1850 planters had expanded the cane country to its geographical limits and over the decade consolidated the industry, expanding holdings in land and slaves along with the application of steam power. In St. Mary and Ascension parishes sugar masters increased their acreage in cultivation over 50 percent and kept up their investment in machinery at $22 per acre all the while. Bagasse burners replaced wood with cane leaves as a cheap source of fuel for steam engines. Planters along the Mississippi shipped hogsheads by rail to New Orleans. Some even integrated trains into production and had tracks laid within their plantations to transport cane from fields to mill. By 1860 cane country was the most heavily capitalized agricultural region North or South. Content with increased production from modest investments in inexpensive steam engines, however, planters neglected to replace the Jamaica Train until the 1850s. Even then most slaves still ladled juice from one open vat to another, much as they had

---

12 Robert H. Gudmestad, "Steamboats and Southern Economic Development," in Delfino and Gillespie, eds., *Technology, Innovation and Southern Industrialization*, 18-40; Thomas C. Buchanan, *Black Life on the Mississippi: Slaves, Free Blacks, and the Western Steamboat World* (Chapel Hill, 2004); Tomich, *Prism of Slavery*, 93 (quotation).

in boiling houses across the Americas since the seventeenth century. While adopting the steam engine enabled Louisiana planters to maintain a tenable ratio of slaves and land as they increased their holdings, they shied away from investments in the fully mechanized mills that increased the scale of production in Cuba.[13]

The modernization of the sugar industry in Louisiana was a decade behind Cuba. By 1830 Louisiana had far fewer slaves, plantations, and mills, and Cuba had surpassed the peaks of production in Saint Domingue and Jamaica. During the 1840s Louisiana planters shifted from animal- to steam-powered grinders and made piecemeal improvements in the boiling house. Meanwhile Cuban planters got started building fully mechanized mills, and between 1840 and 1850 total sugar output doubled to nearly one-quarter of world supply. Slaves tended vacuum pans connected to evaporators and a condenser in a closed system. The apparatus boiled cane juice at relatively low temperatures, condensed it quickly, and increased the quantity and quality of crystallized sugar. By 1860 the sixty-four mechanized mills in Cuba yielded nearly two-thirds the entire output of Louisiana. The Cuban rail network, though far less extensive than the South's, became one of the most developed in the world during the 1850s, with more track per capita than Britain's. Early in the decade Cuba's rails had much the same structure as the network in the South, a series of trunk lines connecting staple-producing rural regions to port towns where crops were exported. While efforts to connect New Orleans to the sugar bowl beyond the plantations along the Mississippi by railroad foundered, Cuba added the beginnings of a radial system connecting ports. Louisiana failed to meet the demand for sugar in the United States, by more than twice the total output of the state in 1855. The largest supplier of the American sugar market was Cuba.[14]

---

13 Follett, "Slavery and Technology in Louisiana's Sugar Bowl," 69-74, 80-81; Follett, *Sugar Masters,* 21-33 (percentage of acreage under crop calculated from figures on 32). John B. Rehder, *Delta Sugar: Louisiana's Vanishing Plantation Landscape* (Baltimore, 1999), 43-57; J. Carlyle Sitterson, *Sugar Country: The Cane Industry in the South, 1753-1950* (Lexington, Ky., 1953), 147-50.

14 Frank Moya Pons, *History of the Caribbean: Plantations, Trade, and War in the Atlantic World* (Princeton, 2007), 220-30; Manuel Moreno Fraginals *El ingenio: Complejo economic social cubano del azúcar* (3 vols.; Havana, 1978), III, Appendix,Table 1; Moreno Fraginals, *Sugar Mill*, 81-127; Oscar Zanetti and Alejandro García, *Sugar*

By another, darker measure,—the wasting effect on slaves,—the Louisiana sugar industry was as modern as any in the Atlantic world. In the South, as in the Americas generally, the slave population on sugar plantations declined without imports of new people. Indeed, situating the natural increase of Southern slaves in an Atlantic context has reformulated the problem. Historians had long assumed the South had the only slave population to reproduce itself. Evidence of growing populations in Brazil and the British Caribbean, however, point to the killing work regime of sugar production as the main obstacle to natural increase. St. Kitts, St. Lucia, Montserrat, and Barbados, where sugar cultivation was in decline, achieved natural increase between 1810 and 1825. Slaves engaged in mixed agriculture in the Bahamas and in Minas Gerais in Brazil, also grew in numbers. In the South, the cane country "stood out as a miserable island of natural decrease," according to Michael Tadman. During the 1840s and 1850s, slave population in the South grew over 23 percent per decade, but the sugar parishes were ravaged by a natural *decrease* of approximately 13 percent. Planters imported twice as many men as women in the domestic slave trade and worked their people hard enough to reduce women's fertility and increase mortality, especially among children. The second slavery in Louisiana casts a harsh light on natural increase in the South as a whole. Outside the sugar parishes, births exceeded deaths, and the slave population grew, but no thanks to a paternalist master class. Slaves achieved natural increase, despite high mortality across the South. Enslaved men and women formed families and brought children into the world with death all around.[15]

---

and Railroads: A Cuban History, 1837-1959, translated by Franklin W. Knight and Mary Todd(Chapel Hill, 1998), 52-54, 65-68, 78, 88-91; Tomich,*Through the Prism of Slavery*, 81-85; Follett, *Sugar Masters*, 23, 40-41, table 1; Follett, "Slavery and Technology in Louisiana's Sugar Bowl," 73-74, 85-88, 90-9; Higman, *Slave Populations of the British Caribbean,* 51.

15 Tadman, "The Demographic Cost of Sugar: Debates on Slave Societies and Natural Increase in the Americas," *American Historical Review* 105 (December 2000): 1534-75 (quotation on 1537). Higman, *Slave Populations of the British Caribbean*, 46-85, 303-17; Laird W. Bergad, *Slavery and the Demographic and Economic History of Minas Gerais, Brazil, 1720-1888* (Princeton, 1999), 105-15, 118 22, 142-49. For the effect of labor as well as diet on the fertility of slave women on sugar plantations, see Kenneth Morgan, "Slave Women and Reproduction in Jamaica, ca. 1776-1834," in Gwyn Campbell, Suzanne Miers, and Joseph C. Miller, eds., *Women and Slavery.* Vol. II: *The*

When scholars talk about modernity, capitalism is rarely far behind. When Robin Blackburn links market relations, consumer society, and colonial slavery, he writes as much of capitalism as modernity. Colonial slavery made a "substantial contribution" to capitalism in England, he argues. Slave societies themselves, however, were "pre-capitalist," for slavery prevented waged labor from becoming the predominant system of labor. In theory wage labor is crucial to capitalism because it transforms relations of production and exchange. Farmers who previously raised crops for themselves or for local sale reorient production towards markets expanding with the ranks of wage laborers, who must buy means of subsistence. Wage relations pare away social obligations between laborers and employers and enable capitalists to increase production, reduce costs, and raise profits. Wage labor, then, generates mobility in both the workforce and capital.[16] As Walter Johnson has suggested though, we need not put the matter to rest with the orthodox answer to a doctrinal question in Marxism. From an Atlantic perspective, "slavery and wage labor . . . characterized the two poles of this single [political] economy." Slavery bestowed a mobile, flexible labor force on the South, as recent work suggests, and thus a critical precondition of capitalism in another form.[17]

Modern Atlantic (Athens, Ohio, 2008), 27-53; and Richard Follett, "Gloomy Melancholy: Sexual Reproduction among Louisiana Slave Women, 1840-60," *ibid.*, 54-75.

16 Jack Goody, *Capitalism and Modernity: The Great Debate* (Cambridge, Eng., 2004); Blackburn, *Making of New World Slavery*, 374 (second quotation), 553 (first quotation); Karl Marx, *Capital: A Critique of Political Economy.* Vol. 1: *The Process of Capitalist Production*, translated by Samuel Moore and Edward Aveling (New York, 1967), esp. chaps. 12-15, 23-33. For a similar argument, see Douglas Egerton, "Markets without a Market Revolution: Southern Planters and Capitalism," *Journal of the Early Republic* 16 (Spring 1996): 207-21, esp. 211. John Ashworth also argues that wage labor distinguished slavery and capitalism but that its significance in the antebellum United States was primarily political. Ashworth, *Slavery, Capitalism, and Politics in the Antebellum Republic* (2 vols.; New York, 1995, 2007), I, 80-121, 165, 195-200, II,1-5, 104-11, 265-303, 453-57.

17 Johnson, "The Pedestal and the Veil: Rethinking the Capitalism/Slavery Question," *Journal of the Early Republic* 24 (Summer 2004): 299-308 (quotation on 305). This argument builds on recent work on the movement of slaves in resistance, the making of neighborhoods, and from the Upper South to the Deep South. Berlin, *Generations of Captivity;* Johnson, *Soul by Soul;* Stephanie M. H. Camp, *Closer to Freedom: Enslaved Women and Everyday Resistance in the Plantation South* (Chapel Hill, 2004); Anthony

Slaves worked as waged laborers in pockets of the South, although not as extensively as has been suggested. In northern Maryland the proximity of freedom in Pennsylvania and the pervasive slave trade to the Deep South inclined slaves and slaveholders to graft elements of free labor onto the terms of slave labor, as Max Grivno has convincingly shown. Wage relations offered slaves an alternative to the risks of trying to escape to the North and provided slaveholders a means of keeping bondpeople at work. Wage labor became increasingly attractive during harvests and as hiring out became more common with a shift from tobacco to wheat cultivation. Future research is required to determine whether similar arrangements prevailed elsewhere in the border South. Such claims about sugar plantations, however, conflate wage labor with work slaves performed on their own time. In Southern Louisiana, as in the cotton belt, planters paid slaves for labor performed after the workday to raise corn, to cut timber to fire the steam engines, and to tend the boiling houses evenings and on Sundays. The difference between payment for overwork and wage labor is apparent in contemporary terms of work for Chinese laborers on Cuban sugar plantations. The Chinese workers' status was certainly comparable to enslavement. Upon arrival many found their indentures sold with provisions explicitly ceding any right to bargain over wages, typically four dollars monthly. These workers "can hardly be said to have been voluntarily selling their labor power," Rebecca J. Scott argues. They were less wage laborers "than debt peons always at risk of being reduced to the status of those alongside whom they worked: slaves." If Chinese laborers in Cuba, who were actually paid for part of their labor time, were not wage laborers, payments for overwork received by slaves in Louisiana had nothing to do with wage relations.[18]

Moreover, the commercial production of food crops with slave labor was more widespread in Brazil and Jamaica than in the South. Planters combined staple and subsistence production virtually everywhere during

E. Kaye, *Joining Places: Slave Neighborhoods in the Old South* (Chapel Hill, 2007).

18 Grivno, ",There Slavery Cannot Dwell': Agriculture and Labor in Northern Maryland, 1790-1860" (Ph.D. dissertation, University of Maryland, 2007); Follett, *The Sugar Master*, 5, 139-42, 195-211, 216-18; Scott, *Slave Emancipation in Cuba: The Transition to Free Labor, 1860-1899* (Princeton, 1985), 28-35 (quotation on 30).

the second slavery. In the South the modest capital requirements of cotton production enabled both planters and yeomen to cultivate a crop mix that secured both profits in the market and subsistence in foodstuffs. Indeed, intercropping corn and plantation staples was pervasive along the Atlantic rim. In Cuba planters raised rice as well as sugar until the end of slavery, yet the dense railroad network enabled them to import food cheaply to feed slaves. In Jamaica, by contrast, slaveholders developed a division of labor in the commercial production of sugar and beef. Cattle-raising employed a substantial sector of slave laborers, a total of 20,000, about one in every eight on the island, in 1832. Owners of "pens," as Jamaican livestock farms were called, with 100 bondpeople on average, were big planters by Southern standards. Until the 1840s cattle-raising was the largest and a still-growing sector of a diversified economy in Minais Gerais, the largest slaveholding province in Brazil. Slaves produced corn and *mandioca* (cassava) in addition to beef for local markets, tobacco plantations in the hinterlands of Rio de Janeiro, and the city proper. In the province of São Paulo planters also employed slaves in the commercial production of foodstuffs. Many slaveholders, who aimed to set up as coffee planters in their own right, produced dietary staples while their trees matured and stuck with the market in corn, rice, and other provisions when it proved lucrative. By the 1830s slaves on coffee *fazendas* were also producing corn in quantity for export. Although the drive for self-sufficiency among Southern planters and yeomen limited the commercial production of foodstuffs, slavery proved compatible with expanding agricultural markets for planters in Jamaica and Brazil.[19]

What was most capitalist about slavery in the South was the mobility of slave property. The power to own laborers was not only the peculiar property right of slaveholders but also their most valuable asset, for it

[19] Zanetti and García, *Sugar and Railroads*, 99-101; Arturo Warman, *Corn & Capitalism: How a Botanical Bastard Grew to Global Dominance*, translated by Nancy L. Westrate (Chapel Hill, 2003); Verene A. Shepherd, "Introduction," 1-18, and B. W. Higman, "The Internal Economy of Jamaica Pens, 1760-1890," pp. 63-81, both in Shepherd, ed., *Slavery Without Sugar: Diversity in the Caribbean Economy Since the 17th Century* (Gainesville, 2002); Bergad, *Slavery and Minas Gerais* (Princeton, 1999), 26-46; Luna and Klein, *Slavery and São Paulo,* 70-106.

enabled planters to increase production in response to increasing demand for staple crops. This capacity was already demonstrated by the peregrine plantation complex before 1800, when slave labor successively established new centers of sugar production on the Atlantic islands off West Africa, on Hispaniola, in Brazil, and in the British and French Caribbean. Slave labor proved extremely mobile during the second slavery as well, yet the trans-Atlantic trade no longer met the demand for labor on sugar and coffee plantations. After Spain outlawed the African trade in 1845, Cuba and Puerto Rico resorted to other modes of compulsory labor. Cuba, as we have seen, imported indentured laborers from China. In Puerto Rico the colonial government compelled peasants to work sugar plantations. In Brazil planters conducted their own massive domestic slave trade after the abolition of the trans-Atlantic trade in 1850. Urban slaveholders and cotton producers in the northeast traded bondpeople to sugar planters in Pernambucco and coffee planters in south-central Brazil. The migration between these regions covered a longer distance than did the U.S. domestic slave trade to the Deep South and may even have broken up a larger proportion of slave families, too. Relatively few owners in Brazil migrated with their slaves and made any attempt to keep families intact. Slavery in the South was as mobile as anywhere, more so by some measures. The proportion of slaves sold out of Northeastern Brazil was briefly, between 1863 and 1872, on a par with that from the Upper South. Yet southern slaveholders transported slaves by both sale and migration, about as many in an average decade as Brazilian owners did during the entire thirty years of the legal domestic trade. This is not to suggest that slave labor was more mobile than free labor during the second slavery. The number of Europeans migrating to the Americas finally surpassed Africans after 1820. Population grew faster in the states of the upper than the lower Mississippi Valley. Still, slavery was sufficiently mobile to provide labor for cotton plantations, which free labor could not do. Slaves, unlike wage laborers, could be bought, sold, accumulated, and bequeathed as property, taken bodily and put to field work, women as well as men. Slavery's contribution to the rise of capitalism, Gavin Wright reminds us, was the power to assign "workers to tasks and geographic settings they would not voluntary have chosen."[20]

Planters everywhere during the nineteenth century mobilized enslaved people to migrate to new lands perforce and compelled them to clear it to begin staple production forthwith, as Laird W. Bergad has observed. In the South the number of slaves in states formed after 1789 multiplied threefold between 1820 and 1840 and then doubled again by 1860. Over 2 million slaves, 55 percent, lived in states that had not existed at the founding of the republic. By the mid-1840s Cuban planters had extended sugar production east across the Matanzas plains over the western part of the island. By 1862 slaves on these new grounds outnumbered those in the Havana region by nearly four to one. In Brazil planters extended coffee production across the Paraíba Valley during the 1830s and west across the province of São Paulo by the 1850s. Between 1819 and 1872 the balance of the slave population shifted from a majority in the northeast to two-thirds in the south-central provinces. Production shifted inexorably with slaves to new regions. By 1833 output of cotton in the Old Southwest had outstripped the U.S. southeastern states, and Matanzas accounted for 55 percent of Cuban sugar by midcentury. In Puerto Rico the *libreta* system, established in 1849 and administered by colonial authorities to compel peasants to work on the plantations, could not maintain the rate of growth in sugar production. Sugar exports, which had increased 20 percent annually for twenty years before the *libreta*, slowed to about 2 percent for twenty years afterward. Nor did wage labor keep up with slave labor on Brazilian coffee plantations. The share of coffee produced by free labor dropped precipitously in São Paulo—in 1829 half of all estates used free labor exclusively; in 1854 a mere 10 percent of coffee workers were free laborers. Meanwhile the number of slaves em-

[20] Gavin Wright, *Slavery and American Economic Development* (Baton Rouge, 2006), 1-34 (quotation on 15), 48-70, 84-89, 122; Barbara L. Solow, "Capitalism and Slavery in the Exceedingly Long Run." *Journal of Interdisciplinary History* 17 (Spring 1987): 711-37, esp. 732; Moya Pons, *History of Caribbean*, 226-28, 233-35; Robert W. Slenes, "The Brazilian Internal Slave Trade, 1850-1888: Regional Economies, Slave Experience, and the Politics of a Peculiar Market," 325-70, esp. 332-33, and Richard Graham, "Another Middle Passage? The Internal Slave Trade in Brazil," 291-324, esp. 297, both in Johnson, ed., *Chattel Principle*; Michael Tadman, *Speculators and Slaves: Masters, Traders, and Slaves in the Old South* (Madison, 1989).

ployed in coffee increased fivefold. Slaves produced staggering increases of plantation commodities: tenfold in Cuban sugar between 1787 and 1830, twenty-five-fold in Southern cotton between 1812 and 1859, and fourfold in Brazilian coffee between 1837 and 1878. Slavery enabled planters to seize preeminence in world markets: the South in cotton and Cuba in sugar by 1830, Brazil in coffee around 1850.[21]

One of the most modern aspects of colonial slavery, "the birth [of] new social identities," to borrow Robin Blackburn's phrase, evolved under new conditions during the second slavery. The legal prohibitions against the transatlantic trade changed the balance within slave populations between the African-born and American-born or creoles. Over the last decade scholarship on colonial slavery has moved away from creolist approaches emphasizing the creation of new African American cultures to a diasporic emphasis on continuities between Africa and the Americas. The shift to a diasporic approach in the study of slavery left historians of the antebellum South, with its increasingly creole slave population, in an awkward position. Their familiar approach to African American culture was falling out of favor, and an exciting new method seemed not to apply to their field. Antebellum historians write less about Africanity than they did twenty years ago and have consequently neglected a critical dimension of modernity in the slave South. The African dimension of slave culture, like all social identities in the making, was a collective exercise in self-fashioning worked out in the everyday encounters of slave society, a profound example of what Blackburn calls "modern traditions of reflexive self-consciousness."[22]

Both diasporic and creolist approaches offer useful tools to historians of the second slavery in the South. Although theoretical debates have often pitted these interpretations against one another, historians have deployed both in practice all along. Creolization posits slave culture as a synthesis of

---

[21] Bergad, *Comparative Histories of Slavery in Brazil, Cuba, and the United States* (New York, 2007), 116-30, esp. Tables 4.1, 4.3, 4.4, and 4.6; Luis A. Figueroa, *Sugar, Slavery, and Freedom in Nineteenth-Century Puerto Rico* (Chapel Hill, 2005), 43-78, esp. 63, 73; Luna and Klein, *Slavery and São Paulo*, 55, 58-59, 77; Stuart Bruchey, ed., *Cotton and the Growth of the American Economy, 1790-1860. Sources and Readings* (New York, 1967), Tables 1A, 3A, 3C F; Blackburn, *Making of New World Slavery*, 498; Tomich, *Through the Prism of Slavery*, 64, 67, 86.

[22] Blackburn,*Making of New World Slavery*, 4.

West African and European practices. Men and women enslaved in the New World, the argument ran, combined varied African languages, religions, and other cultural practices with those of European colonists in the Americas to create common Afro-American cultures. The diasporic approach, by contrast, moves beyond generalized African conventions to trace cohorts of particular African peoples to sites in the Americas. For these scholars the history of slave cultures begins in West Africa and elaborates how enslaved people recreated the cultures of their homelands in slave societies. This approach has found confirmation and gained momentum from concentrations of slaves from specific regions of West and West-Central Africa documented in the Trans-Atlantic Slave Trade Database.[23] Yet historians of the diaspora often write in terms of cultural change and interchange familiar to creolists. Paul E. Lovejoy, who has done much to formulate this research agenda, has recently cautioned against conflating ethnicity and religion, yet he acknowledges how both ",creolized' slaves" by requiring "individuals to subordinate previous identities in favour of a new, shared level of consciousness." The opposition between diasporic and creolist approaches, Kristin Mann argues, has exhausted its usefulness. "Surely, the goal is not to prove that Old or New World influences were more important in shaping the experiences of slaves," she writes. "What we need to understand is how, when, and why slaves were able to draw on material, social, ideological, and other resources from one or other traditions, or from both."[24] Work on

23 Sydney W. Mintz and Richard Price, *The Birth of African-American Culture: An Anthropological Perspective* (Boston, 1992); Paul E. Lovejoy, "The African Diaspora: Revisionist Interpretations of Ethnicity, Culture and Religion under Slavery," *Studies in the World History of Slavery, Abolition and Emancipation* II:1 (1997): 1-23; Voyages: The Trans-Atlantic Slave Trade Database, http://www.slavevoyages.org.

24 Lovejoy, "Transatlantic Transformations: The Origins and Identities of Africans in the Americas," in Livio Sansone, Elisée Soumonni, and Boucabar Barry, eds., *Africa, Brazil, and the Construction of Trans-Atlantic Black Identities* (Trenton, N.J., 2008), 81-111 (first quotation on 81; second quotation on 82); Mann, "Shifting Paradigms in the Study of the African Diaspora and of Atlantic History and Culture," in *Rethinking the African Diaspora: The Making of a Black Atlantic World in the Bight of Benin and Brazil,* ed. Mann and Edna G. Bay (London, 2001), 3-21 (third and fourth quotations on 6). For other examples of scholars who have made important contributions to diasporic historiography and also written in creolist terms, see John Thornton, *Africa and Africans in the Making of the Atlantic World, 1400-1800* (2nd ed.; New York, 1998), 7-8, 183-

slavery in Brazil and Cuba suggests how southern historians can use both creolist and diasporic methods.

The Islamic rebellion of 1835 in Salvador, Bahia, Brazil, the largest urban slave revolt in the Americas, spectacularly demonstrates the complex relationship between old and new worlds in slave cultures. The uprising is an unusually rich example of the correlations between specific struggles in Africa and the Americas at the core of the diasporic model. As Lovejoy has shown, the origins of the rebellion in Bahia lay in the jihad of the Sokoto Caliphate in Central Sudan. As Sokoto expanded its authority and Islam south after 1804, it enslaved many Hausa and other neighboring peoples. Thousands of Yoruba were captured when states where they lived joined the jihad or their villages came under attack. Through the 1830s the expansion of Sokoto thus sent thousands of Hausa and Yoruba men familiar with Islam and war through the slave trade to Brazil. There many became followers of imams who proselytized openly in Salvador and joined the rebellion, fighting in white robes and carrying amulets containing Arabic prayers and passages from the Qu'ran. Yet the 600 rebels were not an ethnic phalanx but an alliance across ethnic as well as religious lines. In Salvador, Lovejoy points out, people of different ethnic origins, including non-Muslims from Central Sudan, were "absorbed into the Muslim community." The uprising is often referred to as the revolt of the Malês, a contemporary word for African Muslims, especially the Hausa, who played a leading role. As João José Reis documented in a path-breaking study, though, Yorubas also planned and joined the uprising in numbers. The rebels' strategy, furthermore, combined Islamic beliefs with slaves' canny understanding of their New World terrain. The day appointed for the revolt not only coincided with Ramadan but also fell on a Sunday and a Christian holiday to take the city unawares.[25]

92, 206-71; Michael A. Gomez, *Exchanging Our Country Marks: The Transformation of African Identities in the Colonial and Antebellum South* (Chapel Hill, 1998), 7-13, 242-43; Gomez, *Reversing Sail: A History of the African Diaspora* (New York, 2005), 1-2, 117, 124-28; Gwendolyn Midlo Hall, *Slavery and African Ethnicities in the Americas: Restoring the Links* (Chapel Hill, 2005), xiii-xvi, 23, 51-52, 165-72.

25 Reis, *Slave Rebellion in Brazil: The Muslim Uprising of 1835 in Bahia*, translated by Arthur Brakel (Baltimore, 1993); Lovejoy, *Slavery, Commerce, and Production in the Sokoto Caliphate of West Africa* (Trenton, N.J., 2005), 55-80 (quotation on 70).

Diasporic approaches remain relevant to the Deep South, for clandestine slave traders continued to deliver ethnic clusters of Africans up to the Civil War. Sylviane A. Diouf traces 110 captives on the *Clotilda*, the last ship known to land slaves in the United States, from the interior of the Bight of Benin to plantations around Mobile, Alabama, in 1860. Attending to their origins among specific peoples yields nuanced interpretations of the shipmates' enduring African culture—how they practiced endogamy, kept a lunar calendar, and conducted funerals, for instance. One couple marked an abiding loyalty to Dahomey on their son's chest with a tattoo of a snake biting its tail, a sacred Fon symbol for "the continuity of the kingdom." The captives also observed burial rites from the Atakora region of Benin. They dug graves narrow and deep, like chimneys, carried the corpse overhead to the graveside, lowered the body upright, and covered it with strips of pine bark in the absence of liana native to their homeland. "Although the people of Atakora in the group stuck as faithfully as they could to their traditions," Diouf subtly observes, "they also introduced some innovations born from their particular circumstances." Probable estimates of Africans imported to the South after 1808 range widely between 6100 and 54,000, yet scholars have found significant clusters near the Savannah River in South Carolina and the Brazos in Texas, and Diouf offers a model of how to study them.[26]

Modifications to the creolization model will also yield insights into modern slave culture in the South. Creolist approaches have much to gain from a new comparative history of slavery in West Africa and the South. Dylan Penningroth has built on the rich literature about West African slavery to compare how law, property, and kinship converged in different ways on the Gold Coast and in the South to incorporate the families of slaves and slaveholders in ideology and practice. As new comparative histories map points of divergence and similarity between slavery in the South and in dif-

[26] Diouf, *Dreams of Africa in Alabama: The Slave Ship* Clotilda*and the Story of the Last Africans Brought to America* (New York, 2007); Eltis, "U.S. Transatlantic Slave Trade," 349-53; Sean Kelley, "Black Birders and *Bozales*: African-Born Slaves on the Lower Brazos River of Texas in the Nineteenth Century," *Civil War History* 54 (December 2008): 406-23. For a rich creolist study of liberated Africans in the Bahamas and Trinidad after the abolition of the British trans-Atlantic slave trade, see Rosanne Marion Adderley, *"New Negroes from Africa": Slave Trade Abolition and Free African Settlement in the Nineteenth-Century Caribbean* (Bloomington, 2006).

ferent African societies, historians of creolization will gain new understandings of the expectations of African slaves and how African American cultures changed over time.[27] Creolist scholars of the Caribbean increasingly attend to the beliefs and practices of particular ethnic groups. Moreover, they treat creolization less as an exercise in assimilation than as a series of radical appropriations subversive of slavery itself. In Jamaica, Jean Besson has shown, slaves adopted and overturned owners' conceptions of private property. Bequeathing village yards and provision grounds to all family members without distinction eschewed slaveholders' rules of primogeniture and belied the principle that slaves were kinless people. Comparable subversive appropriations are readily apparent in literature on the antebellum South, even if they are not framed by recent reworkings of creolization. Many scholars have pointed out how slaves' claims to families and property undermined slaveholders' right to sell their people at will and contradicted the right to human property itself. Douglas R. Egerton has cited the Market Revolution as well as the French and Haitian revolutions as catalysts for the conspiracies of Gabriel and Denmark Vesey, who were also inspired by the Old Testament. They were, he argues, two among many rebel leaders, in and around cities from Cuba to Demerara and Bahia, familiar with market relations and alive to "the power of cash."[28]

Recent studies of the Aponte Rebellion in Cuba suggest how sophisticated conceptions of creolization can illuminate the complex ideologies and multiple wellsprings of revolt. In January and March 1812 two insurrections broke out on plantations 500 miles apart. Here, too, the Haitian Revolution

---

27 Penningroth, "The Claims of Slaves and Ex-Slaves to Family and Property: A Trans-Atlantic Comparison," *American Historical Review* 112 (October 2007): 1039-69.

28 Besson, *Martha Brae's Two Histories: European Expansion and Caribbean Culture-Building in Jamaica* (Chapel Hill, 2002); Egerton, "Slaves to the Marketplace: Economic Liberty and Black Rebelliousness in the Atlantic World," *Journal of the Early Republic* 26 (Winter 2006): 617-39 (quotation on 634); Egerton, "The Tricolor in Black and White: The French Revolution in Gabriel's Virginia," in Doris Y Kadish,ed., *Slavery in the Caribbean Francophone World: Distant Voices, Forgotten Acts, Forged Identities* (Athens, Ga., 2000), 91-105; Egerton, *He Shall Go Out Free: the Lives of Denmark Vesey* (rev. ed.; Lanham, Md., 2004), 42-45, 102-18 135-39, 144-48. For a critique of the evidence of Vesey's conspiracy, including the significance of the Old Testament and Haiti, see Michael P. Johnson "Denmark Vesey and His Co-Conspirators," *William and Mary Quarterly* 58 (October 2001): 915-976, esp. 916-19, 964-71.

galvanized rebels and became intertwined with sprawling rumors that variously reported an emancipation decree issued by kings of Europe or Kongo. Yet the revolt also had its base in distinctly African solidarities among Kongos, Yorubas, Minas, and Mandingas. The rebellion was planned within *cabildos de nación*. These fraternal societies were both diasporic and creole institutions, and as Matt D. Childs suggests, organized by shared African ethnicity, yet combining men and women, slave and free, of varied ancestry. The *cabildos* (a Spanish term used interchangeably for town councils and municipal government) were "an Old World institution modified in a New World setting." Mina Guagni, a Havana society implicated in the rebellion, "based its membership on a shared cultural and geographic heritage rooted in the Gold Coast of West Africa." The rebellion represented an alliance between *cabildos* and hence different African ethnicities. Stephan Palmié has provocatively elaborated radical appropriations of colonial culture in a bound volume of paintings and collages by José Antonio Aponte, a sculptor and retired captain of the free black militia who was accused of organizing the rebellion. Aponte's pictures claimed a place in history for himself and other militia members in his family. One image, Aponte told interrogators, depicted his grandfather, whose "love burns upward in live flames to God, the King, and the fatherland." Aponte used Biblical iconography and a genre of allegorical imagery popular among the Cuban elite in a highly creolized idiom "deeply subversive of the conventions on which he drew." To Palmié, the culture Aponte reflects cannot be comprehended by scholarly dichotomies between African and creole, free black and slave, tradition and modernity.[29]

New models of cultural change are likely to emerge from the present ferment in the field. Neither the creolist nor diasporic model adequately captures religious beliefs and practices in Kongo and the Lowcountry, Jason R. Young argues, although he has learned much from both. His analysis

---

29 Childs, *1812 Aponte Rebellion in Cuba*, 1-19, 95-119 (first quotation on 103; second quotation on 96), 161. Palmié, *Wizards and Scientists: Explorations in Afro-Cuba Modernity & Tradition* (Durham, 2002), 98-107 (third quotation on 102; fourth quotation on 106), 136; Despite a shared creolist approach, the authors have important differences on matters of method and interpretation, including Aponte's participation, which Palmié doubts.

begins with conversion to Christianity in Kongo, especially the use of ritual objects, *minkisi*, to heal the sick, divine criminals, and harm enemies. Understanding religion in the lowcountry means reckoning with Kongo conceptions about human agency, especially how powers residing among the dead can be wielded by the living. *Minkisi* were portals between the lands of the living and the dead, capable of rendering people vessels of the spirit the object contained. In the lowcountry slaves did not simply reproduce Kongo beliefs, rituals, or material culture but creatively changed them with new ritual objects and methods to animate them, such as graveyard dirt, conjure bags, and praise houses. Slaves recreated Kongo burial practices and principles by draining the body of humors and wrapping it in white cloth, taking care to seal and thereby prevent the spirit of the dead from harming the living. Yet mourners also innovated new *minkisi* and portals, such as mirrors, and decorated graves with them. Young uses slave religion, with its "vocabulary of ritual practice," much as creolist scholars have used language, with its structures of grammar and vocabulary, to trace the evolution of African American culture. Slave religion, he contends, can be compared over time at specific sites in Africa and the Americas. When slaves in the lowcountry deployed religious beliefs and practices in struggles with the master class, they also resisted the ideologies that animated their owners and "challenged modernity or, at least, claimed their own space in the modern world."[30]

Southern historians need not reduce the difference between creolization and the diaspora to a choice between tradition and modernity. Creolists have always regarded African American cultures as fundamentally new, brilliant products of vernacular creativity—malleable, protean, and hence thoroughly modern. Historians of the diaspora, for their part, do not treat African ethnicity as mere provincialism. On the contrary, they cast slaves' persistent engagement with African homelands as a popular expression of the cosmopolitanism that defined the Black Atlantic.

30 Young, *Rituals of Resistance: African Atlantic Religion in Kongo and the Lowcountry South in the Era of Slavery* (Baton Rouge, 2007), 120 (first quotation), 108 (second quotation). On using musical structures instead of language, see Richard Cullen Rath, "Drums and Power: Ways of Creolizing Music in Coastal South Carolina and Georgia, 1730-90," in *Creolization In the Americas*, ed. David Buiseret and Steven G. Reinhardt (College Station, Tex., 2000), 99-130.

In recent treatments of the nineteenth-century South, cosmopolitanism is mainly the province of the master class. Planters and intellectuals are now revealed as, far from parochial, a mobile set with broad horizons, acutely aware of events, conditions, and ideas along the Atlantic rim. Historians disagree about whether Southerners‘ engagements with Europe or the Caribbean were most critical. Edward Bartlett Rugemer and Matthew Pratt Guterl argue that an influential stratum of politicians and intellectuals identified the fate of the South with the struggles over slavery and freedom in the Caribbean and Brazil. This perspective brings to light intriguing new figures and recasts others we thought we knew. Octavia Walton Le Vert, for example, grew up on the Spanish borderlands in Florida Territory and married a French surgeon in Mobile, where she translated Cuban poetry and hosted a Monday salon frequented by visitors from the Caribbean as well as Europe. Rugemer boldly argues that the British abolition of slavery was a turning point in American history and that the Southern reaction to it led ultimately to secession. The connections he traces are clearer for the abolitionists than the South, where newspapers wrote less than he leads readers to expect about the great slave rebellions in Barbados, Demerara, and Jamaica that led Parliament to abolish slavery in 1834. The American consul in Jamaica, Robert Monroe Harrison, repeatedly warned of British plots to send armies of Jamaican freedmen to foment insurrection in the South, but his dispatches provoked little response from Abel P. Upshur and John C. Calhoun, the secretaries of state he supposedly influenced. More persuasive is a broad similarity between the lurid thesis of the Jamaican planter Bryan Edwards that abolitionism leads to slave insurrection and Southern responses to northern abolitionism. In debates over abolitionist petitions to Congress, the annexation of Texas, influential figures from James Henry Hammond to Calhoun himself argued that events in the Caribbean confirmed the dangers posed by abolitionists and British designs. Rugemer‘s important book establishes beyond cavil that Southern spokesmen were attentive to the politics of slavery and freedom in the Caribbean, which played a larger part than previously recognized in the antebellum struggle between North and South.[31]

[31] Rugemer, *The Problem of Emancipation: The Caribbean Roots of the American Civil War* (Baton Rouge, 2008); Guterl, *American Mediterranean: Southern Slaveholders in*

For senior scholars, what was most cosmopolitan about Southern intellectuals was their engagement with Europe. Eugene D. Genovese, once the foremost interpreter of a premodern Old South, and Elizabeth Fox-Genovese now argue that "the slaveholders embraced many features of modernity and progress." At the core of "the mind of the master class," they contend, was an intellectually rigorous, morally principled grappling with the contradictions of a slave society in a modern world. Investigations of these conundrums ranged widely in history, theology, philosophy, the natural sciences, and contemporary social conditions on both sides of the Atlantic. The proslavery argument went so far as to defend personal servitude as the most humane condition for all laborers, white and black. This defense of "Slavery in the Abstract" rested heavily on favorable comparisons of southern slaves to wage laborers in both England and the North. These were broad-minded southerners, evangelicals who read deists, conservatives who read bourgeois liberals, slaveholders who read abolitionists. Genovese and Fox-Genovese are characteristically admiring of Southern thought, defending it in spirit, sometimes to the letter. They give the debate with abolitionists over the Biblical authority of slavery, for instance, to the slaveholders—and on the merits.[32]

Where the masters' engagement with the modern world was as ambivalent as it was deep in the Genoveses' view, Michael O'Brien argues modernity came relatively easily to the South. Although Genovese and Fox-Genovese characterize Southern thinkers as most fully formed by classical and medieval thought, O'Brien's elegant profiles recast them as intellectual adventurers immersed in contemporary European ideas and eager to cross boundaries. Abroad in 1829-1830 Jesse Burton Harrison visited Thomas Babington Macaulay and Wilhelm von Humboldt and may have attended Georg W. F. Hegel's lectures on the philosophy of history or at least heard tell of them. Back home Harrison was evidently the first American to mention Hegel in print and an early critic of British philosophy for its narrow

the Age of Emancipation (Cambridge, Mass., 2008), 1 46.

32 Fox-Genovese and Genovese, *The Mind of the Master Class: History and Faith in the Southern Slaveholders' World View* (New York, 2005), 3 (first quotation); Fox-Genovese and Genovese, *Slavery in White and Black: Class and Race in the Southern Slaveholders' New World Order* (New York, 2008), 1 (last quotation).

empiricism. O'Brien's sympathy with his subjects is manifest in a willingness to treat a glass oftentimes half-empty as generally more than half-full. For some on the Grand Tour, England was "an introduction to modernity" and "confusing, often repulsive." Intellectuals, he concedes, "were more associated with the modernizing sector of society" than the South as a whole. Yet figures like Harrison, Louisa McCord, and Francis Lieber vindicate O'Brien's account of an Old South "deeply implicated in modernity."[33]

Writing the history of the second slavery poses a variety of conceptual challenges to Southern historians. It requires pushing past the boundaries of time and space that circumscribe antebellum slavery, back to the early republic, outward to Cuba, Brazil, and the Atlantic world. It behooves us to employ a variety of approaches, creolist as well as diasporic, to slave culture. Such a project demands we think carefully about concepts we have long taken for granted, such as capitalism and modernity. And we will have to surrender, at long last, our Southern exceptionalism. If historians no longer argue this case explicitly, it has been a constitutive concept of the field too long for practitioners to let go easily, and it still undergirds much writing on antebellum slavery. Yet the notion that the South was unique during the nineteenth century does not bear up well under even this cursory examination of contemporary slave societies. If the South was modern and capitalist, so were Cuba and Brazil. If slave labor was perhaps unusually mobile in the South, production for markets was apparently more extensive in Brazil. If slavery proved eminently compatible with technical innovation, biological as well as mechanical, the level of sophistication was higher in Cuban sugar mills. As we reckon with the South of the second slavery, we are likely to find it was neither the most capitalist nor the most modern slave society. We will have to come to terms with a history that was Southern, but not exceptional.

---

33 O'Brien, *Conjectures of Order: Intellectual Life and the American South, 1810-1860,*(2 vols.; Chapel Hill, 2004), I, 17-20 (third quotation on 20); fourth quotation on 17), 90-161 (first quotation on 106; second quotation on 109).